T0354858

TEACHING TENNIS
VOLUME 3

TEACHING
TENNIS
VOLUME 3

THE DEVELOPMENT
OF CHAMPIONS

Martin van Daalen

Library of Congress Control Number: 2017900455
ISBN: Hardcover   978-1-7960-7501-4
                   Softcover   978-1-7960-7499-4
                   eBook   978-1-7960-7500-7

Print information available on the last page.

Rev. date: 12/12/2019

To order additional copies of this book, contact:
Xlibris
1-888-795-4274
www.Xlibris.com
Orders@Xlibris.com
801359

This book is dedicated to my parents
for encouraging me in all my endeavors
and for making me strive to be the best I can be
in whatever I try to do.

FOREWORD BY LYNNE ROLLEY

(After becoming the number 2 player in the US, Lynne has focused on her career in coaching. As director of women's tennis for the USTA, she has helped develop many top players, including Lindsay Davenport, Chanda Rubin, and Jennifer Capriati. Lynne was inducted in the tennis hall of fame in 2008.)

Martin van Daalen has previously written two of the most thorough instructional books for developing tennis players. He provides a clear, simple pathway for improvement and success. Players, parents, and coaches have used his articles and books for guidance through some of the most difficult bumps in the road during their journey in player development.

Now he has produced a third book, *The Development of Champions*. In addition to the instructions provided in his first two books, he delves into the details and expertise of competition. All the excellence achieved through great coaching and practice may not be benefiting a player during the competitive moments. And the patience and passion of a player can disappear quickly if not clearly guided and mentored consistently. According to Martin, competitive skills should be addressed through all levels of development just as the nuts and bolts of hitting the ball.

Volume 3 provides the proficiencies to nurture every competitive player. The love of the battle is an essential skill to learn for every player; and Martin provides the tools to learn the nuances of strategies, tactics, and patterns of play to win at all levels.

Martin also stresses the importance of a support team around the player during this development process. Parents and coaches have important roles and will really benefit from Martin's guidance.

Martin's success record with players has made him a success story in the tennis community. Learn from his experience and enjoy the process by following his simple steps.

Lynne Rolley

Martin van Daalen

FOREWORD BY RODNEY HARMON

(Besides being a successful player on the pro tour and reaching the quarterfinal in the US Open, Rodney Harmon has dedicated himself in becoming one of the top coaches in the US and a leader and respected speaker in the tennis industry. He was the former USTA men's director, helping many players reach their goals, and is now the head coach of Georgia Tech women's team.)

If ever there was a search for a consummate coach, my friend Martin van Daalen would qualify hands down. His passion for our sport is exemplified on the court and, as we know from previous volumes, in his writing.

Of all the forms of communicating a game strategy, a technique, or a coaching philosophy, writing has to be one of the toughest. Yet Martin makes it look so easy.

From a coach's perspective, his style is both descriptive and instructive. His techniques for both players and coaches leap from the page, often evoking his easy, relaxed methods for drawing out exceptional performance and personal bests from his players.

If you are new to the sport or if tennis has been your life's passion, this latest installment in what is now the Teaching Tennis trilogy will teach you something you didn't know before.

Tennis requires skills in technique and tactics as well as the ability to compete against opponents of different ages and skill levels. Through his decades of playing and teaching at the local, regional, national, and international levels, Martin has learned how practice and competition can hone champions.

If you love tennis as much as I do, you will appreciate this consummate coach and his literary gift.

Rodney Harmon

FOREWORD BY MAGNUS NORMAN

(Magnus was one of the top Swedish players, reaching the finals of the French Open and the number 2 spot on the ATP ranking [2000]. He is now one of the leading internationally respected coaches who has helped many top players like Thomas Johansson, Robin Soderling, and Stan Wawrinka, each reaching great heights in their careers. He is also partnering with one of the leading academies in the world—Good to Great, located in Stockholm, Sweden.)

I have worked together and alongside Martin van Daalen on various player development projects, and we still keep in contact on a regular basis. I am proud to have Martin as a friend and colleague to call on for a second opinion of my players, whom I work with on tour. He knows the art of coaching, spending more than thirty-five years working with players of all levels. I really respect his knowledge of coaching—with his tactical and technical knowledge being second to none. What I also admire is his way of translating that knowledge to the players he is working with. In my opinion, that is the essence and the art of coaching. With his third book, *The Development of Champions*, he will assist many coaches in developing their players to the next level and bringing more pleasure and satisfaction to their game.

Magnus Norman

PREFACE

It was my dad who introduced me to the game of tennis when I was ten years old. That summer, he took my brother and me to the local tennis club and showed us how to play the game. We practiced together often until we became good enough to compete in tournaments. I played my first tournament when I was twelve and lost to the number 1 seed (6–0, 6–0). Even though I was very upset, it was at that moment that I decided I wanted to be good at this wonderful sport of tennis.

As a junior, I had a lot of good players to practice with. I also had some great coaches who taught me the basics of the game. Having an older brother to compete with helped me to try harder too. We would spend many afternoons at the club playing singles and doubles matches. There was a great tennis environment with junior and senior players of all ages. And we always stayed after for drinks and conversations.

Growing up in Holland, I played for the most part in the summer because the winters were too cold. Private lessons were expensive, and I was fortunate to receive one or two hours of instruction a week. It took over an hour of travel each way to get there. Practice was never boring to me, so I never minded the travel. From a young age, I was very independent and took charge of my own tournament schedule and took care of all the entries. I couldn't wait for the new schedule to arrive each spring and usually had my plan ready for the year that same afternoon! Sometimes my parents drove me to the tournaments, but I would often take the bus or train to get there. I started making notes of my training, my improvements, and the players I played with. Taking notes helped me to remember the things that went well and what to improve and the specifics about matches and players. I became my own coach at an early stage.

I started getting much more serious about my tennis game around the age of sixteen. Winning many matches and becoming the junior club champion sure helped my confidence. With the limited coaching hours, compared to training today, I had to be resourceful to coach myself by reading more tennis books and making notes of my practice. I also started to do a little coaching on the side to pay for some of the expenses of traveling. After high school, I attended two years of technical college (mechanical engineering) before I realized how much I missed tennis. Little did I know that the mechanical engineering background would help me tremendously in my coaching career.

Europe has professional training for coaches, and I assigned myself the goal of becoming the best coach I could possibly be. The two years of training were extensive and detailed in teaching tennis. Part of the course is an internship working at a club. Together with the other student coaches, we had to learn how to coach students of different levels. The learning process of teaching and evaluating one another proved to be an excellent experience and training in becoming a coach.

When I was twenty, I was drafted in the national army of the Netherlands for sixteen months and stationed in Germany. Being in the army made me tougher and much more assertive in dealing with others. With the rank of sergeant, I learned how to lead others with a calm and determined demeanor. (Later on, I would help organize the first boot camp for top junior tennis players in the US at the US Marine Corps headquarters in San Diego, directed by Sgt. Maj. Keith Williams.)

After the draft, I continued the coaches training course and, at the age of twenty-one, became the youngest national coach in the Netherlands at that time. Even then, I started working on a book of training plans for technique, tactics, mental and physical training for myself. Learning how to take ownership and initiative in my future job was an early asset in my development as a teacher and a coach. After finishing

the second coaching course for advanced players, I was working at three different clubs with most of the top players in the eastern part of Holland and was (playing) captain of the top team for many years.

I decided I needed more international experience and wrote to the famous coach Harry Hopman to request an intern coaching position at his academy in Largo, Florida. The Dutch Tennis Federation granted me a leave of absence to go there for three months to learn new coaching methods. It was a great experience in coaching and playing with the world's best players at the time. Some of the top players who trained there were John McEnroe, Björn Borg, Vitas Gerulaitis, and many other great players from those days. It was a very busy place with up to 250 players training there each week. I trained there myself with Paul McNamee, Kathy Horvath, Jimmy Brown, Andrea Jaeger, and many others. Later, I returned to Holland to continue my work with the federation. I applied a lot of the new coaching techniques in working with the players and in playing tournaments myself.

A few years later, when visiting the US, I was offered a job at the Saddlebrook Tennis Resort. They had recently taken over the program from Harry Hopman, who had passed away the previous year. Working there for six and a half years was very interesting and educational. My task was to work with a variety of top junior players and professionals: Jared Palmer, Ty Tucker, Mary Pierce, Jennifer Capriati, Mark Kratzmann, Shuzo Matsuoka, Pete Sampras, Jeff Tarango, Jim Courier, and too many others to name. During this time, I took on a number of coaching opportunities, which meant traveling on the road with top juniors, pro-level players, and federations including the USTA. One of those opportunities was in Japan, working at a club and coaching juniors of the Japanese Federation. It was a very rich period of experience in learning to cope with all the various international players, customs, and styles of play.

I was also offered a job in Amsterdam as the head coach in establishing an academy, and I was in charge of all the training. I started with only six students. The academy grew rapidly, and within three years, I had forty-five students. It was a very rewarding achievement to build that academy from the ground up. It was a joy to work and develop a talented group of players. One major accomplishment that I was very proud of during that time was winning the top National League for three years in a row.

My next position as director of women's tennis for the Dutch Tennis Federation taught me a lot about management and, unfortunately, about the politics in tennis. Even though I did not enjoy this position as much, it was a great learning tool in dealing with players, coaches, parents, and board members.

After this position ended, I took on a very promising junior, Michelle Gerards, to train her privately for the year. She made tremendous progress, and at thirteen years of age, she won the national indoor championship for eighteen and under. I was sad that I was not able to continue her development. I was invited to join the USTA player development program as a national coach and coordinator of the south region (nine Southern states). I worked for the USTA for eleven and a half years in various positions. When I first started there, I worked under Tom Gullikson (director of coaching) and, later, Lynne Rolley (director of women's tennis) and Rodney Harmon (director of men's tennis). I was always involved with the development of young junior top players. Some of those players were Ashley Harkleroad, Alex Kuznetsov, Chase Buchanan, Rhyne Williams, and Ryan Harrison—to name a few. At one point, I was very involved in changing the ranking system in the US to a point system similar to the one used by the ATP, WTA, and ITF junior ranking. It made sense that juniors in the US play for points just as they do on the international scene. After some opposition to the idea, it finally became a fact and is now an intricate part of the junior competition and development in the US. The new system sparked the competitive spirit in many junior players to play a lot more matches. In addition, it also allowed players to check and calculate their own ranking via the internet. As a national coach, I used to travel to many national and international events, with the Grand Slam junior tournaments being one of the main goals of the year. When the USTA commenced their training program in Boca Raton, I was in charge of the player development group of coaches on the men's side. I oversaw the coaches and the development of the players at the academy, and I assisted with the coaching education of the national men's coaches.

After working privately for a while on tour, I took the position of director of player development in Finland and was able to make an impact to the culture of training and tournament play. At the moment, I am back in Florida as director of programs at the Miami Beach Tennis Academy. The development of advanced players can be a very gratifying experience as a coach. To see your students progress and excel is rewarding in itself. As a coach, parent, or student, this book will assist you to reach your goals. May you have as much fun reading it as I had writing it!

Best of luck,
Martin van Daalen

Martin van Daalen (24)

CONTENTS

1—INTRODUCTION

Teaching Tennis Volume 3 is a comprehensive book for players, coaches, and parents about the specifics of competitive tennis. *The Development of Champions* is the last of the trilogy of instructional tennis books. It will enhance the understanding of methodology and progression in teaching tournament players. After the fundamentals of the game are explained in volume 1, readers are able to build on this information in the second book with specific details on how to develop advanced technical, tactical, mental, and physical skills. Volume 3 is for instructing tournament players of all levels for individual and team competition. It is beneficial for readers to examine these books in order. The books complement one another in the development, progression, and application process while improving your game.

Players are able to improve their competitive game with tips and practice drills. There are detailed instructions on how to play the game by developing a basic game plan with strategies and tactics that fit your personal game style. And it will also show you how to improve the physical and mental part of your game with exercises and multiple examples.

Coaches are able to use this book as a teaching guide to develop intermediate and advanced tournament players. *The Development of Champions* is an extensive and detailed book for coaches, covering all competitive aspects of the game. It includes some short stories and anecdotes from personal coaching experiences to illustrate some of the problems that can occur in teaching and coaching.

Parents can use this book to either assist their children with coaching or use it as a reference or handbook in solving many issues that arise in the development of tennis players. It will provide parents with firsthand knowledge of the many issues that coaches and players deal with and how to solve them.

Martin van Daalen

Sofya Vinogradova, Pearl Navratik, Sammy Nieder

Martin van Daalen

2—COACHING CHAMPIONS

The Definition of a Tennis Champion

"A person who has defeated all opponents in a competition or has shown significant results in a series of events over time."

In the game of tennis, there are many champions. When playing competitions, we can win a local event as a junior or as an adult, but there are many different levels to follow to succeed as a champion. Rankings at each level or age group can also be a way to define a champion. As players, you can move up from local, state, and regional events to national events; and as juniors, you can also advance in the different age groups (twelve, fourteen, sixteen, eighteen). In college, you can advance in positions on your team then to being successful in regional events or in the NCAA final tournament. In international junior and pro events, there are several levels to progress, which all lead to major Grand Slam events. Each level provides champions, and each step requires more skills to advance. Below is the list that shows the progression of levels in the US and in international events:

1. Local (level 9–6, in 2021 this will change to 7-6)
2. State (level 5–3)
3. Regional/National (level 3–1)
4. ITF Juniors (Levels 5–1, B3, B1, A)
5. ITF Juniors Grand Slam events
6. College US (NCAA—D1, D2, D3, NAIA, NJCAA)
7. ITF Pro Future Events (10K–15K)
8. ITF Pro Challenger events (25K–100K)
9. ATP/WTA events (250, 500, 1000)
10. ATP/WTA Grand Slams (US Open, Wimbledon, French Open, and Australian Open)

As you can see, there are many levels to go through to become a top player. But that does not mean you can't become a champion in your own right. Everyone has their own skill and talent level that can make them excel to their top performance. To reach your goals, you have to give it your 100-percent effort and see how far you can go. At the same time, provide yourself with the proper opportunities to succeed.

Developing a Champion

There are many pathways to take to develop a champion. Some of these champions are natural talents of the game, with a good understanding of how to execute their strokes with ease and how to use them strategically. But then there are also examples of hard workers who have used their energy and persistence to learn the game and become successful in their own right. Some players become a champion early as a junior. Whereas for others, it might take a while, and they don't mature until college or right after when they play on the tour. So what are the fundamental components that make them succeed?

1. **Developing good fundamentals of the strokes and footwork**
   Having smooth and efficient strokes and footwork will greatly increase the chance to develop as a player. Sound fundamentals are easier to execute and repeat with automation to greatly increase consistency and confidence. This in turn will increase the execution under pressure to perform in competitive match situations. The simple, rotational, and continuous execution of the strokes is more efficient than mechanical strokes with hitches and/or stops in the motion. The rotational (oval shaped) and continuous motions can use the gravitational force to accelerate the racket head from the top of the backswing. The momentum of the racket and the drop of the arm and racket into the forward action toward the contact point enhances racket head speed and uses less energy. Lesser energy relaxes the arm and grip pressure needed to produce the stroke to increase feel and coordination to control the ball. If you consider how many strokes are hit over the course of a match (average of two hundred to

five hundred strokes over a two-to-three-set match), you can imagine that this will influence not only consistency but also efficiency and stamina of a player. Over the long term, it also can prevent injuries. The proper and smooth footwork of a player can also be of great influence to greater consistency and efficiency in execution of the strokes. You can observe this in how well players position themselves behind the ball before each stroke in a timely and balanced fashion.

2. **Having an experienced developmental coach and mentor**
   Finding an experienced developmental coach or mentor is not an easy task. In a study done by the USTA, it was estimated that 60 percent of all young tennis players in the US are coached by their parents. Having an experienced coach, with knowledge of developing players, will greatly increase your chances to succeed in competition. This person should be someone with an interest in developing juniors to advanced players and who has a proven track record in doing so. As a parent or player, you need to do your homework. You need to investigate their background, experience, results, and demeanor as a coach. These factors become important to find the coach who fits your character traits and whom you respect not only as a coach but also as a person. Ex-players have the experience on how to play themselves but don't necessarily possess the coaching and development skills (or patience) to pass their experiences on to promising students. To develop a champion, you need more advanced skills as a coach:

   - a playing background that provides insight in what it takes to become a player
   - a professional coaching education for high-performance players
   - a trained professional with a passion to gain knowledge and experience of developmental progressions of coaching, tournament scheduling, and advanced training methods
   - an understanding of child psychology and physical development
   - a person who promotes good character and values in his players
   - a coach who takes the time to watch his player compete in tournaments

- a compassionate and patient person who mentors a player to be successful

All these factors combined should make it clear that as a parent, you cannot do this job unless you are a high-performance coach yourself. And even then, it still might be ill-advised if there are too many emotions involved.

3. **Having a good training environment**
   The training environment is set by the coaches and managers who are responsible for the programming at your facility. They can set the stage to create a pleasant training atmosphere that stimulates the learning and developmental process and makes it comfortable and fun for students and parents alike. So how do you create this particular environment in your facility and programs?

   - employ experienced developmental coaches with a passion for coaching
   - employ friendly and knowledgeable office staff
   - be strict on discipline and rules during training but also make it fun
   - have a good mix of training, games, fitness, and match play in practice
   - have developmental plans for all your players and discuss it with all involved
   - create a social environment around the group so they feel like a team
   - go to tournaments or road trips together
   - have other social events together at your facility (club matches)

   When you do all these things in your facility, the staff, members, kids, and parents will feel part of a group that treats everyone with kindness, compassion, and respect to create a pleasant and competitive environment.

4. Continuity of coaching

This is an important factor in the development process. Having one voice and method can greatly help the progress and confidence of a player—especially when working with advanced players in the age groups ten to sixteen (as juniors) and sixteen to twenty-one (as transitional players). In the first stage (ten to sixteen), you are trying to develop all the fundamentals in technical, tactical, physical, and mental aspects of competition. Without mastering this first stage, there is little chance to move on to the second stage. In the second stage (sixteen to twenty-one), you are developing national and international players who are transitioning to college or pro events. This last group is the most difficult to manage, and this is where most mistakes are made. Too many changes at this stage destroy confidence in a player's ability to play. Parents need to consider this before they decide to coach their own child. How long can you fulfill this role? And is it the right choice for your child? Many players change coaches if they, or their parents, see other players be successful with another coach. Especially in tennis, the grass seems to be greener on the other side. Making a change in coaching makes you lose time in development more often and is not recommended. If a new coach starts changing the technique of a player, a loss of confidence is most likely going to occur. With every major change in your strokes, you should count on a loss of at least six months to a year. This is even more the case with older players. The longer a player has been trained to hit the ball a particular way, the longer it takes to change anything. The reason for this phenomenon is the muscle memory that assists in automated motions.

Changes in strokes should only be considered if the current stroke will hamper the player's development and if players themselves are adamant in making the change. In the development of every player, there is a certain plateau where they stagnate for a while before improving again. This is true for virtually every player and can be deceiving to players and parents in thinking they are not making any progress. Only make changes in coaching when you feel the coach has reached their plateau in what they can teach you or when the relationship is breaking down.

5. **Quality of play in practices and matches**

    In order to develop champions, it is crucial to have quality and intensity in your practice sessions. The quality of play is the level of execution of strokes, strategy, physical execution, and mental attitude. The intensity is the level of effort applied in practices and matches. They are both imperative to the development of high-performance players in order to succeed at a national, international, or elite level of play. Coaches can improve intensity by making it clear how fast a drill or exercise needs to be executed by using a grade scale from 1 to 10, 10 being the highest level. In the beginning, you can ask the player if they know at what level of intensity they are in and correct them if they are over- or understating these levels. Very soon, they will learn how to use this in match play to defeat their opponents on intensity alone. The quality can be improved by using video. Players can receive good feedback on their execution and make corrections accordingly. Sometimes you can have them perform in front of their peers as an example. You will see how much more they try to execute with more quality (to impress their peers), and others will follow that example more willingly with more energy and excellence.

6. **Make a developmental plan and proper tournament schedule**

    Once a player becomes more advanced and is playing an extensive tournament schedule, it is time to make a developmental plan. The plan is an outline on how to develop their game to fit their style of play from a technical, tactical, mental, and conditional aspect. This plan needs to be a guideline for the training and tournament schedules. It should contain detail on when to play, when to train, and most importantly, when to rest! The plan needs to be made together with the player, coach(es), and parents. Make it simple and realistic to its purpose and stick to it! Make sure everyone fully agrees to the plan and has had ample input. Usually, the simple and original plans are the best for everyone.

7. **Becoming a student of the game**

    In order to learn how to play the game, you have to study all aspects of the game. You can do this by studying other players and matches to learn about the execution of strokes, strategies, shot choices, patterns, different footwork usages, and strengths and weaknesses of players and how they are exploited. This is where a logbook can be instrumental to make notes on your training, matches, and strategies and the strengths and weaknesses of your opponents for future reference. Reading books and tennis articles and discussing matches with your coach are other ways to increase your knowledge and become a student of the game.

8. **Commitment, passion, and sacrifices**

    Becoming a high-performance competitor in tournaments requires a very high commitment in training and matches to be successful. Players need to be fully engaged and must understand the process of development and longevity of the learning process. This is needed to gain the skills and experience necessary to reach their goals. It takes passion for the sport and great character to become a champion. You have to love the training and hard work it takes to make improvements in small strides (sometimes you don't improve for a while until you master the skill). Amounts of improvements can vary over time and are not always visible. Players can reach a plateau before making another jump in skills and experience before the results are clearly visible. The sacrifices in the tennis sport are not only great on players but also on family members. Becoming a high-performance player takes time and money. You need time to train several times a week for several years and time in playing many tournaments to move yourself up the rankings to get into national and international events. Parents and players are spending most of their free time after school and during weekends and vacations at the training facilities and tournament sites. This can be a lot of added stress on the family in general and on relationships if the main goal is results instead of the improvements and the pleasurable aspects of the game. Also, the financial aspect plays a large role in developing a top player. It is quite expensive to train in a program several days a week with possible private lessons as well. And then you have the cost of travel, entry fees, and coaching. All in all, there's a need for large commitment from all involved.

9. **Having a financial understanding to develop a champion**
    Developing a high-performance tennis player is very costly. Not only in the cost of training with group and private training but also the travel expenses of the sectional, national, or international tournament schedule (this might also be one of the reasons why many parents in the US are coaching their own child). Just playing in the sectional events can be expensive. If the goal is to reach the top of the national rankings in each age group, the costs are much higher. Below is an example of the total yearly cost for an average high-performance junior player at a sectional level:

*   Training   Group training (three times a week,
                   forty weeks) $ 5,000
                   Private training (one time a week,
                   forty weeks) $ 3,000
*   Tournaments Travel to events (sectional and national) $ 8,000
                   Coaching at events $ 8,000
                                           Total $24,000

To make calculations for a transitional player and pro player starting on the tour, the numbers are different from juniors since more training, coaching, and traveling are involved. See an estimate of the cost below:

*   Training   Private training (six days a week,
                   twenty weeks) $20,000
                   Fitness training (three days a week,
                   twenty weeks) $ 5,000

*   Tournaments Travel to events (twenty-five events) $30,000
                   Coaching $25,000
                                           Total $80,000

Martin van Daalen

As you can see, becoming a tennis champion is an expensive venture. Even as a top junior in the US, it takes about $24,000 in order to play the sectional and national events. As a transitional or starting pro player, these costs only go up. There are some advantages if you are a top player in your age group with financial aid from the federations and sometimes even from your section.

10. Enjoying the journey

Learning the game of tennis and excelling to become a high-performance player can be a very enjoyable experience if you allow it to be! Having fun along the way and taking the time to enjoy your accomplishments are very important factors. Too often, elite players can get caught up in a quest for money or to become famous. And granted, it is not easy to stay grounded when you become a champion and you get so much attention from all around you. Especially as tennis players, we get spoiled once we get to travel to national and international events. Seeing all the different sites and events is not there for everyone, so once you get to be in that fortunate position, try to respect it and enjoy every minute of it. Stay humble and stick to your routines and always take some time to explore your surroundings. This will keep you grounded and make you perform better with less stress. Make sure to make friends along the way with other players, coaches, and parents. This will enhance your comfort level in the tennis environment. With less drama and emotional baggage in relationships, you can compete more freely at a higher level. Your competitive life span will end at one point, so don't let the best moments pass you by and enjoy the journey!

3—ARE CHAMPIONS BORN, OR ARE THEY MADE?

There will always be talented tennis players who have obvious skills that seem to make everything they do look effortless, as if they were born to be champions. And those skills can vary from technical to tactical or physical and mental strengths. Most of the champions understand how to play the game, but the true legends of the game separate themselves from the rest with how much they are willing to sacrifice in their lifestyle, willing to train more with pleasure, and willing to work hard to improve. I have witnessed both situations of players who rose to the top through their talents and also of players who got there through their hard work, willpower, and dedication.

The examples of players who were born to be champions seem obvious when mentioning the likes of Pete Sampras, John McEnroe, Andre Agassi, Steffi Graf, Martina Navratilova, Chris Evert, Martina Hingis, Rafael Nadal, and Roger Federer. All these players struggled a little in the beginning but rose much quicker to the top once they reached their teenage years. These players all reached the top hundred in the ranking way earlier than most, and their domination in the tennis sport is now part of history. Their talent lies in the fact that they were able to handle the stress of competition and the global travel from an early age. There are also players who did not progress so fast and had to rely on their relentless efforts. Some of those who are at the top of the rankings at this moment are some of those I have watched up close as juniors. If you had asked me at that time if they were going to be number 1 in the world, I would have had to answer you with "I don't think so." But still they made it. I followed them over time and saw most of them struggle through many problems in their technical, physical, and mental development. You could see how they fixed one problematic issue after another and slowly improved over time. Novak Djokovic was a perfect example of this. As a junior, he was not a top-ranked player; but through hard work, dedication, and willpower, he pushed himself to excel in almost every area of his game. Andy Murray was another one of those examples. Andy made a radical decision as a teenager to move to Spain and train full-time on the red clay courts. His game improved, but his physical conditioning and intensity left much room for improvement. His speed and stamina were especially a problem in the beginning of his career. He hired a personal trainer, and the LTA (British federation) assisted in hiring a hard-nosed coach in Brad Gilbert to toughen him up. All these initiatives paid off in the end with Andy eventually winning the Wimbledon trophy and the Olympics!

Another player I watched up close was Alex (Sascha) Zverev. His family used to come to Saddlebrook every year to train over the winter break. I befriended them since Mischa, his older brother, competed often against Alex Kuznetsov (one of the players on the US team). Sasha worked very hard on his game and spent many hours on court in the morning and afternoon. While playing in the juniors, he wasn't overly talented with his strokes and mentally struggled to keep his emotions in check. But the hard work paid off, and he became one of the rising stars in today's game and is highly ranked on the ATP Tour. So you could say that it is possible to make a champion, but their work ethic has to match their passion and desire!

Roger Federer

Martin van Daalen

10 Things that Require Zero Talent

1. Being on time always for practice and matches
2. Having a good work ethic
3. The effort and intensity you display
4. Your body language
5. Your high energy levels
6. Your good attitude
7. Your passion in practice and play
8. Being coachable and open to instruction
9. Doing extra to improve
10. Being prepared always for practices and matches

Even if you are not talented, you can still succeed. You do need some basic skills like having decent hand-eye coordination and being generally athletic. You will only know you can do it if you try 100 percent. The list above does not require talent; it requires commonsense attitude and a 100 percent physical and mental commitment to the sport. I have seen many players become successful with these attributes. Do you want to be one of them?

Some players have the natural instincts and seem to be born champions. I was a witness to this when I was coaching one of my Dutch girls at Roland-Garros Junior French Open championships. Lara Bitter (eighteen at that time) was playing against a young Swiss girl (thirteen years of age) in the first round. Her name was Martina Hingis. It seemed impossible that such a young girl was already competing at that level. The match started, and you could see right away how she played without fear and moved freely around the court—sometimes taking balls out of the air and coming in to volley at unexpected moments. She struck the ball effortlessly and aimed the ball in the corners with great precision. Lara was obviously much stronger than Martina, and it looked like she would win the match by creating longer rallies and beating her physically. The first set went to Lara, and she was up in score even in the second set, when they stopped the match for darkness. I was impressed and already knew she would be a great player. When the match resumed the next day, the Swiss phenom showed all her talents. She was refreshed and played with even more energy. She didn't seem to have any fear or nerves being down and close to defeat. She played with a higher tempo and attacked Lara whenever she could. Martina ended up winning that match and went on to win the whole tournament. She became one of the youngest players to ever win this prestigious event. Not much later, she won several Grand Slam events and became number 1 in the world on the WTA rankings. She was a born champion! I got to know her personally when she came to train at Saddlebrook Resort, and I enjoyed our conversations. I will always remember that first-round match at Roland-Garros and realized later that I never told her I was there!

Martina Hingis

4—TEACHING AND COACHING

Whenever we are talking about instruction of competitive tennis players, there are two types of instruction: teaching and coaching. They are slightly different in the sense that teaching is generally viewed as the instruction to younger and less-experienced players. These students still have much to learn and need more general and continuous instruction on all topics. Coaching is viewed as more specific and generally for more advanced and experienced players. Teaching can be coaching, but coaching is not always teaching. Teaching is what you do when training at home and introducing new topics of instruction. Coaching is the training and guidance of competitive tennis players through all levels of play.

Teaching

The instruction of tennis players is very interesting but quite complicated. There are many topics of learning with technical, tactical, physical, and mental aspects. It can be very frustrating for students to even learn the basics and fundamentals of the game. It looks really easy on TV when you see top players perform; however, it is much more complicated once you start hitting the balls yourself. You find out very quickly how difficult it is to hit the ball cleanly and control the trajectory of the ball. Once you start moving around the court, you have to coordinate your footwork with your strokes. You have to find the proper contact points and timing of the stroke to achieve this with consistency. And then you haven't even started playing matches yet. Teaching all the strokes and strategies involved can be a very frustrating process for students. You will fail many times before you become somewhat proficient in this game. So teaching has to be fun for it to be stimulating to continue and to be productive. You can be most productive by creating a good mix of teaching, training, and having fun point play. But you can also challenge your students to compete in a different way—for example, you can ask them, Who can show me to do this stroke the best? You can also let them judge one another on their performance. Mixing in some point play to show how the stroke is used in a strategic way can be very instrumental to their tactical development. Be firm in your teaching by keeping the discipline during the training so everyone can get the most out of their lesson.

Coaching

Educating competitive tennis players in match situations and point construction is a different type of instruction. Competitive coaching is a much more diverse role. You can be a trainer in educating the player how to work out on- and off-court. You can be educating the player how to play the game and learn all about strategies and tactics—how to analyze opponents and devise a game plan. Provide feedback after the match and discuss what went well and what needs to improve. Give advice with a long-term training and tournament plan. You can be a possible mentor in guiding the player through their tennis career. Coaching should be a cooperative relationship, and the roles have to be clearly defined. You can be friendly with your students, but keeping a leadership and educational role is imperative to maintain discipline. It is difficult to get the most out of your students when you are not an inspiration and example to them. This means showing you can be understanding but firm and motivational at the same time.

Different Types of Coaching for Different Types of Students

If you can define the type of students you are working with, you will experience more success with a larger group of players. All students learn in a different way. Some learn from explaining the subject; others learn more from viewing an example. And then you also have the students who only learn by feel. In private lessons, it is easier to adjust your training to your students. In group lessons, this becomes more complicated, but it is not impossible. You can give individual tasks to students in a group. Understanding your students will help you communicate better, customize your training and developmental plans, and identify their strengths and weaknesses. The different types of students are the following:

Introvert Students - reserved, shy, soft-spoken, like to blend in
- prefer factual over abstract instruction
- prefer private instruction over group instruction
- like quieter environment
- instruction has to be calm and softer; ask for feedback

Extrovert Students - outspoken, center of attention, like to show off
- prefer energetic instruction in groups
- get easily bored with repetitious drills
- prefer to take initiative in matches instead of retrieving
- like short-attention type of drills
- instruction has to be direct and diverse in topics

Sensate Students - like to digest information before deciding
- hesitate on court by overthinking situations
- thrive on facts and information
- can lead to slower development in the beginning
- success is based on personal results and experience
- instruction with positive feedback and encouragement

Intuitive Students - trust their own instincts above any facts
- prefer to do first and then think about it
- prefer their imagination and creative shotmaking
- look for creative and individual game style
- instruction by showing examples instead of verbal

Martin van Daalen

Thinker Students - prefer business approach to tennis matches
- prefer private lessons versus group sessions
- prefer technical training over mental training
- calmer and less emotional in competition
- instruction with time for feedback and discussion

Feeler Students - enjoy group sessions with their own level and age
- put others' needs above their own
- prefer a good atmosphere on court
- struggle with cheating and gamesmanship
- instruction in organized and calm environment

Judging Students - change is uncomfortable and resisted
- prefer to focus on one subject at a time
- don't like multitasking
- like to master subjects before moving to the next one
- prefer orderly and planned sessions
- like to postpone competition until ready
- instruction has to be organized and structured

Perceptive Students - open to discussion and abstract subjects
- easily adapt to changing situations
- need goals and deadlines to work hard
- take more time to develop mental toughness
- instruction needs to be plan oriented with feedback

Instructing your players by how they perceive the information is important for their development. So instructing them in a personal and individual manner that fits their personality and character has much more impact on their progress. The way their brain operates is important knowledge for coaches to know how their students take in information. Not every player can be set in one of the categories above; it can also be a combination of personalities. Keep this in mind when coaching your players to future successes.

Qualities Coaches Look to Improve in Their Students

1. Athletes who lead by example
2. Athletes who want to improve
3. Students who are reliable
4. Students who show interest
5. Athletes who don't give up
6. Athletes who have passion
7. Students who set goals
8. Athletes who are willing to learn
9. Athletes who have desire
10. Students who learn from mistakes
11. Respect teammates, staff, officials
12. Athletes who listen well
13. Athletes who support their team
14. Students who are good role models
15. Athletes who study the game
16. Students who work hard
17. Athletes who are coachable
18. Athletes who work well with others
19. Athletes who are dedicated
20. Athletes who are organized

As coaches, we should always strive to improve the qualities of our students. Not all your students will learn all these qualities, but the constant attention to detail will make an impact on their overall character.

5—DEVELOPMENTAL ISSUES OF TOURNAMENT PLAYERS

Competing in tournaments as a junior is much more complicated than people at first realize. The competitive tournament system is very complicated, and if you do not grow up as a tennis player, you can make many errors in the beginning. Learning all the different types of progressions in playing red ball, orange ball, green dot ball, and regular yellow ball all have different scoring systems and racket and court sizes. Understanding how you gradate from one competition to the next can be very confusing. Moving up the rankings and going from a district player to a sectional and/or national player takes time and requires traveling greater distances. When looking at a successful player on TV, we underestimate what they went through as a young player—how many sacrifices they made to make it to that point. As an outsider, you only see the glorious results but not the blood, sweat, and tears it took. It is comparable to an iceberg floating in the ocean. You only see the small tip of the iceberg; the rest is hidden from view underwater.

Playing competitive tennis takes a lot of passion, desire, and perseverance to reach an advanced level of play. There are the early mornings in getting ready for your first match, the long hot matches in the burning sun, and the late nights when you finally finish—to start the whole process again the following day. Players have to deal with many disappointments when they first start. They are not physically conditioned; and they often don't understand how to play tactically, are not confident yet, and lose more matches than they win. Staying positive and being encouraging is important for their progress and improvement, which lead to success.

Player Development

The development of players commences from the time they get started as beginners. The basic technical and tactical skills they learn as a novice player can largely shape the results later on as a tournament player. Having smooth and natural strokes helps to play more efficiently, and having a basic understanding of strategy assists players in knowing how to combat their opponents by avoiding their strengths and exploiting their weaknesses. We call these the fundamentals of the game. Below you can find some specifics on junior development:

1. **The Fundamentals of the Game**

   At any level of play, the fundamentals of the game are important skills to obtain and to maintain throughout your tennis career. We are talking about grips, technical strokes execution, footwork, basic strategy, mental attitude, and specific physical skills for tennis. If the fundamentals are not so solid in performance, you will definitely see the results later on in the limitations of the player to hit certain shots properly or be limited in their movement. This affects the shot choices and strategies a player has at their disposal, and they could have a disadvantage in playing points or competing in tournaments (all depending on the level of competition of course). Fundamentals are crucial to the development of champions and should be prioritized and maintained at all times.

2. **Consistency**

   You have to create automated techniques in order to hit the balls with any consistency. This takes many years of training the strokes the same way concerning footwork, setup of the backswing, contact point, and follow-through. When this is trained in an identical repetitive fashion, the muscles start to remember how to perform the motions, and strokes become a reflex action rather than a prethought action. Without consistency, there is very little chance to develop strategies and tactics because the rallies are not long enough to develop patterns to create pressure on the weaknesses of the opponent. Every player has a shot tolerance at which point they start to produce unforced errors. This can be due to physical endurance but can also be patience or nervousness when the rally extends to more exchanges back and forth. Without consistency, you will probably never find out what that magical number is when your opponent starts missing. Consistency is the main objective and strategy to winning matches.

3. **Timing and Coordination**

The timing and racket angle of the contact point determines the height, spin, and direction of the ball and is mostly a matter of rhythm, coordination, and memory of prior experience of contact points over time. Coordination and timing of the ball is best trained when hitting with 60 percent or less of your maximum power. Staying relaxed when accelerating the racket head is more important than most players realize. You can explain this best to players by asking them about their grip pressure. You should not grip the racket tighter than 3 or 4 on the scale of 10. Most juniors do the opposite; they hit the ball as hard as they can, grip it too tight, and end up losing control of the ball and adversely influence coordination, rhythm, contact points, and consistency.

4. **Speed**

Speed is defined by how fast the movement is performed within a certain time frame. Intensity is defined by the amount of energy used in performing the action with power, speed, and tempo. With a tennis court having the same constant dimension, it is possible to train the players to cover specific distances faster. Speed is made up of several components that determine how fast a player can move. They can be trained separately or in combination with one another. Some players may not be able to attain a high quality in every type of speed, but they can all be trained to a certain degree. There are several racket head speed drills you can do with your students. I illustrate some of them as examples below:

• The simplest method in training racket head speed is by using a foam ball. In order to hit the ball faster and use more spin, they will need to increase the speed of the swing and therefore the racket head speed.

- Playing the ball with more spin in general increases the racket head speed. So hitting balls in the service box will increase the speed on the racket dramatically. If you have a player or coach who can play half volleys back to these shots, then even better. You can do the opposite by having players hit winning shots with spin in the corners from the service line.
- Another way is to have players play against one or two net players. The ball comes back twice as fast and will not only increase racket head speed but also increase the intensity of play.

The movement and speed training of tennis players is one of the most important parts of the fitness routine. Weight training alone, although very important to improve power, will not make you a better mover on the court. The weight training is the basis to prevent injuries and to improve speed of movement of the legs, the hips, the trunk area, the shoulders, and the arms (preferably in that order). Players need to use the power from the ground up (kinetic chain) to produce power rather than try to muscle with the shoulders and the arms. This is why movement and speed training is so important. The speed training helps to get there on time and hit the ball with control; and the movement training helps to set up, recover, and change direction with ease. There are a few factors that will positively influence the movement and speed training for tennis:

- make the movement and speed training exercises tennis-specific
- time them to monitor and stimulate progression
- use the racket as much as possible for improving balance

There are some tennis-specific movements and speed tests you can perform to provide feedback to students. This feedback is important for students to gauge improvements. It will not only provide a continuous stimulating effect for players to keep improving but will also give them goals to work for. Goals will set a target to work toward, and testing the tennis-specific exercises regularly shows the progressions made over time.

Martin van Daalen

5. Intensity of Performance

This is a heavily underrated topic that changes the dynamic and outcome in tennis matches quite dramatically. Intensity is not only physical but also mental. The intensity is defined by the speed, power, concentration, stamina, tenacity, and aggression of the player in training and point play. You can imagine that the level of intensity will influence the quality of training and increase the pressure on opponents in match play. The level of intensity will determine the level of improvement in practice and development, but it also has a large impact on the level of play in competition. To become a champion, it is imperative to learn how and when to increase the intensity without forcing the situation and creating unforced errors.

6. Strategy

Teaching students a strategy during point and match play gives them an advantage over other junior players who are playing solely on feel. There are several components to strategy:

- You need to be able to analyze the strengths and weaknesses of your opponent.
- You need a basic game plan to start the point with structure.
- You need to recognize patterns of play and know how to use them to your advantage.
- You need an understanding of shot choices and how and when to use them.
- You need to understand scoreboard pressure by applying pressure at specific times in the game or set.

Analytics

Recognizing the strengths and weaknesses of your opponent is one of the key components of strategy. It is like reading a book and recognizing the meaning of the word in an instance.

Basic Strategy

A basic strategy, or battle plan, means understanding how to start points with high percentage patterns and shot choices from both sides of the net. Either serving or returning, players need to have a plan and method of play.

7. Emotional Control

One of the more difficult things to learn is emotional control during competition and tournaments. Everyone gets nervous before a tournament or a match. Some of it is a healthy stimulation of competitive anticipation, but it can also be fear of losing, which can heavily influence the performance. Players will often feel their body freeze and feel it slow down. Others will overhit their strokes and lose coordination in an effort to compensate. Learning how to stay calm and to enjoy the competition is the key to controlling your emotions. Visualization and extra physical exercise before the match can be very helpful.

When I was coaching Mischa Zverev in Miami, leading up to the Australian Open, we would go and watch his younger brother, Sascha (thirteen at that time), play in the Junior Orange Bowl. He was struggling with his emotions in a bad way. He would get upset every time he would miss a ball. He would hit his racket and scream in anger. It was very unproductive, and he would play much longer matches than necessary. His parents were at their wits' end and asked me if I could help. I would talk to Sascha after he split sets and try to calm him down, but I must admit, I was not so successful. So I had to try another approach. I said, "If you promise to stay calm during the match, I will let you train together with us next time." I was not sure this would work, but I did know that he had been asking me before. He seemed to calm down and won his match. After the match, we discussed this some more and gave him some tips on how to stay calm and to focus on the next point. He ended up going all the way to the finals and lost to a Korean player. Sascha went on to win many events in junior ITF and pro events and is a highly ranked player on the ATP Tour.

When he was fifteen, I saw him at the place he was training in Tampa. The first words out of his mouth were "You owe me some training sessions." Obviously, he had not forgotten my promise!

**The Lotto Team from Popeye Gold Star in Amsterdam
Training weeks in Saddlebrook (1997)**

8. Training Situation

The training situation is one of the most complicated in player development. It is not easy to find a top-notch development center that will cater to all your needs as a developing player. There are many training facilities and academies that don't necessarily have development as their first priority. Some of the things to look for in development training centers are these:

- The coaches should be proficient in their own playing skills and must be experienced in developing players, not just coaching.
- You should look for a mentor/coach who will take responsibility for your development and coaching at events.

- There should be a good ratio from coach to student (1:4) in order to get enough playtime and instruction for each player.
- Preferably, there should be a separate conditioning coach who will work on the physical development off and on court (depending on age).
- Every tournament player should receive assistance in their tournament schedule so they can better plan their training schedule.
- Private training from your assigned coach will help you develop much quicker and enhance your focus on topics of improvement.
- The price of the training should be reasonable in accordance with the level of competition the student is attending.

In general, you can recognize good development centers by the number of players they are developing on a regular basis. But don't be shy to ask around and get information from players and parents on the type of training center and programs they provide. You will find out fast enough if students are enjoying the instruction and how much they respect the coaches. Having experienced coaches who have done the development many times before with success is a good indicator.

9. **Education**

In observing junior tennis at the moment, more parents are making the decision to homeschool their kids. And in this case, I am talking about kids playing at the higher echelon of competition in sectional and national tournaments. Education for serious competitive tennis players is important to have a chance on a scholarship in college. Being homeschooled does not disqualify you for a scholarship, but it also does not help you since college coaches know that it is difficult for these students to attend classes again. Most homeschooled kids struggle with the number of classes they have to follow and the assignments that come along with these. Then there is also the question of why you would homeschool at a young age when there is no necessity to do so. Unless you need to travel internationally, there is no need to change your education to homeschooling.

As a national player, you can still participate in all the national tournaments since they are played mainly in the weekend or during vacations. International Tennis Federation (ITF) tournaments are different since they require the whole week of play. Also, from a training standpoint, players don't really mature physically enough until fifteen to sixteen years of age to warrant training twice a day. Most players have not reached puberty before this point and won't have the hormonal release to take advantage of growth and body (muscle) building. After-school training sessions can be just as valuable and effective and can avoid overtraining and burnout at an early stage of their tennis career. If results in international events improve, you can always make a choice to go that direction and homeschool from that point forward. At least you will have given your child a decent chance to be successful at tennis and at getting a college degree.

10. Junior Competition

Playing junior tennis tournaments is different from any other sport. The matches can last between 1.5 and 2.5 hours, and there are often multiple matches each day. Officially, the tournament can have you play two singles and a doubles match each day (even two singles and two doubles if the doubles matches are one-set matches each). In the beginning, the matches are not so physical yet; but as soon as you reach the sectional level, the matches are very competitive. The length and speed of the rallies increase, and endurance becomes a larger factor—especially when playing multiple matches each day and having to perform at a high level multiple days in a row. The experience teaches you how to prepare for the tournaments and becomes a routine after a while. Players learn how long it takes to travel to the event, how long they need to plan for their warm-up, how to scout their opponents, how to form a game plan and strategy, and how to get ready for their next match. The more tournaments you play, the more you will gain confidence on how to organize your day. These are some of the details most juniors forget:

1. Towel
2. Extra clothing
3. Warm-up or jacket
4. Sports tape and under wrap tape (for blisters)
5. Hats or cap
6. Sunscreen
7. Balls for warm-up
8. Grips rewrap
9. Drinks (electrolytes for recovery)
10. Snack for during play
11. Lunch

The towel is very important to give players an opportunity to pace themselves in between points and to calm their nerves to think about what game plan to use on the next point. Extra clothing can help you to shower and feel fresh again after a tough match. It clears your mind and lifts your spirit for the next match. A jacket and warm-up pants also can come in handy when eating lunch after in an air-conditioned area. Sports drinks can help you sustain your hydration and endurance throughout the match and make sure you don't lose performance during long hot matches. Snacks during matches can assist in keeping your blood sugar up to fuel your energy in long rallies and long matches. Also, it will help you with your recovery after the match, as you are fueling your body during match play.

12. Coaching

Competing in junior events is difficult enough as an inexperienced player, so it is up to parents and coaches to give the player enough space to relax before, after, and in between matches. In an effort to help them, we end up cheering too much, talking too much about their game, giving too much feedback/information to focus on, and making them nervous and anxious in the process. So how should we coach players?

Cheering and clapping for your player can be good as long as it does not distract them too much. In many cases, it takes their focus and concentration off the court to the side of the court. You will see them start to look into the eyes of the cheerleaders and often become desperate when things don't go their way. Since the focus is not on the court, they expect to get the answers from the sideline instead of seeking for the solution themselves. Coaches and parents have to learn how to be supportive without distracting the player. Don't say too much, don't clap too loud or overly long, and make encouraging remarks only!

Talking too much to a player, positively or negatively, can be very distracting to a player's performance. If the comments are positive first, it is easier to bring up comments about topics that need improvements. Limit the amount of the comments even though you have more information to share. Prioritize feedback on the most important topics instead of giving too much information. Players will not remember more than two things anyway once they get back on the court.

Before the match, the directions on how they should play their match should be short and concise. The longer the conversation, the more confused a player will be. You can have them repeat it to make sure they understood the plan.

In between or after matches, give some feedback on what went well first before commenting on the aspects of their game that did not go so well. It is so easy to directly focus on the bad aspects of the match. Wait a little after the match to give them a chance to relax and shower before getting into details right away. Ask the player first about what they thought of their performance before offering advice. Getting their feedback first will give you a good indication of their feelings and gives you, as a parent or coach, a good indication of where their reality is concerning what actually happened. After their comments, you can give a short recap. Remember to keep it positive but realistic and finish with some uplifting comments for the next match. Once you have given your info, give them some space or talk about something else rather than keep on talking about the same topic. After a tough match, not every player wants to talk nonstop. Some find a quiet spot or like to go and talk to their friends. This part is an important time for them to relax or have lunch until it is time to warm up again. Teaching your students to cool down after competition can be very helpful for their recovery. It helps them to relax and to get rid of any bad nerves or anxiety. If you are not an experienced coach, I would advise you to do less rather than more in communicating with the players. You can still be very encouraging and helpful in organizing their day of competition without interfering too much with their focus and concentration and letting them enjoy the experience of the event.

I was coaching Timothy Neilly (fifteen years old) at an ITF event in Boca Raton, Florida. He was doing well and excited to play, but he still needed to gain more confidence at this level. He came to me before his match and admitted to me that he was quite nervous. "Why are you nervous?" I asked him. "Well, I was watching my opponent play, and he is very aggressive," he replied. "What do you mean by aggressive?" I asked. "He is playing over there," he mentioned. "Come and see for yourself." So we walked over to the match where his opponent was playing in the previous round. When we got there, I understood what he meant. Not only did the boy play very aggressively but he was also very aggressive in his demeanor. He would call out "*Vamos*" on every point won and shake his fist at the opponent (even though this is actually against the rules). After watching this for a little while, I said to him, "OK, this is what I want you to do. When you play with him, I want you to do exactly the same thing. You say '*Vamos*' every time you win a point." "Really," he said, "that's what you want me to do?" "Absolutely," I confirmed. As he played his match, he followed my instructions exactly as discussed. He would call out "Vamos" loudly after every point won and shake his fist at me as a victory salute. His opponent looked surprised at first. But then he looked frustratingly and shockingly at his coach. After that, he started making comments in anger at his coach. And it did not last long before he had completely lost confidence in his game. Timothy won the match and came smiling off the court.

When players use excessive language and cheers to encourage themselves, they are doing this because they have low confidence and self-esteem. Just knowing this should help players to break down their opponents. One method is to copy their method, which will become more distracting to them than to you. Find a way to take charge of the situation by finding something to distract your negative thoughts and turn it into a positive thought or action. You will feel empowered and gain confidence in your game. Tim later won the Orange Bowl 18 and is now coaching players at a club in Boca Raton, Florida. We still see each other at junior events.

Confidence and Character Building

One of the most important aspects of competition is confidence and the character needed to execute. It is almost impossible to build confidence without building the character of a player first. The core values and sportsmanship have to be prioritized from the start before confidence will improve. Players have to become proud of their own accomplishments and hard work to improve their game. Results will always follow those who have passion and drive to excel in every aspect of the game. The mental aspects can be the last to develop as juniors mature, and they rarely happen at the same time. Coaches, mentors, and parents can play an important role to assist in developing confidence and character. Coaches and mentors can do this with positive feedback and encouraging remarks. Parents can do this with the education they provide at home (core values) and not being too critical with their child's performance. Making the added comments is a common thread in the tennis culture. It seems a good idea to help the coach by copying a comment you heard the coach say, but you might find the opposite effect. Players take comments about their game very differently from a parent than from a coach. You actually will undermine their confidence and hurt their self-worth.

Ranking Progression

If your goal is to become a competitive sectional, national, or international player, you have to understand how those rankings work and how to play certain events to get ahead. If you solely play for your ranking, your game could suffer since your thoughts and focus will be constantly on results instead of improvements. If your focus is on getting better and improving your technical, tactical, physical, and mental skills, results will follow automatically. But it helps to have a good understanding of how the rankings work so you know what tournaments to schedule. In the beginning, when playing only sectional events, it is fairly easy. You can choose appropriate age and level tournaments close by and compete locally. As you progress in the ranking, it will give you access to higher-level sectionals with participation from the best players in the district or state. Those tournaments in turn give you access to play regional or national events. ITF junior events are international junior events. They are played all over the world, and the age group is thirteen through eighteen.

Junior Opportunities

There are several opportunities available for junior players to play international tennis or to be part of a sectional or national team. These opportunities arise when you reach the top of your age group in the section or nation. You could get invited to be part of the team in playing other sections or representing your country at international team events. They are valuable experiences to enhance your confidence and game in general.

College Tennis or Pro Tennis

The game of tennis is constantly evolving and progressing, and it has become increasingly more difficult to break into pro tennis and even more difficult to become an elite player in the top 100 ranking. Unless you make it to this group of players, it is virtually impossible to have a long-term career and to properly support yourself financially to afford the cost of travel, coaching, hotels, and such. But that is not even the hard part of this rise to the top. Players will often experience three to five years of international travel and hardly have any income from prize money or sponsors. It used to be easier for juniors to get sponsored or to sign with a management company, but those golden years are over. Looking at today's international rankings, you will find many top players who first attended college before starting their pro career. This is no coincidence. It has a lot to do with the increasing difficulty of breaking into the top ranks and the increasing years and finances it takes to achieve this. So unless you are an early developer and reach the top echelon of pro tennis as a teenager (top 350–200 WTA or ATP), it makes total sense to plan to go to college for a few years to take advantage of the financial support, competitive system, and training they can provide. Below are some of the advantages that college tennis provides:

- The top colleges provide great programs for aspiring pro players to compete and train for little or no cost of their own and obtain a college degree in the process.
- Most of the top colleges produce pro players and assist them with coaching and expenses in traveling to pro events and improving their rankings.
- It is possible to attend college for one or more years and start your pro career when your ranking and/or results are significant enough. When your pro career is over, you are able to pick up your studies where you left off and finish your degree on the same scholarship.
- The competitive schedule and physical program are especially very valuable for developing players. The competitive schedule in college is very taxing physically and provides much match experience. The physical training is a great benefit to players between ages of eighteen and twenty-two and contributes in a big way to their stamina and strength.

- In receiving a part or full scholarship, you are saving $200,000 to $400,000 in cost you otherwise would spend over the four years of education and training.

As you can see, the pros definitely outweigh the cons in this respect. There are very few players anymore who can make the jump early to the pro tour.

Transition to Pro Tennis

The transition from junior to pro tennis is a huge leap. Every step before this is a jump of one level at a time—one level for each age group, one level from sectional to national tournaments, and one level from national junior to international junior competition. However, the jump from junior tennis to pro tennis is comparable to taking a jump of three levels all at once. All of a sudden, juniors have to play with maturity and against players of all ages and strengths (and most of them are with much more experience). Unless you have some weapons that can neutralize your opponent, you just don't stand a chance—unless you play with another junior player in the same event who is also trying to break through to the pro ranks. So being successful on the pro tour requires players to be technically, tactically, physically, and mentally mature above their age. This is not an easy task for an eighteen- or nineteen-year-old. It requires a full-time dedication.

6—PROGRESSIONS OF COACHING

Not unlike going to school, tennis development has its own progressions of learning and coaching. You can divide it into five groups of coaching:

1. The fundamentals of the game (beginners and intermediate players)
2. The development of intermediate players (recreational and competitive)
3. The development of advanced players (sectional, national, and international)
4. Transitional and college players (junior pro and college players)
5. Pro players

Each level of coaching has an expertise that is specific to age, competency, and goals for the sport, with different levels of players and coaches. To give an example, you would not use a kindergarten teacher for a high school or college class. The purpose of each level is completely different in what you can expect from the students. The beginner classes are more geared toward the introduction to the game with fun and entertainment rather than tournaments and competitions. However, the competitive spirit is always a great way to get kids excited and is a method to elevate their intensity.

Progressions of Learning

At every level of teaching and coaching, it is advisable to have a learning progression. This needs to be organized in the method and drills that are used to teach every topic. To ensure the fastest learning curve and enhance confidence in your teaching, you should start with the easiest methods to execute the drills. Master each drill or skill with plenty of practice and in point play before moving on to the next competency level. Go from easy to more complicated executions and have multiple steps available that lead to continued success. Make sure to repeat these from time to time:

1. Easy drills to complex drills
2. Multiple steps of advancement/improvements
3. Master with point play in practice
4. Try it out in actual tournaments and analyze the performance
5. Repeat the exercises to enhance these particular skill

All drills and exercises should follow a technical guideline that has a progression of learning in the following order:

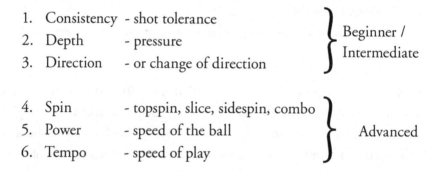

1. Consistency - shot tolerance
2. Depth - pressure
3. Direction - or change of direction

} Beginner / Intermediate

4. Spin - topspin, slice, sidespin, combo
5. Power - speed of the ball
6. Tempo - speed of play

} Advanced

The first three points, 1 through 3, are for beginners and intermediate level players. The points 4 through 6 are aspects and skills for advanced players. You can imagine that every new skill has to be practiced with consistency first before trying any of the other skills. The same goes for coaching at tournaments and team events; teach them to have consistency with their strokes and to know basic strategy first before going into more complicated strategies and patterns of play.

Basic Strategy

All players at any level need to know a basic strategy that gives them a plan to be better prepared and to rely on in difficult situations. Having a basic plan is better than having no organization in your strategy. It provides you with more confidence and the experience of having done it before. Eventually, this will lead to automated responses and reflexes that become very useful once the game speeds up, with less time available to think of every action. The basic strategy also provides a higher percentage play from repetitions and practice. Below is the basic strategy that should be learned from an early age:

1. Know the strengths and weaknesses of your opponent
2. Keep a high first-serve percentage (preferably 70 percent or above)
3. Hit the return to the middle of the court (preferably to the weakness of the opponent)
4. Play second/third ball to the weakness of the opponent
5. Accelerate to the open court to surprise the opponent
6. Attack the weakness again
7. Engineer the patterns of play to use your strongest shots as a weapon

Coaches should teach students this basic plan to increase their consistency in point play and tournaments. After this skill is mastered, it becomes clearer how to start points and play with margins and high-percentage play in pressure situations.

Strategy-wise, there is also a progression to learning that is consistent with the skill level of the player. These are some other factors that become important skills once the player reaches an advanced level of play:

- styles of play and how to play against them
- weapon development
- patterns of play
- shot choices
- tactical situations
- tactical positioning / anticipation
- percentage play
- analysis of opponents

Physical Progressions

Physically, players also need to be trained in progressions. You have to start simple and develop easy-to-learn skills before demanding more complicated skills. After the skills are practiced and have become more consistent, you can slowly increase the direction or change the direction with more spin and speed. Below are some physical progressions in order of difficulty:

1. Coordination
2. Balance
3. Flexibility

} Learning Skills

4. Endurance
5. Agility
6. Strength
7. Speed

} Practice / Competitive Skills

As you can see from this list, it makes sense to first practice the timing and rhythm with coordination, balance, and flexibility of the physical aspects before delving into agility, endurance, strength, and speed. Some examples of physical aspects and progressions of drills in two different levels of play can be seen below:

- Intermediate - consistency in making twenty-ball rally
  - consistency of three consecutive fifteen-ball rallies
  - alternating fore- and backhand twenty shots (up middle)
  - playing points after four shots down the middle

- Advanced - consistency of five consecutive twenty-ball rallies
  - alternating fore- and backhand thirty shots (crosscourt)
  - cross and down the middle drill (points)
  - cross and down the line drill (points)

As you can see in the examples above, the advancements are in sequence, from easy to more complex. There are multiple progressions possible with various drills and exercises. If you find progressions that work well for you and your students, you would be advised to document them for future use.

Mental Progressions

Just like the technical, tactical, and physical progressions, there are also mental aspects to progressions in every level of play. Some of those aspects are these:

- motivation
- focus and concentrations
- discipline in execution
- emotional control
- problem-solving
- character building

Motivation of a player is the drive they experience from the passion and love for the game and the willpower to succeed. Setting goals for themselves can enlarge their motivation through a pathway and direction with clear objectives in making steps forward toward their goals or prize.

Focus and concentration is the attention span to details of the game in order to execute them with greater precision over time. With matches lasting two or three hours, concentration and focus are necessary to be successful. These mental aspects need to be trained on a daily basis in practice and further developed through many competitive matches. The calmer the player is under pressure, the more they will be able to concentrate on the task at hand (ability to focus on strategy).

Discipline of execution is the restraint, control, and consistency a player shows in execution of footwork, strokes, and strategy. The amount of discipline in footwork and strokes influences the consistency of execution, while the discipline in strategy influences the pressure players can sustain on their opponents by consistently attacking their weaknesses without letting up.

Emotional control is the power and learned skills to stay calm under pressure. Players have to keep control over their emotions inwardly and outwardly so they can perform to their best ability under the most stressful situations. Every junior player goes through a development in learning the importance of emotional control in order to execute with more success. In the beginning, they might struggle with this. It takes a lot of training to master this aspect, but if you do finally obtain this skill, you realize how crucial it is to becoming a champion.

Problem-solving is an ongoing mental aptitude to become a champion. As a recreational player, it is not a critical skill; but for champions, it is crucial to solve a dilemma or crisis to turn a situation in your favor during a match. This could range from a tactical decision to win an important point, game, or set to dealing with a disagreement of a line call with an opponent or referee. How you handle yourself in these situations can determine the outcome in the end.

Character building is the development of a player's personality, moral fiber, spirit, disposition, and temperament. Many coaches in multiple sports consider this aspect the most important for the development of champions in their sport. This aspect takes the longest to develop and requires good parental supervision, experienced coaches, and a healthy training environment with good role models all throughout this process. The mental progression goes from easy to very complex skills and might be the most important to learn. They also drive the consistency of execution and discipline to perform under pressure. Think about the mental skills champions must possess to perform in large stadiums, in front of thousands of spectators, and the many changing situations and having interviews before and after competitions while maintaining a good attitude and composure. This takes time to learn and experience to perform well.

7—COMPETENCIES AND LEVELS

Coaches should know the skill sets of each player according to their level of development and age. When you know the technical, tactical, physical, and mental skill sets, you can easily determine the next progression of learning. If this is done correctly, progressions are made more easily and confidence will be increased. Below is an outline with all the skill sets in each level of play:

Beginner

Technical	Tactical	Physical	Mental
• fundamentals of the strokes • forehand, backhand, serve • basic footwork (split step, stepping in, recover with side steps)	• consistency • positioning • fundamental strategy • recovery	• endurance • coordination • basic movement skills	• focus on one topic • concentration • score-keeping

Intermediate Player

Technical	Tactical	Physical	Mental
• consistency in execution • forehand, backhand, serve, return, volley	• basic strategy • player analysis • open court and center pattern • defensive strategy	• footwork speed • arm speed • start, stop, change direction	• motivation • goal setting • match play setup and organization • discipline of execution

• short- and deep-ball footwork, sliding • topspin ground stroke	• serve to backhand and return to middle (neutralize)		

Advanced Junior

Technical	Tactical	Physical	Mental
• specialty shots and footwork • drop shot, overhead, lob, approach shot • spin, slice, top slice, and kick serve • weapon development • net game development	• patterns of play • shot choices • styles of play and tactical solutions • offensive and defensive tactics • tactical positioning • percentage tennis	• speed • power • flexibility • balance • agility • endurance	• focus on strategy and execution • problem-solving • emotional control • character building • travel

Transitional Player

Technical	Tactical	Physical	Mental
• weapon development • second-serve spin • absorbing and transitioning power	• risk management • anticipation to tactical situations • camouflage • put-away shots	• power development • speed endurance • flexibility • balance	• mental endurance • dealing with pro events and stadium-crowd settings

• efficiency of strokes and movements • tempo and rhythm changes	• approach shot tactics • playing against net player		• dealing with agents, interviews, etc. • managing travel • media training

Professional Player

Technical	Tactical	Physical	Mental
• consistency of execution • technical execution in patterns • technical execution of specialty shots • technical execution in pressure situations	• tactical analysis of opponent • discipline of tactical execution • pattern combinations • shot choices • point setup routines	• training on the road • injury prevention • speed training • flexibility (yoga) • massage	• stress management of stadium play at pro-level events • media training

In order to become a champion at every stage of the development, players should obtain the competencies or skills of each level to achieve a balanced and well-rounded game. The amount of skills needed in each level is quite substantial and makes the sport difficult to learn. As you go from being a sectional junior player to a transitional player, the skills become more physical, tactical, and mental.

From Junior to Pro

The most difficult level to obtain is the transitional level (in going from junior to pro events). Every step before is a gradual increase in skill level, whereas the step from international junior player to transitional player is much larger. Most players have great difficulty dealing with this phase when they try to make the jump to professional tennis too early. They are often not physically or mentally ready for this transition and fall back in performance and ranking. Having good supervision and guidance at this time is crucial to maintain or stabilize their position for the second year before moving on. This is also why so many make the decision to go to college for a while until the ranking dictates to make the jump to full-time tennis. Later in this book, we will address the aspects to consider when turning pro and how to go about this in different ways.

Junior Champions

Preparation

Developing future junior champions takes careful planning and longtime dedicated training and coaching at tournaments. Players and parents have to be guided and coached how to think and react to each new situation that arises, and there are many! In order to be more successful, I can list a few points that can assist you in their development:

1. **Prepare your future game by developing the fundamentals.** This means getting your basic techniques solid on all your strokes so that you can depend on them in critical and stressful situations. This can start early while you don't have the strength yet (ages eight to twelve). This is also a good time to learn the basic strategy and learn the discipline in executing it. This age is a good time to start working on a physical program to build stamina, coordination, flexibility, and balance that will stimulate the process once you are ready for strength and speed exercises (ages twelve to eighteen).

2. **Develop consistency in all aspects of the game.** This means training the coordination and muscle memory of the strokes and

footwork to enhance the confidence in striking the ball at the correct contact points with regularity (timing). But it also means the training of consistency in direction in finding the proper targets with a margin for error (large targets). And then there is the consistency in executing strategies and tactics during match play.

3. **Learn the different specialty shots with rotations to the ball.** As soon as the players have mastered the fundamentals, it is time teach them how to use topspin, slice, and sidespin to control the trajectory of the ball and to develop specialty shots in their game (ages eleven to eighteen). The spin also assists with keeping the ball in play when increasing the speed and in slowing it down when trying to hit an angle shot, a drop shot (or drop volley), or a lob.

4. **Play plenty of practice matches and tournaments.** Never avoid practice matches as they give you the experience needed to use your technical skills in a tactical situation. This is when you learn how to use the different strategies and tactics against different opponents. Choose opponents with diverse styles of play so you get trained on how to combat them. Play many tournaments to harden yourself in competition and in playing many matches in a row. Winning matches is good, but the end goal should be to win tournaments. This takes practice and patience. Be prepared to work hard and stay calm at all times because only then do you have a chance to reach your goal.

5. **Learn the patterns, percentage plays, and proper shot choices.** Strategies and tactics become more important as players progress. Learning the patterns of play will not only assist them in consistently applying pressure on their opponent but also in recognizing patterns used against them and anticipating future attacks. Percentage plays are strokes that have a larger margin of error in their targeting and have a great chance of success in neutralizing a tactical situation. Proper shot choices

are percentage plays that require a certain trajectory, speed, and spin to become effective in offensive, neutralizing, or defensive manner. These three tactical aspects take a lot of time to learn and will usually take the whole junior phase at different age levels to master.

6. **Develop your own style of play.** Your style of play has to develop over time when you grow into your body and become more aware of your strengths and weaknesses. As a player, you should try various game styles to see if they fit your technical, physical, and mental traits. Only then will you be able to determine what game style fits you best. And then you still have to practice it and develop it as a weapon against your opponents.

7. **Develop your weapons.** Every champion has to develop weapons in their game. These weapons can be the technical execution of a powerful forehand or serve, but it can also be the mental or physical attitude and energy performed on court in match play. All top players have many weapons they rely on. In some cases, they are so powerful that even if you see it coming, there is little you can do to defend yourself.

Sofya Vinogradova, Mikey Zoi, Sammy Nieder

Training

The training of juniors is different compared to transitional or professionals and should be gauged according to age and level of play. The differences lie in the topics to be trained, the duration of the training, and the intensity to be used. When you are training for too long or using topics that are not suitable for their age or level of play, you are just wasting time; and in some cases, you can even put their development backward.

The training of juniors should be a fun pastime and should be enjoyed by coaches, players, and parents alike. As a coach, it is important to know what players like. They like training to be tough and fun but also like it organized and structured. Players enjoy to be challenged and play any kind of games. You can do all those things and still get your objectives done by keeping a certain degree of discipline so the training runs smooth and never gets out of hand.

Training and Parents

Parents like to see the improvement of their children but should never become a disturbing factor to the training. When kids are very young (eight to ten), it can be helpful to have parents on court for private lessons; but after this age, they progress better without involvement of parents on court. In many cases, the kids progress better when parents are not watching at all since they feel less pressure to be judged. It is also not advisable to clap or make any comments (positively or negatively) on the performance during training. It is perceived by other students as bad form and creates resentment among the students and other parents. So as parents, if you want your kids to be successful, the golden rule is this: just observe, make no comments, be encouraging, do not be judgmental (leave that to the coaches), and stay off the court!

Training Content

The training content is instrumental for the progress and development of players; so a good mix of technical, tactical, physical, and mental aspects should be covered. The best way is to make a lesson plan for your groups and private lessons in covering the content that is suitable for their age and level of play. For example, you don't start teaching a kick serve to an eleven-year-old tournament player if their normal serve is still lacking technical consistency and they are still making many double faults. Especially with junior players, it is crucial to have a good progression in the lesson content. Making it simple in explanation and going from easy to more complex exercises will stimulate confidence and increase consistency in strokes and strategy.

Training Intensity

The intensity in the training is measured by the duration of the sessions each day or weekly and the energy and speed of the exercises. When junior players are still young and have a lower level of play, they have less sessions per day and in total in a week than when they are tournament players and older in age. You cannot train every player the same way or train every day with the same intensity. As coaches and parents, we like to see high intensity all the time; but unless you have done that yourself, you know that that is not always obtainable as a young junior. As players mature, they are able to reach a higher level of intensity, stamina, and energy output on a more regular basis. Nevertheless, it is advisable to limit the amount of training sessions in the middle and end of the week and before tournaments.

Level	Sessions	Duration	Match Play
Beginner	2–4 sessions per week	1–1.5 hours per session	2–3 sets every 2 weeks
Intermediate Junior	3–4 sessions per week	1.5 hours per session	2–4 sets per week
Advanced Junior	6–10 sessions per week	1.5–2 hours per session	2–4 sets per week
Transitional Player	10–12 sessions per week	1.5–2 hours per session	4–6 sets per week
Pro Player	10–12 sessions per week	1.5–3 hours per session	4–6 sets per week

Coaching Juniors at Different Ages and Levels

Coaching juniors to become champions at different age levels takes experience at progressions and knowledge of junior development and their skill requirements at each level and age. To do this well, you have to make a developmental plan for each player—understanding their strengths and weaknesses at each age and level of development. This might be different at ages for boys and girls as they have a different rate of development. You can divide them into the following stages of development:

1. Local (level 9–6)
2. State (level 5–3)
3. Regional (level 3)
4. National (level 3–1)
5. ITF Juniors (levels 5–1, B1, B2, A)
6. ITF Juniors "Grand Slam" events

There are local, state, and regional events in age groups from under twelve to under eighteen. With ITF events, you have to be thirteen years old in order to participate. In ITF events, there is only one age group ranging from thirteen to eighteen years of age.

Age-wise, you can distinguish the following age groups of development:

1. Eight to ten years old (beginner starting from red ball to green dot)
2. Eleven to thirteen years old (intermediate junior player)
3. Thirteen to sixteen years old (advanced junior player)
4. Fifteen to eighteen years old (high-performance junior player)
5. Seventeen to twenty-two years old (transitional player)
6. Sixteen years and Up (pro player)

Skill Requirements

The skill requirements are all a little different in the age groups. As juniors progress and improve, they gain in strength, speed, and skills and are able to take on more complex training subjects. The different levels all have specific skills to succeed at their own stage of development. Moving up to a higher stage requires players to learn and master new and more advanced skills. Not everyone will progress to the next level. This depends largely on the basic available skills and the drive and passion of the players to push themselves forward to excel. Below is a list of skill requirements by age groups:

Juniors (Ages Eight to Ten)

Technical	Tactical	Physical	Mental
• fundamentals of the strokes • forehand, backhand, serve • basic footwork (split step, stepping in, recover)	• consistency • positioning • fundamental strategy • recovery	• endurance • coordination • basic movement skills	• focus on one topic • concentration • score-keeping

- *Technical.* The focus of this age group should be on the basic fundamentals of the forehand, backhand, and serve. Coaches often are doing drills with beginners in introducing a baseline shot and approach shot and a volley or overhead. The reality is, they will never use it in competition for at least two years. So three of the four shots are useless to them in point or match play! That's a waste of their practice time (three-quarters of their time is used on shots they don't need yet). The basic footwork should be taught with stepping in toward the ball. This will enable them to pick up short-ball situations much easier. Don't teach beginners an open stance. It makes them lazy in their movement and hinders them from learning weight transfer and moving forward. They are not strong enough to do this motion correctly, and they won't learn the hip and shoulder rotation properly. Stepping in teaches them the proper distance to the ball.

- *Tactical.* Consistency is the most important skill to learn for a beginner. It provides them with the ability to keep the rally alive and apply pressure on the opponent. Consistency is a technical skill, but it is also a priority as a tactical skill. The only way a novice player understands the importance, necessity, and quality of consistency is to count the amount of times the student can make the ball bounce in a certain target area. In the beginning, that might be the whole court; but later on, this will change to half the court or even a certain area. The positioning of a player needs to be explained—where to stand when serving, returning, and in playing the point. It is quite different from singles to doubles play, and there are many factors that determine where to recover when rallying the ball back and forth (recovery). The fundamental strategy for beginners is to play as many balls back over the net and to find the weakness of your opponent (consistency, weakness). As a coach, you should always ask the students if they have figured out the weakness of the opponent. This also shifts their attention from themselves (and their possible inadequacies) to their opponent, looking across the net and starting to read their opponent and anticipating possible shot choices.

- *Physical.* The movements and footwork of beginners are not so sophisticated, and they are not fast or strong yet. It makes more sense to focus on coordination, endurance (longer rallies), and basic footwork. Young juniors need to learn to increase their endurance not only physically but also mentally if they want to prepare themselves for competition. The intensity of the movements is not high yet, but it can be improved with the introduction of games or point play (with some assistance from the coach).

- *Mental.* The attention span of beginners is quite short. Therefore, it is important to give them one topic to focus on and construct several games that all amount to the same goal of improvement: consistency of performance. When young players are focusing on winning, they can concentrate much better and are often more willing to exert themselves. This way, you can get many of the training aspects accomplished all at once. It also teaches them to keep score (often problematic at a younger age).

Intermediate Juniors (Ages Eleven to Thirteen)

Technical	Tactical	Physical	Mental
• consistency in execution • forehand, backhand, serve, return, volley, overhead • short- and deep-ball footwork, sliding • topspin ground stroke	• basic strategy • player analysis • open court and center pattern • defensive strategy • serve to backhand and return first serve to the middle (neutralize)	• footwork speed • arm speed • start, stop, change direction	• motivation • goal setting • match play setup and organization • discipline of execution

- *Technical.* As an intermediate junior, it is possible to add return, volley, and overhead to their arsenal of strokes. The consistency of their execution becomes more important when playing tournaments. Since players cannot hit winners so easily (strength), they resort instead to playing much longer rallies to win points. The up-and-back movements become more prevalent. Footwork and sliding techniques need to be introduced when playing on clay courts. As they get older, they slowly start hitting the ball faster and topspin needs to be added to keep the ball in play. Adding topspin brings a variety of new shot choices to their game. Players are able to not only accelerate the ball more but also vary the height over the net and make it bounce up high (out of the strike zone of the opponent), play a lob over the net player, play an angle shot, or play the ball low at the opponent's feet when at the net. Teaching the separate topics and then trying it out in a game is the best way for students to learn the multiple ways to apply it in the future.

- *Tactical.* Learning a basic strategy is crucial to give students a standard method to play (see chapter on strategy). You can use the basic strategy in many ways. You can use it to start the match; it gives you more structure. You can use it when you are nervous or simply if you don't know what strategy to use against that particular player. Besides the basic strategy, players have to gain skills in analyzing their opponents so they can better form a game plan. Easy patterns need to be introduced so that students can learn how to be offensive and defensive. Learning how to neutralize the opponent with the serve (playing a body serve or aiming to the backhand) and return (playing the return to middle of the court, preferably to the backhand side) is a basic aspect to master for this level. All these skills together give juniors the tools to start progressing in sectional or national events.

- *Physical.* Intermediate players are ready to train in a more physical way, and intensity should slowly be increased. This is the time to start working with a physical trainer as well or to incorporate physical training to the tennis sessions. Footwork speed needs to improve in order to cover the court better. This includes moving with urgency toward the ball, stopping in a balanced way, and changing directions to recover for the next ball. The topspin in the strokes requires players to increase the racket head speed and therefore also the arm speed. Physical improvements at this age can easily be achieved by making competitive games or by using circuit training. From time to time, test the players on their improvements and record their results so they can compare their results in one- or two-month intervals.

- *Mental.* Match play becomes more important to practice the competitive skills of execution under pressure and the discipline of the (basic) strategy. A tournament schedule is helpful to plan what tournaments to play and how many to schedule each month and to organize your training plan and rest periods. Setting performance goals is an excellent way to stimulate players to make improvements for future results.

Advanced Juniors (Ages Thirteen to Sixteen)

Technical	Tactical	Physical	Mental
• specialty shots and footwork • drop shot, overhead, lob, approach shot • spin, slice, top slice, and kick serve • weapon development • net game development	• patterns of play • shot choices • styles of play and tactical solutions • offensive and defensive tactics • tactical positioning • percentage tennis • risk management • score management	• speed • power • flexibility • balance • agility • endurance	• focus on strategy and execution • problem-solving • emotional control • character building • travel

- *Technical.* With this level comes the introduction and development of the specialty shots and the necessary footwork belonging to these shots. The examples of specialty shots are these: drop shot (playing the ball as short as possible behind the net with backspin), overhead (or jump overhead), approach shot, drop volley, kick serve, etc. Juniors at this level are very much interested in experimenting with specialty shots but have to learn discipline to use them in the proper situations. When using them too often, their game becomes sloppy and unstructured and could have an adverse effect on the results. This will give opponents the opportunity to take advantage of the situation and take control of the rallies in the match. Weapon and net game development are important progressions for advanced players. Consistency alone is not sufficient; applying pressure by attacking short-ball situations and the strength of the strokes start playing a larger role. Every advanced player has some weapons to force errors or to make outright winners. They rely on those individual weapons in competition. It can be a technical stroke; but it can also be a tactical, mental, or physical weapon. But there are some weapons that are universal in all advanced players. Most have a strong serve and forehand and can make outright winners with both these strokes.

- *Tactical.* This stage of tactical development determines, over time, the style of play for each individual player through their strengths and weaknesses of ground strokes, net play, serve and return, shot choices, movement, and the comfort level of execution. This is also the stage to progress from sectional and national tournaments to international (ITF) events. In playing international junior events, players have to develop their tactical, physical, and mental skills in order to compete against possibly older players since the ITF junior age group is from thirteen to eighteen years of age. Becoming more mature and experienced in these areas becomes very useful in playing these events. Players who succeed in developing good tactical skills and discipline in the execution of their patterns and shot choices will be more successful and will progress faster in results and their rankings. The best way to improve tactical skills is to practice patterns and shot choices and play tournaments on a regular basis while reevaluating your performance all the time. Staying calm quickens improvements.

  Because players are becoming stronger and are able to go for more winners, they also have to learn better risk management. This means knowing when to play the rally and when to go for the winner and not being scared to do what is needed. It also means that once you make the decision to accelerate the shot, you should also add extra spin and use larger targets. You should know when to follow it up by going to the net and finishing off the point. Score management is the understanding of when to increase the intensity in the point, game, or set to take advantage and create scoreboard pressure on your opponent.

- *Physical.* This component of development becomes the cornerstone to improvement at this level. The strokes can only further progress by improving the strength, speed, balance, coordination, endurance, flexibility, and agility of movement. Usually there is already another growth spurt and the release of hormones during puberty. These will greatly enhance the physical performance with training these specifics during this age group. Students of this level are very receptive to physical training, if and when they experience the progress. They respond positively to group training and competition in physical skills. Results can be monitored by regular testing on- and off court (see physical training).

- *Mental.* Due to the increase of physical and mental pressure during competition, there will be a necessity for more mental strength and maturity in this age group. Besides the inner mental skills players may possess, the way to increase mental strength is through increased physical activity, training on focus by redirecting the priority on tactical execution, learning to increase emotional control during point play and focusing on body language, learning how to solve problems by discussing tactical situations and how to solve them, and ongoing mental training through character building and showing players how they can be tougher in competition.

Transitional Player (Ages Seventeen to Twenty-Two)

Technical	Tactical	Physical	Mental
• weapon development • second-serve spin • absorbing and transitioning power • efficiency of strokes and movement • tempo and rhythm changes	• risk management • anticipation of tactical situations • camouflage • put-away shots • approach-shot tactics • playing against net player • score management	• power development • speed endurance • flexibility • balance • agility • explosive movement development	• mental endurance • dealing with pro events and stadium court settings • dealing with agents, interviews, etc. • managing travel • media training

- *Technical.* In general, this technical stage is ideal for further weapon development to keep up with the power increase that occurs in this age group. The baseline strokes need to be trained with high intensity. The second serve is a telltale sign of the strength of the server, either to force a defensive return or at least to neutralize the opponent.

- Learning how to absorb power and redirect/transition it to the opposite direction is an advanced skill that involves weight transfer, coordination, and timing of the contact points. The efficiency of the strokes is a technical aspect that provides powerful strokes with minimal expenditure of energy. It requires much training and can only be obtained with great timing of the contact point in front of the body, weight transfer, and timely release of racket head acceleration. This all needs to be coordinated with the recovery footwork. The tempo and rhythm changes are used to speed up and slow down the exchanges of the rallies. These are all designed for tactical purposes. These can be performed by having one side train for offensive strokes and the other for defensive strokes (for example, topspin against slice).

- *Tactical.* As the speed of play increases, it becomes more important to anticipate the actions of the opponent. Anticipation is trained by paying attention to the possible directions of the ball, the movements of the opponent in the setup of the feet and body, and the contact points. It takes some time and experience in playing against many different opponents before you get a feel for this skill.

  Risk management is a tactical skill that is regulated by percentage tennis. Understanding what percentage tennis is can assist you in the choices you make concerning targets, speed, spin, and tactical situations in neutral, offensive, or defensive plays. Camouflage of the shots is a highly advanced skill designed to hide the intention or direction of the winner shot or to wrong-foot the opponent. Score management becomes even more important to master to more easily defeat opponents and to apply pressure at the proper moments during the game's sets and matches. The tactical situation of playing against a net player has several aspects in learning. You can pass directly or indirectly by preparing the passing shot (think of playing at the feet first and then pass or lob). The approach-shot strategy has multiple points to consider. The approach can be after the serve, on a short-ball situation, or after a return. The strategies in this transitional level are crucial to the development of a college or pro player.

- *Physical.* The speed and intensity have to be optimal and explosive in order to compete at this level. In order to play at these speeds, the movements have to be organized with speed and power with great explosiveness, balance, flexibility, and agility. For players in college, the physical training is scheduled regularly on a weekly basis. Players can take advantage of these training sessions through weight training, running on the track, and agility on court. For aspiring pro players, they should organize their physical training in a similar fashion. Their challenge is to continue their training on the road while playing tournaments. The program has to be adjusted in intensity and duration in coordination with their match schedule.

- *Mental.* The mental aspects for college players and aspiring pro players can vary quite much from each other. In college, everything is taken care of and the school staff organizes travel. As a young pro player, there are not only mental aspects on the court during play but there are also many aspects off court in organizing practice courts, traveling, dealing with agents and management organizations, signing up for events, playing in front of large crowds, and having to deal with interviews before and after match play. These mental stresses are difficult to deal with, and most players don't anticipate this. Coaches should try to prepare players as much as possible and teach them how to enjoy the journey rather than fight the system.

Pro Player (Ages Sixteen and Up)

Technical	Tactical	Physical	Mental
• consistency of execution • technical execution in patterns • technical execution of specialty shots • technical execution in pressure situations	• tactical analysis of opponent • discipline of tactical execution • pattern combinations • shot choices • point setup routines • point management	• training on the road • injury prevention • speed and agility training • flexibility (yoga) • physical preparation and recovery	• stress management of stadium play at pro level events • media training

- *Technical.* There is a big misconception that all pro players have perfect techniques. However, this is far from the truth. Many young pro players still have to work really hard on the fundamentals of the strokes—especially when their coach as a junior player was not a technical coach. The technical execution has to be refined during the patterns, the specialty shots, and under-pressure situation to fully control the trajectories of the ball with movement and tempo situations. Once the speed of the movement and play increases, the level of accuracy and degree of ball control (spin, slice) goes up quite significantly. Coaching on the pro tour and working with pro players is quite different compared to working with players still in development. There is less focus on technical issues and more focus on tactical and physical issues. Mental aspects come more into the mix in learning how to deal with stresses on tour and how to think about problem areas in a positive way. There could be times that you work on a technical issue, but that should probably be done in the off-season.

- *Tactical.* Tactics and strategies at this level are all about analyzing the opponents at hand so you can make a game plan.

Martin van Daalen

You can divide the game plan in several parts: (1) strengths and weaknesses of the opponent, (2) serve and return tactics on where to play and why, and (3) how to play the rally with patterns and shot choices and what to expect in return from the opponent. Use the same method of coaching and delivery in your message. The only thing changing in the information is how to play. Keep the information concise and to the point instead of a long story. A good method is to have the player repeat the information to make sure they remember and understand the information. You can add some tips to the players about certain things you know they struggle with tactically and/or things that cause them unforced errors. For instance, "When you are up in score, don't slow down" or "When you play down the line, choose bigger targets." Giving too much information can be counterproductive. Some examples I have seen are the coaching tips received during matches on the ITF and WTA tour.

- *Physical.* Most pro players have a physical training program, and the top players even have a full-time trainer on staff. The weekly program of pro players is quite heavy, and physical training is integrated on a daily basis and during breaks in the tournament schedule or off-season. Daily routines have to include stretching or yoga, warm-up and cooldown program, and massage or physical therapy (in the case of small injuries). Most pro players have a routine on how they schedule their day. This is an example:

1. Stretching program before breakfast
2. Visit to trainer for therapy or massage on problem areas
3. Physical warm-up in gym or on court (twenty to forty minutes)
4. Hit on court in warming up strokes (forty minutes)
5. Match (1.5–3 hours)
6. Cool down, massage, and stretching after the match
7. Interviews with the media

As you can see, this is not to be underestimated, and this schedule only had one match. If the player plays doubles, the physical schedule is even more complicated.

- *Mental.* The mental aspects for pro players are very complex and vary from player to player. The player has to be mentally mature to handle the stress and daily routine of training, playing, the media, the crowds, and the fans. And the mental preparation and planning of a tournament and each individual match is much more detailed. Being able to stay calm and controlling your emotions are essential and will help in your execution of your plan. However, enjoying the process and the challenges of each opponent and seeing how much you can rise to the occasion is what creates real champions. This takes mental training, much experience in matches, talking about your experiences, and getting feedback and good advice and support from experienced coaches or mentors. Over time, this shapes the character of a player. The character of a player helps them to be strong in difficult situations when things are tough, and having an endless positive outlook is the only thing that pushes them onward to victory. Players without character have trouble dealing with stress and will be much more vulnerable in difficult situations. This shows in how they behave on court and may even lead to outburst of anger or confrontational situations.

Recap

Even though you have all this information available for each level, moving too fast and introducing advanced material too early to players who are not ready can be detrimental to their development. First they have to master each subject at each level before moving on to the next level. You can also overwhelm students with too much information. When they cannot perform the task or you have to make too many corrections, they feel like a failure. Confidence is fragile and can easily be destroyed at a young age.

Novak Djokovic

8—INTANGIBLE SKILLS

(CHAMPION SKILLS)

These type of skills (or talents) are the indefinable skills of a player that make them ultimately suitable for advanced match play. You could also call them champion skills. They are the aspects that make a player special to perform their strokes with ease and make it look so effortless on how they set up points. Below is a list of those intangible skills:

Hand-Eye Coordination

In tennis, this coordination is actually between the eyes, body, footwork, and hands. The coordination between the eyes, footwork, and hands is crucial in making the timing for the correct contact point with the ball. First of all, the eyes have to be trained on a daily basis to observe many different types of information. The player has to be able to read the timing of the strike of the opponent's ball in order to react on time to move to the oncoming ball. The eyes have to read the type of shot, the speed, the spin, the trajectory, the direction, and the spot where the ball will bounce and track it to the possible contact point. Observations and calculations have to be made at a split second. Then players can react and move their body to the correct spot to strike the ball. The eyes have to coordinate with the feet, body, and hands to swing the racket at the correct angle, distance, and speed and make contact out in front of the body for optimal control. Since every shot is made with a variety of speeds, spins, and trajectories, you can imagine the skills needed to execute this at increasing speeds and spins. To have the footwork and body coordinate with the arms and hands in this fashion makes the tennis sport so difficult to master at advanced levels. Training of these skills is definitely possible and requires players to groove their strokes until automation and rhythm is established. This is best trained at medium speeds without using more than 60 percent of the maximum power. Testing has revealed that this is the best way to obtain maximum coordination.

Hitting the Sweet Spot

There is an area on the racket strings that produces the most speed, control, and spin to the ball. It is located a little higher in the center of the racket. Players will feel this contact as a lighter pressure of the ball on their racket. We call this the sweet spot or hitting clean shots. Top players all possess the skill of finding this sweet spot on a regular basis. When the ball is struck with force and acceleration in this spot, it makes a different, distinct cracking sound. When struck with the correct timing in front of the body, the speed differential is very noticeable.

Juniors often underestimate the importance of this contact point on the strings and don't focus as much on this aspect of their strokes. I myself was not aware of this skill until my coach made me aware of how many balls I was hitting off-center, also called shanking. He taught me how to focus longer with my eyes on the ball and how to track the trajectory of the ball, especially after the bounce, until the ball contacts the strings. The contact point in front of the body assists in viewing the ball better through the strings. It is still in your viewing angle as it approaches toward you instead of in your peripheral vision on the side of your body. This skill provides great advantages at higher speeds, in taking over the speed and tempo of the opponent's ball and changing the tempo within the rally. Top players use this phenomenon on a regular basis. Training of these clean shots is a daily training routine. This skill should become a recognizable and comfortable feeling (rhythm) when you are striking the ball correctly. It will create more confidence and commitment in your strokes. Once this confidence is established, it will provide more options with your strategies, patterns, and shot choices to take more initiative in your game.

Consistency

This is a skill that needs to be obtained at any level of play. Consistency is not only important for the strokes and rallies but is also needed in strategy, physical energy and intensity, and mental stability. When players are inconsistent, they become frustrated and irritable and eventually will hurt their performance. Consistency of the strokes will provide more confidence and commitment to your game and increase the pressure on your opponents. It will also give efficiency of play and reduce energy usage and time spent on court in matches. Consistency of strategies, patterns, and shot choices gives confidence in your game plan and gives you a positive outlook and feedback on your matches. Mental stability and a calm demeanor saves energy and is a successful method to increase consistency long-term. More energy means more physical intensity during the rallies. You can see this method displayed in many great champions.

Point and Match Management

The management of points, games, and sets becomes an important winning factor for competitive players. Understanding how and when to apply pressure is a skill that needs to be learned and mastered over time. These are the several pressure points in each game that provide advantage:

- The first point in each game is always a nervous point to play for every player. It often causes tentative play, which could influence the remainder of the game. Winning it or losing it is a difference of two points. Some players are aware of this factor, but many see this as a nonconsequential point. But you could have a different outlook on this first point and see it as an opportunity to apply the first pressure on your opponent and to have more freedom of play in the following points. Rafael Nadal is one of those incredible competitors who uses this most of all and has probably the highest first-point winning percentage on tour.

It almost seems as if the game is all decided in that first point of the game. He plays with incredible intensity and uses extra spins and margins with his targets to set up the point before he strikes. Once he is ahead in score, he plays the following point with more speed and freedom to apply additional pressure.

- The middle of the game is usually the pressure point that provides a game point. The score of these pressure points are 30–0, 30–15, 30–30. Winning the next point brings you within one point of winning the game and delivers huge pressure on opponents. Applying more intensity in your play and playing aggressively to larger targets gives you more chance to win this point and the game.

- The end of the game is a scoring situation to take advantage in the set. The scores in the games are 40–0, 40–15, 40–30, and advantage after 40–40. Even when leading in score, players can become nervous. They usually start thinking too much about the pressure of winning and losing instead of thinking about how they are going to play the point. Imposing your strengths on the opponent's weaknesses is the key to success. So this should be your main focus of concern. Very often, juniors become so nervous that they are not able to focus on strategy; and instead of taking advantage of the pressure on the opponent, they create the pressure on themselves. This results to not always closing out the game right away and extending the battle unnecessarily. Not only is it very inefficient energy-wise but it also chips away at the confidence and commitment of play. You have to learn to stay committed to your game plan and increase your intensity on these points instead of slowing down and playing tentatively. This killer instinct is something you need to develop and nurture if you want to become a champion.

- Playing three- or five-set matches also is a management skill. You have to learn how to play long high-pressure matches. You have to know when to speed up and when to play the rally, tire your opponent, or force them to make mistakes. Finding ways to get an advantage over your opponent in playing strategically and efficiently to last the duration of the match becomes an art form. Finding the opponent's technical, tactical, physical, and mental weaknesses is the key to winning long matches. It definitely helps to increase your physical stamina so you can think more clearly under pressure and not have to worry if you can last in longer rallies as the match is extended to three or five sets.

- Playing high-percentage tennis and understanding risk management is an important part of match management. Building the rally with pressure but at the same time playing high-percentage shots is the skill of champions.

Athletic Ability

The physical ability and attributes of a player increase the options in match play. They are a combination of coordination, strength, endurance, speed, and flexibility. All these physical components are important to play at a high level and should be trained on a regular basis. If there is a weak link in any of these aspects, you can be sure your opponent will figure it out and will try to take advantage of it. If you are looking to become a champion at any level, you should always make sure to be in top shape and work on your athletic ability.

Intensity

Speed kills in any sport, and tennis is no exception to this rule. Intensity of play affects the speed and tempo of play during the points quite dramatically. Intensity of movement and tempo of play provide the pressure players feel, and it can affect their demeanor or style of play. Increasing the intensity can give you an offensive game style that doesn't necessarily mean you are taking more risk. Just increasing the intensity actually gives you the opportunity to run your opponent around the court and take time away in their decision-making. Intensity can also affect the opponents to become more tentative or choose to take more risk. Either way, this is a positive development in making your opponent play differently. Using this intensity on the pressure points in the games and sets is especially a skill that needs to be learned and mastered in advanced playing styles.

Competitive Character

A true competitor develops their willpower and persistence to win in match play. It is a skill that is trained through hard work and building character and a big heart. A competitive character is built through tough trials in matches where you learn to stay positive and keep believing in your skills. You learn to fight and never give up no matter what the score is or what difficulties you have to overcome. Your demeanor is calm, but you show your aggressive nature in your shotmaking and/ or your voice. In tennis, this is quite normal, and you will hear the players either blowing out hard or grunting while striking the ball. This skill also includes the ability to make the necessary adjustments in solving strategical problems and understanding point and match management (as seen above). All champions develop their competitive nature in their own way, which identifies them in their own style of play. Sportsmanship is an important part of character building and treating others the way you want to be treated. Competitive characters become the traits of champions.

Focus

The ability to focus on many different aspects for an extended time makes this an incredible difficult sport to play. The eyes have to focus on tracking the ball in order to hit the ball clean. The focus has to be there with the footwork and motions of the strokes in order to hit the appropriate shots. Decisions have to made fast in order to create the proper speed, spin, trajectory, and direction. Decisions also need to be made on strategy and making the proper shot choices in similar tactical situations. Discipline in basic strategy and making these shot choices in offensive, neutral, and defensive positions requires great focus skills. It takes great concentration and stamina when play is extended over several or more hours. You can actually train your focus by practicing longer rallies and playing points under pressure situation. For example, you can practice games or sets with a different score (0–15, 0–30, 15–30, or 30–30) or start sets at 2–2 or 3–3. By practicing the different scores, you can simulate similar situations in match play. All these games will increase your ability to play these pressure situations better and increase your focus. You can recognize these skills very clearly when watching pro tennis.

Body Language and Demeanor

Your appearance and attitude during match play help to control your emotions. At the same time, it provides tremendous pressure on the opponent. Positive demeanor and body language makes it impossible for the opponent to read your inner fears. They will get no energy from you if you don't show what you feel. It might actually throw them off if they don't see you get frustrated or irritated. By keeping calm, you also save energy and can play more efficiently. Emotional control is one of the major skills to learn for any competitive player and is difficult to learn for juniors. So start early to learn routines that will help you concur this skill. When going to your towel after every point, you learn a rhythm of play and give yourself a chance to recover and think how to play the next point. Stay calm at all times.

Routines

These are customs and habits that players follow in sequence to create a familiarity and rhythm in activity and rest. The routines give your mind and body time to recover after each point to think about what strategy to use and to calm down physically after every intense rally. It is no coincidence that you see so many top players follow exact methods. Some routines and habits are as follows:

- training and preparation routines (consistency)
- prematch routines (focus, match attitude, warm-up)
- going to the towel after each point (recovery)
- show no reaction after losing points, turn around right away and start thinking about the strategy of the next point (emotional control)
- fist pump after winning points (positive expressions)
- walking back to the back fence before getting ready to play (preparation and think of strategy)
- looking at your strings in between points to keep focus (focus)
- analyze previous point quickly and make strategy for next point (tactic)

All these factors become important for high-level match play. They add to the demeanor and attitude of a player to make them more competitive. Bad habits are the ones that are hard to shake and should be avoided at all times—for example, hitting your racket on the ground or crying out loud when you miss a shot. Both show the opponent your frustration and help them revive their energy to beat you. Routines can help you prevent those bad habits and channel your frustration in a more positive way by using physical energy in the next point. Work on your routines!

Anticipation

This skill is based on the recognition of patterns, shot choices, and tactics. Players get their experience from reading the body movements, preparation of the stroke, and contact points with the ball. But it can also be the memory of what the opponent usually does in those situations with patterns and shot choices. Reading opponents is an advantage to get a head start in moving to the ball just before the opponent will strike the ball versus waiting till you see the ball come over the net. This difference in time is crucial in preparation to strike the next ball. If you have great anticipation, you are able to reach more balls and prepare more easily with balance and poise. If you are rushed on every shot, your movements will have to be more aggressive with the urgency to reach the ball on time. This takes much more physical and mental energy and reduces chances to win in long matches. Players with good anticipation skills play much more efficiently and can play with more initiative since preparation of the shots is easier and calmer. Being rushed in your shot preparation gives you less time to set up your shots with balance and causes errors. Train your eyes!

Strategic Mind

A good strategic mind gives players the advantage of making decisions on how to play and solve tactical problems. Understanding the various strengths and weaknesses of opponents and how to exploit them is a huge advantage and skill to learn. Some players are naturally talented in understanding strategy, and they execute these instinctively through specific tactics. But it is not impossible to learn strategies and tactics through trial and error and practicing patterns and shot choices to situations. Being a student of the game and discussing strategies, tactical solutions, patterns, and shot choices will definitely assist in the learning process and gaining experience. A strategic mind also includes knowledge of different styles of play and finding the tactics to combat these opponents. In all these tactical situations, there will be exchanges of rallies with offensive, neutral, and defensive shot choices. The tactical decision-making can vary on the score in the match (game or set) in taking initiative in the rally with offensive, neutral, or defensive plays. Solving the problems during play becomes the norm and will eventually become a reflex and an automation since they are reoccurring tactical situations. Keep training the many different tactical situations and their solutions to train your strategic mind.

Martin van Daalen

Problem-Solving

Solving the various problems during play in an efficient way is important to maintain dominance and initiative in a match or tournament. There are several different problems that can occur. These can vary from tactical problems to verbal exchanges with opponents, officials, or referees. How you solve these problems can influence the outcome in points and matches. Experience in these matters can help, but in learning how to deal with these problems, it is important to stay calm and poised in your demeanor and mental state. If these problems upset you too much, they can change your mood and, more importantly, make you think of the problem rather than think of the strategy you should be using. Talk about all these aspects with your students so they learn instant methods of dealing with them.

Weapons

The weapon development is an advanced skill that all champions possess. These are usually developed during the ages fourteen through eighteen and further mastered during the transition period in college or pro tennis. The obvious weapons are the serve and forehand, but there can also be other weapons in a special shot, a special tactic, or the physical skills a player has. For advanced male players, the serve is a dominant weapon that can deliver instant points. They are difficult to defend against. These types of players rack up many points with direct winners (ace) or indirect winners on a weak return of serve. The forehand is the second most developed weapon and can have devastating effects on the rally through forced and unforced errors of the opponent. It does not matter if your weapon development is a technical stroke, superior footwork, or the style of play; you need to make it a priority to enhance your game. Take the time to work on your weapons separately to enhance consistency in tough situations under pressure.

Specialty Shots

The specialty shots are the strokes that are based on fundamental techniques but advanced to a special shot through inventiveness and experimentation. They are not necessarily part of the basic technical training, but they developed with the competitive nature and athletic ability of a player. Below is a sequence picture from Roger Federer with the execution of a special shot—the backhand overhead:

Roger Federer—backhand overhead (specialty shot)

9—WEAPON DEVELOPMENT

What does weapon development mean in your game? The definition of a weapon in tennis is the strength in your game or stroke that forces your opponents to play a neutral or defensive stroke in return. The best weapons are of such a force that even if you know it is coming, you still can't find a good answer to them. Two strokes that are good examples in the modern tennis game are the forehand and the serve. I have listed some examples of weapons below:

- technical   - forehand, backhand, serve, net play
- tactical   - consistency, game plan, patterns, game style
- physical   - strength, stamina, footwork speed, and agility
- mental   - competitiveness, character, focus, willpower

These are some good examples of weapon development you can see in top players on a regular basis. Not everyone has all the weapons or the same weapons, and not all the weapons are developed to the same degree. Some are better at one than the other. Nevertheless, if you want to be a champion, you will need to develop some of the weapons listed above.

Development

In order to create a weapon of any sort, you have to first determine what affinities each player has to certain weapons; are they able to develop it based on the technical, physical, and mental qualities they possess? Players also have to show they are ready to take their game to the next level and have the strength and speed of motion to perform these skills. It is advisable to follow a method of progression in learning new weapons:

1. **Physical Weapon Development**

   The physical development has to be the first aspect to consider before any technical training of any weapon can commence. The strength, speed, and stamina have to be sufficient to sustain the execution. There are three major growth periods in the development that can assist with the strength, speed, and stamina. The first major growth is around the ages of twelve to fourteen. The next one occurs when they are fifteen to seventeen, and the last one is from seventeen to twenty-one years of age. These growth periods are initiated by hormonal changes in the body that also influence the growth of muscles, tendons, and ligaments. It is important to understand the effects so that the type of training can be adjusted to enhance progress. Before the first growth period, it makes less sense to spend much time on weight training to increase muscle mass since the hormonal changes have not started yet. This growth period starts at a different age for each person, and you can see this clearly with the difference in height and size. So at a younger age, it makes more sense to spend time on other physical aspects: stamina, flexibility, coordination, etc.

   Example

   Once the first growth period has occurred, it is possible to add other factors like strength training (using their own body weight), speed training, and agility (by training explosiveness of movement). At the second and third growth period, the strength, stamina, and footwork trainings are taken to a much higher level (using external weights and training on a track). The physical development at each growth period makes it possible to increase the workload and improve strength and speed of movement and motion to develop the weapons necessary for progress.

2. **Technical Weapon Development**

   This part of the development is the mechanical form and motion that makes it possible to execute the stroke in a more forceful way. To properly develop these strokes, you have to understand a little bit about mechanics and motion—how they are initiated and how the forces are released most efficiently to produce the most racket head speed. Let me give you an example: if you told a student to just hit the ball harder, they would grip the racket tighter and try to muscle the racket to swing faster. This would have the opposite effect since the muscles on both sides of the joints would squeeze and contract at the same time and, subsequently, slow the motion down instead of speeding it up. To speed up the motions, you have to learn several technical methods:

- *Loading.* You load the motion by bending the knees and rotating the body parts in the opposite direction to stretch the muscles and tendons and use the elasticity to increase the pressure before release. In the case of a tennis stroke, the loading is used by lifting the arm(s) and racket in the backswing so that the release can occur with acceleration with the assistance of gravity.

- *Weight transfer.* By transferring your body weight against the direction of the oncoming ball, you can increase the mass against the ball. The timing and coordination of the weight transfer has to happen right after the bounce of the ball. The foot is placed forward to transfer the weight from the back to the front. The speed and type of spin of the oncoming ball is obviously a big factor in the timing of the weight transfer. This weight transfer is an important factor in the learning process and imperative to the weapon development. That is also why this needs to be taught from an early age. Many coaches/parents try to start teaching open stances and bypass this very important stage of development, therefore holding back / slowing down proper weapon development at a later stage. Once the method and feeling of weight transfer is mastered, it will be much easier to teach weight transfer with open stances. The weight transfer is the initial start to the forward and rotational motion that forms the strokes. It also facilitates an easier rotational motion by stepping forward. This opens the hips and shoulders to extend farther forward and make a longer follow-through.

- *Kinetic energy (ground force).* By bending the knees before impact and then extending the knees just before impact, you can create a ground force (kinetic energy) that accelerates the body parts and rotational swing of the strokes. It will accelerate the hips and shoulders, and subsequently, the racket head to create a very efficient release of the racket against the ball.

- *Rotational force.* The rotational force (swing around the body) generates the racket head speed to increase the impact on the ball. If the loading, the weight transfer, and the ground force happen in coordination, the racket head speed will increase dramatically during the swing—especially when unloading (releasing) the stroke in a relaxed fashion. The racket head speed can further be increased by bending the elbow and accelerating the wrist in sequence during impact with the ball. You can compare this rotational force with swinging an object on a string around your body and then letting the string swing around a pole. The faster you swing it around your body, the faster the speed of the object (in this case, the racket head).

- *Contact point.* These are the points of contact of the racket with the ball. The racket head speed is highest when out in front of the body right before it swings around for a follow-through. The timing and coordination of this contact point is achieved by years of training and by the experience of training and playing on many types of surfaces. It is crucial to find consistency in the contact points so you can control the speed, spin, and trajectory of the ball and therefore gain consistency in the strokes.

- *Recovery.* The recovery is the motion that restores the balance to the stroke after contact with the ball and returns the body back in position to hit the next ball. It plays a crucial role in weapon development since it keeps the body in balance and can also generate further speed to the ball if executed in sequence correctly (loading–weight transfer–ground force–rotation).

Example

Teaching a forehand to be a weapon can be done in progression. First you have to make sure that students understand the concept of stepping forward, using the weight transfer, and finding the proper contact points with a faster follow-through to create racket head speed. Setting the stage to hit the forehand more forcefully without muscling the ball takes time and patience from coaches and students. The first drill is to teach players to hit winners from inside the baseline, up to the service line, and within the service box. You can set parameters on how hard the ball needs to be struck in order to hit the back fence after the bounce. (When struck softer, the second bounce of the ball will fall short of the back fence.)

You can turn this into a game by having three players try to hit winners inside the baseline against one opponent trying to return the winner. If they hit a winner, they get a point. If the returner touches the ball, they get one point as well. However, if they are able to win the point, they get two points. As players get stronger, they should be able to hit winners from deeper in the court. Obviously, you make many variations to this drill, and players have to learn to not hit every ball with the same speed. Alternating a rally speed with a winner speed is an important skill to develop.

Example

Teaching a more powerful service motion is another weapon. You can start by hitting serves from the service line and setting up targets close to the baseline. This method gives players more confidence to hit the ball harder since they are able to see the target over the net. You can follow that by challenging players to hit the back fence after hitting a target area. The height the ball reaches on the fence gives you a measure of the speed and spin of the service action (see picture).

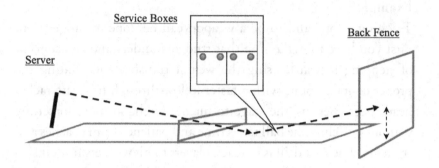

Server Service Boxes Back Fence

3. Tactical Weapon Development

This type of weapon development has all to do with the skills of how to play the game in order to win points. Understanding the strengths and weaknesses of the opponent and yourself is imperative to have a plan on how to combat your opponent.

- *Basic plan.* Having a basic plan and the discipline to execute it is the first tactical weapon. For so many times, you see players of all levels stray from this basic plan and miss balls unnecessarily before even starting the rally.

- *Consistency.* A basic plan also provides consistency, the second tactical weapon. Just by following a method, you are continually making shots to predetermined targets. The players who can execute this sequence of shots with the highest success rate have a huge advantage over most other players.

- *Patterns of play.* The patterns are important tactical skills in moving the opponent around the court. You can open the court for winner situations or force errors from your opponent. Recognition of these tactical situations becomes a skill and a powerful weapon.

- *Shot choices.* These are the decisions a player makes to direct and shape the shots with spin or slice to control the ball trajectory in tactical situations to create defensive, neutralizing, or offensive strokes. These shot choices become a weapon when the discipline of execution improves by hitting the appropriate shots at the right time to the proper targets.

- *Court positioning.* This is a tactical aspect that requires you to recognize the patterns of play and shot choice possibilities of the opponent in order to choose the proper court position to strike the next ball. It requires lots of experience on the possible strike angles and physical movement skills to recover on time with efficiency.

- *Taking initiative.* Once players understand the concept of basic strategies, they need to learn to take initiative in the rally. This does not only changes the tempo of the rally but also changes the patterns and keeps your opponent off-balance. Physically and mentally, it will give you an advantage to take initiative. Mentally, it gives you the feeling of being in control when you take initiative in the rally instead of waiting and letting things happen to you. Physically, it is easier to take initiative and be the first to move your opponent around the court than waiting and reacting to shots (not to be confused with going for winners that cause unforced errors). The fraction of a second you lose each stroke you wait costs you more energy to sprint harder to catch up and reach the balls in the corners. All this extra energy adds up a lot over the course of a whole match and is not an efficient way to play. The trick and tactical skill here is to keep your opponent in a neutral or defensive position. Make them feel the mental and physical pressure. Give them less time to set up for each next stroke and make them feel rushed for them to go for more risky shots under pressure situations.

- *Creativity.* This is a much more difficult tactical skill to learn. It requires quicker thinking ability and decision-making. It's a natural talent for some but can also be learned over time in playing more matches and gaining experience from studying patterns and shot choices from opponents. Creativity in shot choices can get you out of trouble in difficult situations or create winning shots that your opponent is not expecting at all.

Example

You can teach the discipline of execution and the consistency of the basic strategy by making players repeat the sequence of shots that follow the serve and return (with both possibilities of starting the rally to the weakness or the strength to open the weakness). By making them aware of this sequence and training it at regular intervals, they will have a much lower percentage of unforced errors and become more confident in their tactical skills. Eventually, this will develop as a weapon.

4. **Mental Weapon Development**

This aspect of the game is usually the last one to develop and is even harder to acquire as a weapon. Mental development can be shaped by the player's natural demeanor and character, but it also can be influenced by the coach and the training environment. We recognize competitive greatness through mental skills when players have poise, self-control, character, confidence, grit, determination, intensity, and the guts to be brave and take initiative when needed to go for their shots. The game of tennis is also quite unique in giving players more time to think. The pauses in between points, games, and sets give the players a moment to reflect on their performance. This short time for feedback can be positive, negative, or neutral. It is better to generate positive or neutral thoughts than negative ones. Sometimes that moment (twenty-five seconds in between points) is just long enough to generate some negative thoughts, but in order to become a champion, it is imperative not to express those emotions in a negative way. It brings your confidence down and helps your opponent gain more confidence in return.

Emotional control. This could be one of the most important skills to develop as a mental weapon. It confuses your opponent to see you stay calm under every circumstance and keeps your head clear in order to think of your strategy. The other way around, a player cannot develop their full potential and learn all the mental skills mentioned above without learning emotional control first. Your mind will not be open to learning if you are always negative and frustrated. This skill is subject to maturity, understanding the importance of mental toughness, and willingness to learn and to endure hardships to improve. You will see players develop mental skills much easier as their passion for the game increases and as their physical fitness becomes a weapon. When you are more fit, it is easier to stay calm and dominate players a different way. You can train mental skills through physical toughness.

Example 1

To become a top tennis player, you need exceptional physical skills in speed, coordination, strength, stamina, and flexibility. Getting to that level requires endurance, grit, and determination. Your mind is taxed to a higher degree when you physically train your body more.

Problem-solving. Whenever you play competitive tennis, you will be confronted with problem-solving on an ongoing basis. You have to keep your focus and keep your brain active to solve questions that arise concerning shot choices, positioning, movement, strategies, patterns of play, and constant adjustments made to actions from the opponent.

Example 2

A great way to train players mentally is to create handicaps for them to solve and also to increase the pressure in any way possible. You can do this easily by playing points or practice matches with a starting point with a different score. Here are some examples of those:

- 30–30 in the game or 2–2 in games to increase intensity and urgency of play with less time to afford errors in the game or set, players will be forced to play under more pressure and urgency to perform from the start of play.

- 0–15, 15–30, 30–15—these scores in the game can be used as a handicap in playing against slightly weaker players and feel the pressure to win under these circumstances and seeing all points more as a challenge instead of pressure.

Example 3
To train players to have emotional control during point play is difficult enough, and usually, they are not open to reasoning when they start getting frustrated. A good method is to deduct a point every time a player shows any signs of physical or mental emotion. This can be as simple as a verbal emotion or a slight tap of the racket on the ground. The key is to be firm and consistent with all players. That way, they know the rule is applied to all, and they will change their ways quite dramatically.

10—PARENTS AND COACHING

Many parents are coaching their children in practice and in competition. The USTA estimates that 60 percent of parents are coaching their own children. That percentage is very high in comparison with Europe or Asia. Part of it is the culture of sports and parents being very involved in sports through college. The other part is that tennis is more expensive to play in comparison with the other continents.

Coaching your own child is possible but not always recommended. It can work but can also seriously ruin your relationship with your son or daughter. Be careful not to be too overbearing in trying to correct every problem. It is natural to want your child to succeed, but trying too hard is what parents do differently than coaches. When it is not your child and as a professional coach, you are able to take your emotions out of the situation and react objectively. Below are some examples of good tennis parenting and bad tennis parenting:

Good Tennis Parenting	Bad Tennis Parenting
supports the coach	argues with the coach
lets the child make decisions	constantly shouts instruction
encourages their child	criticizes their child
lets their child have fun	overpressures their child
praises their child and cheers for everyone	compares their child to other players
is a role model	demonstrates negative behavior
respects officials	is abusive toward officials
respects the opponents	argues with opponents/parents
supports the coach's decisions	disagrees with coach's decisions
gives their child autonomy	tells their child how to play
wants their child to learn lesson from tennis	wants their child to win at all cost

I am sure that if you are involved with the competitive system, you will recognize many of these situations. If you are a parent who was never a tennis player, you will make many mistakes in the beginning. But the positive side is, you have many years to learn since the developmental pathway of a tennis player is quite long.

Communication as a Parent

The interaction and communication of parents can have a great effect on the players' enjoyment of the tennis game and the rate of progress. There are many factors that can play a role in the enjoyment of the game. However, one of the most important factors is how parents interact and communicate with their child, the coaches, and the other parents and players. The form of interaction and communication sets the tone and perception of the game. To fully enjoy the game, it is important that children not only set their own goals on the level of intensity of the training but also on how they feel about their relationship with others. To create passion for the sport, it has to be their decision, not the parents, on how much they want to train and play. Passion is created when the drive comes from the player rather than from the parents or the coach. Parents will know their children are enjoying the sport when they are looking forward to going to the tennis courts.

Coaching Your Child with Success

It does not matter if you have hired a private coach to coach your child. As a parent, you will always be involved in some part of the coaching. You might not always realize it, but the moment you make a comment on the practice or a match that was played, you are already coaching. The content of the communication and the method of delivery can be of great influence to the progress and enjoyment of your child. If you have hired a coach for his expertise and knowledge, try to make your comments stimulating and supportive. Otherwise, it will undermine the instructions and directions of the coach and possibly create conflicting ideas with your child.

When coaching your own child, it can be very difficult to find a good balance between pushing them to excel and enjoying the experience. Players have to learn to create their own passion from within rather than yours as a parent and/or coach. Even more so with parents, children will be sensitive to the body language and tone of the instruction since they associate it with the way parents speak to them when reprimanding them. Making training and playing an enjoyable experience for both the parents and the child through proper communication is the key to a healthy relationship and gratification of playing the game. The key here will be your patience, word choice, timing of the instruction, and body language. As parents, we are more impatient with the progress and attitudes of the players than a neutral person might be. Players learn faster when in a calm environment. If the word choices are too direct, too frequently repeated, and not systematic to the progressions of learning, players will easily become frustrated. Players have to learn to use their own memory instead of yours as a parent and coach. By letting them make mistakes, you provide them time to improve and gain confidence in each progression. By pressuring them too soon, you are basically going from step 1 to 10 without the proper progressions in between. Your tone of voice and body language tell all for your child. He or she can read you more than you think. They will be able to tell if you are happy, excited, or frustrated very easily; and you should always keep this in mind when coaching your child. Hiding your emotions when coaching matches will be the biggest challenge of all, but your emotions should not become a distraction to your child.

Communication with Coaches

The communication of a parent with a coach can assist in the level of confidence and commitment of your child's training. Parents can have a positive but also a negative influence on the relationship between the coach and their child. This will depend mostly on how parents communicate with the coach. Proper discussions should consist of an inquiry and feedback as to how your child is responding to the training. It is not always wise to talk to the coach about training progress and matches in front of players, unless it has a stimulating effect. As a parent, observing the training and match play can sometimes be difficult without interfering with the content of the training and method of coaching. Too much interference, comments, or derogatory remarks can undermine the relationship with the coach. It can easily be perceived as criticism in their method of coaching and might have an indirect effect on the relationship between the coach and your child. Choosing the proper coach and method of coaching you prefer is a better starting point for a healthy relationship for all involved. Understanding your role in this relationship and how to communicate as a parent is instrumental to the progression, success, and enjoyment of the sport.

Communication with Other Parents, Players, and Coaches

Many parents, players, and other coaches can be very sensitive to remarks made by other parents and players. Just knowing this fact should make you aware of your language when speaking to other parents, players, and coaches. Keep your comments positive and neutral about training and competition without making any additional comments about the performance of the opponent. It will ensure that no ill feelings and stigmas are created toward other parents, players, and coaches. These ill feelings and stigmas often will increase the pressure in playing with other players versus having a healthy competition.

Communication as a Player

Players need to learn how to communicate with parents, players, and coaches as well in order to learn and improve. The players who communicate better will have an increased opportunity to learn and improve and do this at a faster rate. The listening and focusing skills of players have a large influence in comprehending the topics and executing them in drills, exercises, and match plays. Asking questions and discussing problems are part of the communication necessary in understanding the full aspects and complexity of the strokes, strategies, patterns, physical aspects, etc.

Assertiveness is an important aspect in the communication of advanced players. It will assist the player to take charge of difficult situations and show confidence in dealing with each confrontation. Players have to stand up for themselves in speaking up right away when making line calls, keeping track of the score, and dealing with faulty decisions of referees. As players mature, they have to take increasing responsibility for the organization of their tournaments and schedules, training, practice partners, doubles partners, etc. and making these decisions with ease.

Parents and Coaching

My mother used to drive me to most of my tennis tournaments when I was still a junior. As a parent, she would watch the matches and not say anything, not even to cheer me on. In fact, she would not make any facial expressions at all. Because of this method, I was never distracted and was able to concentrate on the task at hand. My thoughts stayed on the court and on my opponent. I never realized how valuable that was to me until I was coaching myself.

I was sixteen years old and playing an open tournament in the south of Holland that particular afternoon. I was in the heat of the battle against an experienced player three times my age. He was trying every trick in the book to get me distracted by making remarks and by talking to me during the changeover. He obviously did not want to lose to a junior. When he saw that it was not working, he took it to the next level and started making dubious line calls. I protested, but there was no referee. Finally, on the third one, I stopped and protested again about the bad line call. Finally, I looked over at my mother on the side of the court and said, "Did you see that call?" Her answer was a simple "I can't say." This answer threw me off since I had expected my mother to defend me in that situation. I became frustrated and mad and ended up losing that match in a close third set.

On the way back home, my mother would usually talk about all other subjects except tennis. Whenever I lost, like that time, I would not say anything and would still be boiling inside with frustration. After ten minutes of listening to her talk about all other subjects, I finally said to her, "Why did you not say anything? Did you not see he was cheating on me? Did you not see that call?" Her answer was "Yes, I did see the ball, but I am not the referee, and I am not allowed to make that call, especially because I am your mother! You did not lose the match because of those bad calls, you lost the match because you got mad and distracted." I was perplexed at first, but I later realized she was right. That was exactly what had happened. I would have to learn to deal with it differently in the future.

These experiences as a junior taught me some valuable lessons as a coach about parents and coaching:

- When you parents are coaching your child, be even more careful about cheering and supporting your child. Players are more sensitive to remarks and body language from parents and are easily distracted in their match. Their focus will be on you instead of the execution of the strokes and the strategy.
- When coaching your own child, give them more time after the match before discussing the match, especially when they just lost. Preferably, you should wait for them to ask questions. Children are more sensitive to remarks from their parents but will accept it more easily when given time to think about it. More importantly, they will accept your suggestions more readily when they ask for your opinion rather than when it is provided unsolicited.

Martin van Daalen

11—DEVELOPMENTAL PLAN

As the player starts taking the game more seriously and develops a passion for the game, coaches and parents should organize a plan for the future. This plan should be a developmental plan on how to engineer a player's game to fit their style of play. In looking at the strengths and weaknesses of the player from technical, tactical, mental, and conditional aspects, the coach can derive short- and long-term goals. By making it realistic to the player's capabilities, you can ensure that goals will be met and that confidence will improve future results. This results in a training plan, a tournament plan, and a periodization plan. Make sure everyone fully agrees to the plans and has ample input to the content. That way, there is no confusion later on. Usually, the simple and original plans are the best for the player. Here is an outline of a developmental plan:

A. **Strengths and Weaknesses**

   The coach can be instrumental in making a proper evaluation of the strengths and weaknesses of a player. These aspects should not just cover the strokes but all aspects of the game: technical, tactical, physical, and mental. That way, you have a more realistic picture of what to work on when setting some priorities in training for the short-term and long-term goals. The strengths and weaknesses should be evaluated according to the level of the player—going by their age, physical and mental development, and playing experience (see form).

B. **Goal Setting**

   To achieve anything, it is important to know what you want to accomplish. This is also the case in trying to improve your tennis game. When you have a clear picture of your goals, you will be more motivated and driven to reach your objectives. These goals have to be reasonable and obtainable so they will push you forward to your next goals. They have to be challenging and cannot be too easy or too difficult in reaching your target. If it is too easy, players will become bored and disinterested and not motivated to work hard. If the target is too difficult to reach, players will become frustrated, and it might affect their confidence. Once goals are met within a reasonable time frame, they will enhance the confidence of players and make them feel in charge of their own improvements. It becomes their game! Whenever you set goals, it can be helpful to use a guideline and a method. The goal setting is best performed by using the SMART method:

Specific   (specific to your goals)
Measurable   (gives feedback to improvements)
Attainable   (keep it within reach for confidence)
Relevant   (has to be common sense)
Time frame   (set a time to reach your goal)

There are several different goals for players to consider when making choices on the various goals, and they all have their own specific purpose:

- *Outcome goals.* These are goals that can be set to winning certain events, matches, or rankings. This particular set of goals is most common among players and parents since they are result-oriented. It can, however, also be a hindrance to improvement when the goals are set too high or when winning alone increases the pressure of reaching these goals. It takes the focus away from improvements to the game, and the score becomes a constant pressure. Especially with players who are not as confident, it is crucial to have performance and process goals rather than outcome goals. When choosing the target of these outcome goals, be careful not to reach too high when setting these particular goals. It is easy to reset a new goal once it has been reached.

- *Performance goals.* These particular goals are set with a certain execution in mind. There could be many different forms of execution. It could be how a certain stroke is performed, reaching a higher percentage in the execution, or the execution of a strategy or physical output in intensity during a match. But it could also be an improvement in mental control with a change of attitude. All these are performance goals that can be obtained under the guidelines of the SMART method. Sometimes these goals can be set for a practice or a match, but it can also be set for a short- or long-term plan. Using these specific goals can be very stimulating to players and are usually experienced as a challenge rather than added pressure, especially if the targets and timeline are chosen properly.

- *Process goals.* To achieve measurable success in reaching a performance target, it is essential to have a method or a process. This process is a step-by-step approach to perform a skill, a strategy, or a tactic. The process goals provide you with a method on how to reach the targets with a specific outline. This could be by using a specific technique in the execution of a stroke or footwork. Or it could be a method to improve a pattern or strategy in a specific situation. All these process goals help the player to think their way through the execution and perform better under pressure. Having a method or process to reach a performance level will enhance a player's confidence in their ability to execute far more than having no process at all.

- *Short- and long-term goals.* Besides immediate goals in practice and in matches, it is important to plan for improvements and targets for the future that cannot be obtained instantaneously. We can divide these short- and long-term goals according to the difficulty in learning and/or priority.

Short-term goals should be the priority subjects from the strengths and weaknesses to stabilize and/or improve the player. It does not mean that you only work on weaknesses. It could be to stabilize or improve a subject. Short-term goals should be scheduled in a time period from three months to a year. These are usually not complex changes or adjustments and can be successfully accomplished in a shorter time span. This can be a technical adjustment that needs to be addressed before moving on to specialty shots or a tactical application of the stroke. It can also be a physical problem that needs to be improved before a player can execute better. These adjustments totally depend on the specific problem areas of each individual player.

Long-term goals are more complex systems of learning and therefore deserve more time to develop. They should be scheduled over six months to two years' time span. After that period of time, the coach should make a new developmental plan (best to be updated each year). This is because of the difficulty of the subject and/or the time needed to acquire experience in the subject. Other factors could be physical strength and speed improvements. These will influence the tactical capabilities. Growth, maturity, and discipline play an important role in the speediness of learning.

These evaluations result in three plans:

1. Training plan
2. Tournament plan
3. Periodization plan

1. A training plan will give an outline of the content and specifics of the training with an individualized approach for each player.
2. A tournament plan will provide a tournament schedule that is based on the amount of training and ability of each player to obtain the best results in matches.
3. A periodization plan is a schedule of training designed for better performance during specific time periods throughout the year.

We will examine these plans individually in the following pages.

Strengths and Weaknesses
(Sample)

Player :	
Date :	
Coach :	

Strengths	Weaknesses
Technical	
- forehand	- backhand
- first serve	- second serve
- net play	- return
Tactical	
- first strike capability	- consistency
- patterns	- shot choices
- weakness recognition	- patience
Physical	
- strength	- endurance
- speed	- flexibility
- change of direction	- coordination
Mental	
- aggressiveness	- patience in execution
- determination	- fear of losing
- competitiveness	- confidence
	- focus

Analysis of Strengths and Weaknesses

By looking at this form after completion, you can make a certain conclusion (analysis) of this player by looking at the strengths and weaknesses. The bullet points in each box are telltale signs of the makeup of the player—how he or she likes to perform under all four aspects of the game. Let's examine this example of this player more closely:

Technical

This particular player has a strong forehand and first serve and a good net play. These are all strokes that indicate an aggressive player who likes to use his weapons. Certain strokes are less developed (backhand), possibly since this player might be running around the backhand more often to strike with the stronger forehand. This can be a habit developed over time to cover up the weakness of the backhand, or the backhand has become weaker because the player has relied more on the forehand. Good net play development is a logical continuance in finishing off the ball after the point has been set up well. Weapon development in players becomes more visible when strength and speed increase in their game.

Tactical

In looking at the strategy, this player has an aggressive style of play and likes to put the opponent on defense. It indicates a first-strike capability with short rallies. This can be an advantage in creating errors from the opponent but can also create errors for the player when being impatient and forcing a situation too much. The patterns will be designed to quickly force the opponent on the defensive. This style of play creates many opportunities to take advantage in hitting winners or forcing the opponent into making errors. As long as the player works on his or her patience in building the rallies and developing the consistency for the long rallies, they can be very successful with this game style.

Physical

The strengths of this player show that some of the components are very suitable for this game style. However, some of the components need to be improved in order to play with stronger opponents. This game style does not automatically train some of the weaknesses that are visible in this player. The longer rallies will promote a more fluid and coordinated effort from the player and automatically improve the endurance overall. The flexibility of the footwork needs to be improved to perform under pressure.

Mental

Sometimes the aggressive and competitive nature of a player can drive them to become impatient and too anxious in scoring the point rather than letting the point develop and unfold on its own. When a player is winning, they will think less and points will add up quickly with the coordination flowing more naturally. As soon as things don't run smoothly, they can lose focus and their game can unravel very quickly. It is easy to lose confidence when thoughts of losing become more frequent. For these types of players, it is important to think proactively and ensure they stay patient and on task. Their focus should be on the process of how to create the patterns and shot selections rather than on winning or losing.

Short-Term and Long-Term Goals
(Sample)

Player : Date : Coach :	
Short-Term Goals	**Long-Term Goals**
Technical - improve backhand consistency - improve second-serve target - improve backhand return	- improve backhand power/spin - improve kick serve - add slice backhand return
Tactical - improve overall consistency - improve length of the rallies	- improve shot choices and targets - improve and add to patterns - improve offensive tactics
Physical - start a running program - develop a stretching program - improve coordination - rhythm drills	- interval training - dynamic warm-up routine - endurance/rhythm drills
Mental - improve concentration/focus - practice point play	- practice with different scores - practice coming from behind - practice longer rallies

Analysis of Short- and Long-Term Goals

The short-term and long-term goals provide coaches with a priority list of topics. With the short-term goals ranging from three months to a year and the long-term goals ranging from six months to two years, coaches have a good plan of what to work on. Topics might overlap one another somewhat with the possibility to train both at the same time.

Technical

The first priority would be to improve the basic consistency of the backhand and the return of serve. These two aspects alone will assist the player in their confidence in their game. They will feel more relaxed about their strokes since they can rely on their backhand without the urgency to produce winners with the forehand. There will be a buildup of the rallies. After these goals are developed, it is possible to move to the long-term goals with the development of the specifics.

Tactical

With the improvement of the consistency and automation in the strokes, players are able to watch the strategies and tactics of the game much more. They will shift their focus from their side of the net, with the execution of their strokes, to the other side of the net to what the opponent is doing. This change of focus will only occur when players mature and become more confident. This will open long-term opportunities to develop patterns of play, different shot choices and targets, and offensive tactics.

Physical

When players already possess good physical abilities, it is possible to develop the weaker areas. Short-term, it is advisable for advanced players to start a running and stretching program to develop some good routines and a base. As they improve and start feeling the effects in practices and matches, you can improve the specifics with on- and off-court drills and routines. As players mature, the duration of the matches lengthens and shortens because of the capabilities of the player. For example, a fourteen-year-old player might have much longer matches at a national level than at a local level. This changes as power improves and points become shorter (sixteen years and up).

Mental

The mental training is usually the most difficult to enhance. The first few development years prove to be very important to instill good mental habits. Young players are able to focus for a shorter period of time, but the best juniors are able to focus longer and achieve better consistency at an early age. Improving consistency alone will force them to focus longer and improve multitasking capabilities, a necessity in playing matches. Point play will provide feedback on all the aspects and improvements. It provides valuable information on what needs to improve and shows the weaknesses clearly. Playing practice matches with different scores can alleviate many fears. Players need to learn not to focus on the scores but on the task at hand with the strategy and tactics. By practicing different starting points in games (1–3, 3–1, 3–3 or 15–30, 30–15, 30–30), you can create an urgency on how to play these crucial and pinnacle situations. Players will become used to these situations and on how to deal with them with focus and confidence.

Training Plan

In order to make a training plan, you need to gather all the information to make an analysis of the player—where are they in their development in relationship with their age and concerning their technical, tactical, physical, and mental aspects. What are their strengths and weaknesses in relation with their playing experience? And then you also need to take into account their character, motivation, training activity, and talent level. Communication with the player and/or parents (with younger kids) is the key to gather information on future tournament plans and goals they might have.

- **Age**

  In order to make a training plan, you need to take the age of the student(s) into consideration. You would not train a fourteen-year-old the same way with an eighteen-year-old. The subject matter needs to be appropriate to the age and skill level of the players— concerning technical, tactical, physical, and mental aspects.

  Example

  If you try to have a fourteen-year-old hit with older and stronger players, they might develop injuries and, more importantly, will probably develop technical problems in hitting balls late and muscling the ball in trying to keep up. Patience is important here!

- **Gender**

  The subject matter is mostly the same in coaching different genders. But remember that girls develop quicker and are more mature at a younger age. Girls start playing stronger events at a younger age.

  Example

  Girls start playing international events on average two to three years before boys do. With this in mind, your training and tournament plan with advanced players needs a specific approach, and gender can make a big difference in your planning.

- **Playing Experience**

  The skill level and match experience are important factors to consider before organizing a training plan. As a coach, you do not want to jump ahead too far and introduce subjects that the players are not equipped to execute. On the other hand, if the subject matter is too easy, the students will become bored and not try as hard. The key is to find the proper level exercises to keep their interest and motivation for improvement.

Example

A player without much match experience will lose more first-round matches than an experienced competitor. This affects the training plan, the amount of training, the intensity, and the tournament plan in scheduling.

- **Strengths and Weaknesses Analysis**

  A good analysis of the strengths and weaknesses, in relation to the points mentioned above, assists the coach and player in staying on task. Otherwise, it becomes so easy to get distracted and jump from topic to topic in training. A good coach will spend more time on the weaknesses that need improving while at the same time trying to maintain or strengthen the strong points in a player's game. The key is to organize this all in a training and tournament plan that has a progression of new subjects and repetition and/or improvement of old subjects.

  Example

  Sometimes you can focus so much on one stroke (backhand) that the stronger stroke (forehand) starts suffering. Keeping a good mix of improving the strengths and the weaknesses promotes confidence in training.

- **Training Activity**

  The training activity needs to include training intensity and training frequency (how many training sessions per week). The progression and intensity of a training plan depends on the subject matter and improvements in prior lessons. The coach has to analyze the intensity of the training and the improvements of the students. The intensity of the training can be by quantity in time or by the level of intensity performed. If necessary, adjustments can be made to the training plan in intensity and subject matter.

  Example

  Your training plan needs to be appropriate/realistic to the amount of training (activity) and the amount of matches a player is performing each week. Otherwise, the confidence will be undermined over time.

- **Tournament Plans**

  The intensity and subject matter need to be coordinated with the tournaments and/or competition of each student. Close to competition, the intensity of the training might be higher, but the duration will be shorter. The training will be focused on strategy and mental preparation rather than technical issues.

  Example

  Closer to the competition in tournaments, you want players to be fully comfortable with the execution of the strokes. Consistency should become stability and automation. Coaches should adjust the training plan keeping confidence in mind.

- **Character and Motivation**

  These two factors come into play concerning the intensity and commitment of both the player and the coach to a training plan. In order to have the most improvements, players should take ownership of their game in convincing the coach of their commitment to improvement. Character and motivation become the driving force in becoming a good competitor.

  Example

  The passion for the game and motivation to train hard should not just come from the coach but should show in the character of the player in driving the coach. Players often will exhibit this by starting to train on their own in developing their game and improving each time you see them next. The coach cannot want it more than the player!

- **Goals from the Student**

  It is important to know what goals your student has for himself or herself. These goals can be outcome goals, performance goals, or process goals. It should be no surprise that most players will choose an outcome goal rather than performance goals or process goals since they are usually result-oriented. The coach needs to communicate and investigate what the goals are from his students and inform them of the other goals available before making a training and tournament plan.

Example

A player's goals can differ from his coach. This can heavily affect the motivation, effort, and outcome of the training and tournaments.

- **Financial**

  Making a financial picture of the cost involved can be an important factor in making a training plan. Most often, parents and players are not aware of the cost involved in training advanced players. But coaches can play an important role in assisting to receive financial help from sponsors, local clubs, and state and national associations. Making a budget to the cost involved makes it clear for all parties involved.

Example

Training an advanced player in the US can cost a total of $30,000 a year. This can be even more if international travel is involved, with coaching salaries and expenses.

Training Plan Content

The content of the training should be methodical and logical in progression. A good mix of topics is advisable to ensure that you train an all-round player. (It also keeps it much more interesting for the student.) All the topics should be integrated with technical, strategical, physical, and mental aspects to provide a sound combination that makes sense when explaining these to students. It is also possible to teach the other way around in using a tactical objective in justifying a certain technique. The training content should be constructed from information that is gathered from the various assessments:

1. Analysis - the assessments made from the technical, tactical, physical, and mental performance of a player

2. Short-term plan - the short-term plans for corrections and improvements
3. Long-term plan - long-term plans with a vision and plan for each player
4. Corrections - adjustments needed for improvement
5. Lesson plan - prior lesson plans play a role in the lesson content for future lesson plans

Corrections

This should be a list of subjects that need correction (short-term or long-term) and, more importantly, a plan on how to correct them. The wording of how you are going to improve something is crucial. For instance, to improve the topspin forehand of a player is different for player A to that of player B. Being precise on what actually needs to be improved in that specific stroke for that specific player is the key. After that, you need a way to deliver the correction with a method of correction! (See correction form below.) To determine what needs to be corrected is not always as easy as it seems. Some technical issues can be hidden and are not always easy to detect with the naked eye. Taking some video of your student and using slow motion can be a very helpful tool.

Correction Form (Sample)

Subject	Needs Improvement	Method
Technical topspin forehand	contact point	square off shoulders
Tactical backhand slice	trajectory/target	aim for a specific target
Physical baseline footwork	recovery	stepping out left and right

The form above shows some examples of the subjects, the improvements that need to be made, and the method of correction that should be used.

There are many methods that will solve the problem. Finding the right one that fits each specific player is the key.

After gathering the information from the evaluation of the player, the coach combines the information in one training plan form (see training plan form). In the training plan form, you can decide on what day you want to practice the subject and how you want to deliver the subject with a certain method of approach. This method of teaching maintains a consistency in the transfer of the messages to the player (communication).

Training Plan Form
(Sample)

Week	Day	Subject	Improve/ Correct	Method
1	Monday	FH + BH consistency	technical	contact point method
	Tuesday	service + return	tactical	shot choice / targets
	Wednesday	third-ball situation	tactical	shot choice
	Thursday	FH + BH patterns	physical	footwork/recovery
	Friday	net play	technical	contact points
	Saturday	point play	tactical/mental	focus on execution
	Sunday	off	-	-
2	Monday	FH + BH topspin	technical	trajectory
	Tuesday	point play	technical/tactical	execution / shot choice
	Wednesday	serve + return	technical	contact / footwork
	Thursday	volley	technical/ physical	closing on the net
	Friday	approach + volley	tactical	patterns
	Saturday	point play	tactical	tournament
	Sunday	point play	tactical	tournament
3	Monday	off	-	-
	Tuesday	BH slice	technical/tactical	defensive / drop shot

	Wednesday	second kick serve	technical/tactical	trajectory
	Thursday	drills	physical	stamina/footwork
	Friday	point play	tactical/mental	third-ball situation

Documentation

Once a plan is clear in front of you, coaching a player will become structured not only in teaching technical subjects but also in spending time on tactical, physical, and mental aspects. By documenting the plan and making notes on future training plans, the following step is to make a lesson plan. This contains the notes of the topics and how you set up your lesson for that day.

Stan Wawrinka

Martin van Daalen

Tournament Plan

A tournament plan is made after all information is gathered from the player concerning their ranking, tournaments played in the past, and the goals of the player and the parents. There are two different types of goals to consider:

- **Performance Goals**
  These goals can include subjects to improve the strokes, the strategy, and the physical or mental aspects in execution.

- **Outcome Goals**
  These goals are focused on trying to win a match, a certain tournament, or even to win a certain number of rounds and matches. It also can be a certain ranking goal.

These goals result in a detailed tournament schedule. The schedule needs to be a semiannual or annual plan that includes all the tournaments throughout the tennis season. In making the schedule, both outcome and performance goals should be added.

Scheduling

The scheduling of tournaments needs to be done with the goals and the development of the student in mind. The number of tournaments and level of the events are important to not only gain as much experience during play but also improve the player's ranking. Every aspiring advanced player should strive to play three levels of events: (1) the lower level to win tournaments, (2) the middle level to be competitive (at least quarterfinal), and (3) the higher level to gain experience. To achieve the goals from the student as well as the coach, you need to retrieve your steps backward through the tournament calendar in scheduling.

Level

There are several different levels of tournaments suitable for advanced players:

Eighteen and Under	Eighteen and Over
1. Nationals	1. Open events
2. ITF/ETA junior events	2. Future events
3. Open events	3. Challenger events
4. Future events (pro)	4. Tour events

The open events are prize money tournaments held in almost every state that are open to every level and age. These events are an excellent training ground for young advanced players to gain experience in play. (Note—To maintain amateur status for college, only accept expenses and fill out official expense form from the tournament director.)

Rule 1
A good rule of thumb in scheduling events is to never move on to the next level of major competition until the player has dominated the level they are competing in.

Rule 2
A win-loss ratio to keep in mind is at least 2 to 1, but a 3-to-1 ratio is preferable in order to keep confidence high (very important with juniors).

Quantity of Tournaments

The number of tournaments is related to the level of play and where you are in the development process as a player. In playing lower-level events, competitors will play many more matches than higher-level events. In making a tournament plan, take into consideration playing fewer events if you are making major changes to your game. Give students time to get adjusted to the changes in practice matches first. In general, the players should play two or three tournaments in a row to acquire a rhythm of play and then practice two to three weeks before playing tournaments again. A good mix between practices and tournaments will create improvements and confidence.

Week	Section/National	ITF/TE Juniors	Pro Events	Practice
1				home
2	local event			home
3				home
4	sectional event			at event
5				home
6				home
7		ITF event		at event
8		ITF event		at event
9				home
10			pro event	at event
11				off
12	local event			home
13				home
14		ITF event		at event
15				home
16	sectional event			at event

In organizing the scheduling, always keep these in mind:

1. **The age of the player** needs to be appropriate for the tournaments. Keep in mind that the age limit at ITF junior events is thirteen to eighteen, whereas the age limit in national events is to play up until the month of your birthday.

2. **The ranking of the player** and the entry level of the event go hand in hand.
   Check the entry list and rankings from last year to find out if entry is a possibility.

3. **Qualifying events** are another possibility to enter events (watch dates). They also provide extra practice in match play.

4. **Event dates** are important so events don't overlap. This is more important when entering qualifying events with several events played in a row.

5. **Entry dates** are usually three to four weeks prior to the tournament. But they can vary, so make a note on the tournament plan of the entry dates.

Planning

Making plans depends not only on above aspects but also on the budget available for training and travel. The tournament plan should be made ahead of time from six months to a year. The type of plan can be determined for the most part by the level of play.

Lower-Ranked

If you are a player at the bottom of the pack, you have to consider the tournaments you are able to enter. You can look at the cutoff (last-ranked player in the draw) of last year and look at the ranking of the players who entered for the event. This way you can make an estimation if you can make it to the competitors' list.

Middle-Ranked

If you are one of the middle-ranked players, you have various options. You can enter middle- and high-level events in your own age group and also try to gain experience by playing up in a higher age group. For this level, it makes sense to have two plans, one for each possibility of tournaments you are able to play. The proper balance is needed to keep the confidence in your game while trying to venture out and learn to play with stronger or older players. There should be a good mix of winning some easy events and playing some other tournaments where you reach the quarterfinal.

High-Ranked

If you are a high-ranked player, you obviously have all the options open. You can play all the middle- and high-level events and play up in sectional, national, or even international events. Your tournament plan should be a mix of events where you can win but also challenge yourself to improve your game.

Periodization

Always try to keep in mind how many tournaments you are intending to plan for the year and keep sufficient time for training and build in rest periods. Each player can vary in the number of tournaments they play, depending on how far they go. A better method is to keep track of the number of matches played. That way, you can plan the rest needed after each event and how to build up the training sessions in the type of training, the amount of training sessions, the length of the training sessions, and the intensity level of the training sessions. If you do not pay attention to periodization, you could have situations of overtraining occur, which will negatively influence the player's performance. You could also push the player too hard, and the fatigue could cause injuries. In the next chapter, you can find more information on this topic.

Periodization

This is a plan to gauge the frequency, the volume (intensity), and the duration (time) of the training quarterly, semiannually, or annually. This is crucial for three reasons: (1) this method achieves the most optimal training program, (2) it creates peak performance at important events, and (3) it prevents players from overtraining. The plan should contain the following aspects:

1. **To gauge the frequency (per day or per week) of the practice.**
   With the frequency, we mean the amount of practice units per day and per week. The more units per week, the more the intensity needs to be lowered and the duration adjusted.

2. **To gauge the volume (intensity) of the practice.**
   With the volume, we mean the intensity or load of the practice. With a higher load in the practice, the less frequent you can schedule training units, and the duration will have to be adjusted.

3. **To gauge the duration (time) of the practice.**
   With the duration, we mean the time of the practice units. With a longer practice time, the frequency of the training units and the intensity will need to be lowered and adjusted.

4. **To determine the type of training sessions.**
   It is important to train all aspects of the game with a combination of technical, tactical, physical, and mental training sessions. These topics can be new topics of learning, but it should also include training and repetition of old topics to increase consistency and confidence in the player's skills. The type of training is also determined by the competitive phase of the player or team. A lot of this depends on what you are trying to accomplish during the training and what the purpose of the training is. Are the players preparing for the season close to competition, are they training during competition, or are they recuperating after a match play?

Training Sessions

The training sessions should have a good buildup. It should contain a proper warm-up, topics for practice, and a competitive part with tactical, mental, and physical aspects and a cooldown. By making a periodization plan, you can keep track of all the aspects involved over time and make sure all topics are included in a proper ratio. By adjusting the frequency (training units), the volume (load/intensity), the duration (time), and the type of training, you will be able to create different types of training sessions that benefit the players' progress and performance to reach their peak performances when it's needed the most. This plan is simpler with juniors in an after-school program compared to full-time students with a more advanced level of play. A periodization plan becomes a necessity when working with top players who compete on the national or international stage.

Peak Performance

A peak performance can only be obtained when the mind and body are working in perfect coordination. This means, the player is in top shape, has great rhythm in their strokes, has good consistency in their game, and is feeling positive, eager, and confident to compete in the upcoming events. No player can reach his or her peak performance all the time. You could make an analogy between a race car and a top player; you cannot run the engine at full pace all the time. The engine would overheat and burn out. The same goes for athletes. You need to pick some areas during the year where you plan the peak performances and get the most out of your player. (With many top players, the peak performances are geared toward the top national and Grand Slam events.) As a coach, you should not underestimate the mental stress that match play has on the mind. Keeping a player mentally fit is even more important than keeping them physically fit. Rest periods should be organized at regular intervals. The rest periods can include doing other light activities (active rest) like stretching, yoga, jogging, or other sports (swimming and biking). The different types of training can be divided into these training phases:

1. **Preparation Phase**
    In this practice period, the coach tries to work on the fundamentals (technical) of the strokes and build up the basic endurance and strength of the player. There will be some match play, but it is not the main focus. (Frequency and duration are high; volume is medium.)

2. Precompetition Phase

In this practice period, there will be some more specificity of training with the focus more on the strategy and mental aspects. There is more match play as the player gets closer to competition. (Frequency and duration decrease to medium as the volume increases to high.)

3. Competition Phase

In this practice period, there is only specific training with the full focus on tactical and mental issues. There are only short intense practice sessions and lots of point play. (Frequency is low, duration is low, and volume is high.)

4. Recuperation Phase

This practice period is an active rest period in order to recuperate for the next preparation phase or precompetition phase. (Duration is low at first but medium later; frequency and volume are low.)

Training Compensation

With the body exerting energy through training, the body will adjust during the rest period by supplying more energy than what was previously available. This cycle of enhancement is called training compensation or super compensation. If the training units follow one another too fast, without proper rest for the muscles and nervous system to recover, the reverse will be the case; and there will be less energy available. In this case, you can have a form of overtraining. (See graph below.)

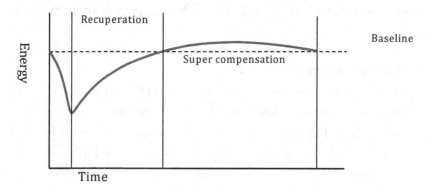

Overtraining

Starting to train too much (or too early) in the recuperation phase will cause the energy levels to stay below the baseline. The compensation of energy exertion will not occur, and the baseline of energy capacity will be at a lower level. In repeating this cycle too many times, the player might reach a state of overtraining. Undertraining might not make you reach peak performance, but overtraining can lead to illness and injuries due to fatigue. Here are some signs of overtraining:

- chronic fatigue
- irritability
- less interest in tennis
- weight loss
- slower reflexes
- reduced speed, strength, or endurance
- poor performances
- possible injury increase

If a coach or parent suspect there is a form of overtraining, it is wise to talk about this as soon as possible. When you develop good communication with your players, they will let you know when they feel tired or stale. The best remedy is to lighten the training or give the player some time off.

Active Rest

Another method is to have an active rest with light physical activities that do not tax the player physically or mentally. In many cases, the light physical activity can also reduce the mental stress and restore a calm, peaceful mind and relax the muscles and body. Some of these active rest activities are stretching, yoga, biking, swimming, jogging, other light sports, or even some massage.

Periodization Plan

Year

Player :

TRAINING AND COMPETITIVE SCHEDULE

Date of birth

Primary Coach

PHASE 1

Wk begin	TOURNAMENT	Rating	TRAINING	Rest	TECHNICAL	TRAINING CONTENT			Volume
						TACTICAL	PHYSICAL	MENTAL	

PHASE 2

Wk begin	TOURNAMENT	Rating	TRAINING	Rest	TECHNICAL	TRAINING CONTENT			Volume
						TACTICAL	PHYSICAL	MENTAL	

Martin van Daalen

Coaching and Development

As a national coach, I have taken many groups of players through the developmental stage from juniors to pro levels. It is a very enjoyable and gratifying experience to see them all progress through different phases. The toughest part was to find the proper level of tournaments to play. They needed to be challenged with competition but still win enough matches to gain confidence in their game. There is, however, no substitute for learning to win tournaments! A good win-to-loss ratio for matches would be 2 to 1 or even 3 to 1. There is a certain point when juniors need to make a breakthrough to advance to the next level in juniors. This happens again when breaking through the international level of the juniors and again when breaking through the pro levels. Below you will find one of those experiences I had in working with one of the boys' groups. I supervised these groups from the age of thirteen all the way to eighteen years of age.

I remember taking Rhyne Williams to the future events over the summer in Detroit. We went a couple days early so he could acclimatize and get used to the clay courts over there. We went out to practice that morning and were almost done with our session when a young man came over. He introduced himself as Milos Raonic. Rhyne was sixteen at that time and quite big for his age, but Milos was seventeen and definitely taller than Rhyne. He asked if they could play a set that afternoon, and we agreed to meet later that day.

They warmed up for about thirty to forty minutes and were ready to play a set. When Milos was serving, he was definitely dominating Rhyne in the beginning. His serve was so fast, and he made some aces early on. His ground strokes were not so consistent and still needed some improvements. When missing some baseline shots, he would get very mad and hit his racket on the ground multiple times. I gave Rhyne the task to try to get as many returns back as he could and told him this: "Rhyne, you can beat him with your ground strokes, so if you get the return back in the court, you have the advantage." He seemed to like that advice and went to work. After being down 1–3, he slowly got back into the set and ended up winning 7–5. Milos did not like this at all and smashed one of his rackets on the ground and completely broke it apart. We both looked perplexed at this spectacle and said our thanks to Milos and left to go back to the hotel. In the car, I said to Rhyne, "Never follow that example. If you don't stay calm, you never know if you could have won or not."

As it ended up, Rhyne was opposite Milos in the draw and had to play with him in the quarterfinal. I only gave Rhyne a simple strategy against him: "Remember what happened before when you played with him. He got mad, and you were able to win with your baseline strokes." Rhyne won the match in three sets and went on to win his first future event of his still young career. His first major breakthrough on the pro tour! Rhyne went to college and played on the ATP Tour. His injuries prevented him to continue. Rhyne is coaching on tour, and we have stayed the best of friends.

Milos Raonic went on to become one of the best young Canadian tennis stars and still, to this day, is considered a formidable opponent. He was at one time even top 10 in the world and is still top 20 in 2019. He obviously learned to control his emotions!

12—ANALYSIS OF TENNIS PLAYERS

As players become more advanced, it becomes even more crucial to make an extensive analysis in order to make proper instructions and corrections. Due to the various techniques, combined with the multiple styles of the players, the complexity of the instructions and corrections increases. It takes much experience and a good eye to find the proper methodology and approach to training the fundamentals, let alone the specialty strokes with different styles of play. It provides a better starting point to make improvements or corrections for appropriate instructions.

Analysis Goals

An analysis of a player can have different purposes. It is not only to determine the errors for correction from a technical point of view but also involves the tactical, physical, and mental aspects of the game. The different analysis goals are these:

- **To determine the level of competency of a player.** This is important for the method and level of instruction needed to improve the student. It is also a factor for pairing players with the proper level of practice partners for optimal training.

- **To determine the strengths and weaknesses for improvement.** A coach has to analyze how their technical game has been developed in combination with the tactical, physical, and mental aspects. Most often, these last three are overlooked in the analysis or dealt with at a later date. Just keep in mind that with advanced players, it is usually not the strokes that are holding them back in their development. More often, it is the tactical, physical, and mental aspects that need improvement in execution during matches.

- **To detect the errors for correction.** When a player experiences a problem during play, it can take a simple instruction to correct an error. However, it can also be a deeper-lying issue that causes the error. Learning how to conduct an analysis is crucial in preventing many errors with instructions and corrections.

Aspects that Can Influence the Analysis

There are several factors that influence the decision-making that eventually leads to an accurate analysis. These factors are the following:

- *The experience level of the coach.* It takes years of experience in coaching various players to develop the knowledge needed to make the correct analysis of a player. And even then, you have to know what to look for!

- *The time frame of the analysis.* Make sure that what you are trying to analyze is studied at the right time during the execution and over the right length of time to eliminate any other factors that might influence your decisions. Make sure to analyze with similar ball speeds and trajectory conditions so you can make proper comparisons.

- *Observing all aspects of the player.* For example, when observing a technical aspect for analysis, it is important to observe the player as a whole. The tactical, physical, and mental aspects of their game will influence the execution of the stroke with their personal style and can lead to an unnecessary or inaccurate analysis.

- *The personal style of the player and of the analyst.* Always consider the personal style of the player in making an analysis and make sure to leave your own personal style of play out of the equation. It is very easy to be influenced by your own style of play in making your students play like you. Just remind yourself how many different styles of players there are and respect them all.

Analysis Types

In making an accurate analysis, one has to know all the aspects involved that influence the decision-making of a coach. It is important to have a method that reduces the chance of mistakes and pinpoints the problems for correction. The analysis or observation should not be limited to practice but also be continued through match play and off-court training. As a coach, it will provide you with a much better picture of your player. There are three types of analyses to consider:

A. Pre-analysis   - made at the start of the practice or exercise (This method is mostly used to enhance a subject during practice with the intent to make regular instruction.)

B. Continued analysis - during point play and match play (This method is used to make mental notes of the instructions and to communicate these later with the student.)

C. Post-analysis   - after the correction is made (This method is used to check if the corrections hold up over time and if the student keeps executing the subject correctly.)

Error Detection

When making an analysis, you might come across errors in technical, tactical, physical, or mental execution. It might just be one error that is detected, or there might be several in the same execution of the action. There are two types of errors:

Primary errors. These are errors that are basically the root of the problem in executing the action. Sometimes the primary error is hard to detect, with multiple errors being a factor. This is where experience and knowledge of the fundamentals is crucial to make a detection.

Secondary errors. These types of errors are most often created by the primary error(s). It is very common to see players develop secondary errors in an effort to stabilize other errors in their execution, sometimes even to the point of becoming a personal style.

It is important to determine the difference in these two types of errors in order to focus on correcting the primary error first before tackling the other errors! In order to make the proper error detections, coaches should study the fundamentals and key positions of players. This will provide you with the best chance in making an accurate analysis of the possible errors and also in determining the method of making correction.

Methodology of Analysis

Step 1—*Determine first your goals as a coach and those of the player and/or parents before making any analysis.* There is no need to make an extensive analysis if no changes are desired by the player and/or parents other than to improve and play the game within their style of play. Your goals have to match the ones from player and parents.

Step 2—*Determine if your analysis is based on fundamentals or on the personal style of the player.* This can be of influence in making a proper analysis that is not based on your personal preference as a coach. Sometimes coaches will make corrections so that every player hits the ball the same way they do or how they would like them to play. However, it is possible that this is not suitable for that particular player. Changing strokes or making corrections to players needs to be based on the execution and productivity, with the player's personal style of play. It is very easy for coaches to fall in a pattern of making an analysis that leads to corrections based on personal preferences. Knowing the differences between the fundamentals and styles of play is important.

Step 3—*Stabilize the technique first before making an analysis.* Before you can make any analyses or corrections, you need to stabilize the strokes or situation first in order to get a correct analysis of the player. The follow-through on the strokes is usually a dead giveaway on the stability of the stroke production. It will usually indicate that either the grips or the contact points are not correct. Even in observing a tactical, physical, or mental situation, it is difficult to make a correct analysis when players are not hitting strokes out of stable positions. Questions will arise if the execution was meant to be like that or if it was a one-time occurrence.

Step 4—*Observe the subject of interest one aspect at a time.* Trying to get the whole picture of the player is important at first, but after the general observation, you have to break it down in parts. Break it down in technical, tactical, physical, and mental parts before looking at the specifics of each subject.

Step 5—*Determine primary and secondary errors.* By deciding on the root cause of the problem, you can eliminate additional and unnecessary correction that could make things worse rather than better. Once you have found the primary error(s), you can plan how to correct the problem.

Step 6—*Make sure to do a post-analysis.* This post-analysis is performed to make sure that the analysis was correct and the problem was resolved. It is also to see if the proper corrections were used and if they held up over time.

Competitive Analysis

To make a competitive analysis, or scouting report, you have to take in all the aspects of your opponent's game. This means both strengths and weaknesses in the technical, tactical, physical, and mental components. To make a good report, you should break it down the following way:

A. Technical

Determine the strengths and weaknesses

1. Serve and return
2. Baseline strokes
3. Approaching the net
4. Net game
5. Playing against the net player

B. Tactical

1. Serve and return
   - where does opponent like to serve (first-serve percentage)
   - where does opponent like to return
   - where does opponent go on offensive or defensive positions

2. Baseline game
   - what is the consistency and style of play
   - what is strength and weakness side
   - what are the patterns of play

3. Net game
   - strength and weakness in approach shot, volley, and overhead
   - how often does opponent come forward

C. Physical

Physical makeup

- age
- height
- strength
- speed
- stamina
- movement

D. Mental

Mental makeup

- concentration
- attitude, demeanor, and character
- emotional control

All these factors together generate an overall picture of how the opponent plays the game. Knowing all these specifics is important to make a basic game plan (strategy) and devise the execution of that plan with several tactics (specifics). The tactics are the multiple execution plans you can use to put pressure on the opponent. Using the different options of those tactics will keep the opponent guessing what tactic you are going to use next, and it will keep them off-balance. (See strategy and tactics in next chapter.)

Victoria Azarenka

Martin van Daalen

13—STATISTICS

Statistics are the facts and numbers that represent the results of matches and players. Most of the statistics of matches gives you the amounts of first serves, unforced errors, winners, amount of points won, etc. They can be statistics of a whole match or multiple matches or even in comparison to other players. These numbers of the game can be very useful if they are very specific and detailed. A report on a player can tell you what their preferences are and where they are making their mistakes. At the big tournaments on tour, these stats are recorded at every match, and you can get a printout of them after the match.

With these stats, we can make a comparison between some of the top players. Let's analyze Novak Djokovic for instance. What makes him so good, and why is he ranked no. 1? After his injury a few years ago, he bounced back and has been winning Grand Slams, just recently beating Roger Federer in the Wimbledon final (2019).

> I personally used to follow his progress as a junior when I was a national coach for the USTA. The group of boys I was in charge with were the same age as him and Andy Murray and such. As a junior, he was not the best player, and you could not see any indication he was going to be that good. Even later on, when he turned pro, he struggled with many of his strokes and footwork. I would have to say that he is one of those players who achieved his accomplishments and results mainly through hard work, diligent training, and sheer willpower.

Novak Djokovic's strokes and footwork are now considered the best in the business. Besides being very consistent, he can strike with every stroke from all over the court. There are many other players who have won Grand Slam events—Roger Federer and Rafael Nadal, to name a few. But Novak has been the most dominant player over the past five years. And the stats are there to prove it. If we go more in-depth with the statistics, the analysis shows why he is the only player with these numbers (results taken from Tennis Profiler).

The first analysis is to compare shot results with the general average of the ATP Tour. For instance, during the Australian Open final against Rafael Nadal, Novak won sixteen points with his forehand, with a total of 142 points in that match. So his ratio of forehand points is 11.27% (16/142), and this result is above the general average of ATP players.

The second analysis is to compare Novak with his rivals. Let's take the previous example with Nadal in the Australian Open final. Djokovic won sixteen points with his forehand against fourteen for Nadal. So he made 14.3% more points with his forehand than Nadal in this match. These stats are one of the factors that show why he won.

The third analysis was made by using several strokes in comparison with his rivals. The strokes analyzed were the serve, the return, the forehand, the backhand, and the volley. The number of errors will be compared with his rivals when he played with them.

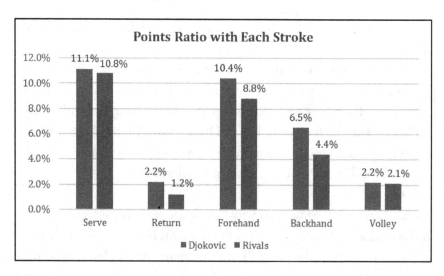

As you can see in this chart, Djokovic makes an average 3% more points with the serve, 83% with the return, 19% with the forehand, 45% with the backhand, and 4% with the volley in comparison with his rivals.

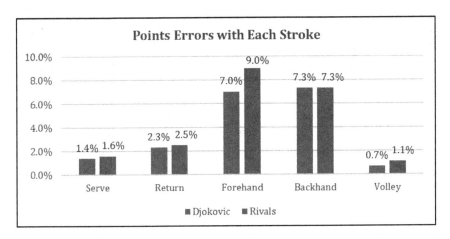

As you can see on this second chart, Djokovic makes an average 8% less errors with his serve, 9% with his return, 23% with his forehand, 1% with the backhand, and 36% with his volley than his rivals. These results are averages and can differ from match to match. It depends largely on who he plays with on any given day.

Let's compare his results with the rest of the big four who dominated the tour (Nadal, Federer, and Murray). Let's see on the ten shot comparisons how many each of the players have better than their rivals.

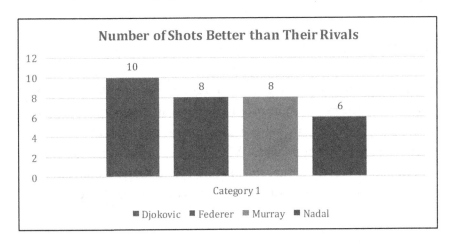

Out of the big four, Novak Djokovic is the only player to have better stats than his rivals with every possible shot. Roger Federer makes an average 2% less points on his return and 13% less points with his backhand than his rivals. Andy Murray has an average 11% less points with his forehand and 56% less points less with his volley than his rivals. Rafael Nadal makes an average 12% less points with his serve, 38% less points with the return, 10% less points with the backhand, and 53% less points with the volley.

Novak Djokovic is so good because he is such a complete player, capable of not only being more consistent but also being dominant in each part of the game. He can play close to the baseline and jump on returns and baseline strokes. Besides these weapons, his retrieving and counterpunching skills are one of the best in the world, and it allows him to make less errors than his rival in the rallies with every possible shot. His offensive skills have always been the basis, and it developed throughout his career. He comes in more frequently against some players to get an edge, but his volley is very reliable. He is not among the fastest servers in the world, but against the best baseliners, he often dominates them with more aces and service winners.

Novak Djokovic is not the most popular player, but if he continues to dominate in this fashion, it would not be surprising to see him eventually win more Grand Slam events than Roger Federer or Rafael Nadal.

Four-Ball Rallies

In studying stats on the length of the rallies, there are definitely some conclusions to be made. Some players are better in shorter rallies (one-two punch), whereas others are better at medium or long rallies. However, the most common rally length on the ATP/WTA Tour are exchanges that are won in four strikes (7–8 total shots). This means, if you train your serve and return in combination of 3–4 shots and can do this all the time, you have a large chance to win many matches. Don't forget that many players make mistakes on returns or in the next two balls.

First Set Percentage Wins

There are also stats available on the first set percentage wins. On average, players have 75 percent chance of winning the match after winning the first set. This percentage fluctuates more in women's tennis since they play more three-set matches. This winning percentage goes up to 85 percent after winning the first set and with a break of serve in the second. Knowing these stats should make you even more aware on how to prepare for matches and where to have your focus and energy:

- prepare with longer physical warm-up and hit to start matches stronger
- focus on beginning the match with aggressive and consistent play
- apply extra energy in the beginning of second (or third) set to force a break

In 2015, the ATP Tour's highest performers of winning first set percentage were Andy Murray (0.984), Novak Djokovic (0.972), and Roger Federer (0.970)—which was not so strange, considering they were also dominating the field at that time.

One of the players who follows this strategy rigorously is Rafael Nadal. His first set winning strategy has been very successful. His percentage of won first-set matches is very high on clay courts, but here is the strange stat on him: his percentage of matches lost on hard court after losing the first set is very high in comparison with the other top players. On clay, it actually is the highest, which is not so surprising since he grew up on clay and his style of play was modeled on this service.

I was texting with my friend Magnus Norman before the match in Australian Open (2014). He was coaching Stan Wawrinka in the final against Nadal. We were discussing his strategy, and I texted him the stats on Nadal's losing first set percentage on hard court and stressed the importance of winning the first set. I said, "Whatever you give him as a strategy to play, winning the first set against Nadal is crucial to winning the match." And I added, "If he loses the first set, you almost can shake hands after that. But if he loses the first set, he has a low percentage of winning matches." I don't know what he ended up telling him, but Stan won the first set 6–3 and went on to win his first Grand Slam in stylish fashion (6–3, 6–2, 3–6, 6–3).

Winning Percentage Points

There are many types of stats you can follow. They range from the amount of Grand Slam events won to overall tournaments won on the ATP/WTA Tour. You also have stats on how many times players have reached the semifinal of major events. No matter what stats you choose, there are some bottom-line skills that set players apart at the top in every level. They are the percentage points won on serve and return. To be more specific, they are percentage points won on first and second serve and return. You can see the specifics below:

- first-serve percentage points won
- second-serve percentage points won
- first-return percentage points won
- second-return percentage points won

Why are these four things so important? They represent not only the percentage of serves and returns but also how the points are set up and won. The combination of serve and return percentage with winning percentage says it all in the sense of playing skills. Some players are good at one of them but bad in another. So how do players use stats to improve their game? Some of it depends on their skill level, but there are definitely some ways to improve by becoming aware of the stats first and then showing how to improve them later. I will give you some examples on how these percentages (stats) vary, why they are important, and how to improve them.

Juniors (Twelve to Eighteen)

As a junior, you might have a low first-serve percentage and consequently lose a lot of serve games, with most players attacking your second serve. In junior tennis, it is not uncommon to see players hit a hard first serve but have a low (30 to 40 percent) first-serve percentage. The reason is, they like to hit it hard, like the pros on TV, but don't add the proper spin and are not tall enough to get it inside the service box. Every junior player, at one point or another, goes through this phase. The attitude on second serves is to attack and create pressure. Together with a low first-serve percentage, it makes it difficult to win service games in general. The opposite is the case for return games. So in general, juniors win return games easier than service games. That's why you see so many junior matches lose serve games.

So what is the answer for junior players?

Teach them to use more spin on first serves. This will create a higher first-serve percentage. Second, teach them how to play the third-shot situations better to keep initiative and pressure on their opponents. These methods will lead to more holds of service games and a higher first-serve percentage wins in points.

Transitional Players (Seventeen to Twenty-Two)

As a transitional player, you have to think of college-bound players and players starting to join future and challenger pro events. These players should be able to have a higher first-serve percentage in speed and placement, but they might not be skilled at returning all return shots. To have a good return for high-level speeds, you need to develop not only fast footwork and reflexes to reach the serves in the corners but you also need to get experience when to hit the return and when to block it back. In some cases, the ball speeds are so great that blocking the ball out in front is sufficient to hit the ball back. Controlling the ball at those speeds takes time to learn. This level player usually has a decent first-serve percentage wins, but the second serve can lack in speed and spin. Opponents will look to take advantage to attack the second serve and decrease the win percentage on second serves.

So what should transitional players focus on?

Transitional players should focus on improving their second serve and their return skills. Starting the point by pressuring the opponent is a sure way to keep initiative with the opportunity to apply pressure on the following shot (third shot).

Pro Players (Sixteen and Up)

As soon as your player hits the pro circuit, they will be confronted with serve and return percentage wins. The first four strokes in pro tennis are the most crucial to win points. This goes not only for serve and return but also for the commitment of consistency of the following shots. If players have a weakness in the first or second serves or returns, it will definitely be exploited. If a player slows down in the following shots of the rally, the opponent will immediately try to take initiative to apply pressure. In pro tennis, they have a golden rule: "Taking no risk is taking too much risk."

This doesn't mean that pro players take risky shots all the time. Not at all! They play with commitment to big targets to eliminate risk on the one hand but are not scared to go for the winner whenever the opportunity presents itself. That's why you see the serve and return winning points percentages fluctuate so much. This has mostly to do with the age, experience, and skill level of the players. You can see the difference in stats of a match from a top player against a less-experienced player to be quite lopsided. The top player could have a high winning percentage not only on first and second serves but also on return. The average player could show a high percentage on first serve but lower on second serves and return percentage points.

Stats Factory

There are now companies that specialize in analyzing stats for professional players. They do all the manual labor in analyzing all the videos of your matches and the videos of your opponents. They analyze the pattern and shot-choice habits and provide the service of compiling all the data so you can study it beforehand.

Recap

Stats are great for transitional and pro players. They are less valuable for juniors except for first-serve percentage and where you make most mistakes. For juniors, it is more valuable to see this because consistency can still be a problem. In the end, all players need to learn to develop and win rallies of medium length. Those are the most prevalent in all matches. Having a basic strategy and practicing patterns and shot choices will solve this problem of stats.

I told a young junior I would keep track of his first service stats because he was not believing his numbers. He did indeed change his first-serve percentage and went from around 30 percent to about 85 percent. The problem, however, is that he started pushing in his serves just to make the numbers in the stats and still was having trouble winning his service games. So I had to explain to him that "Those numbers are not the ones you are looking for. You want to know your stats (in this case, first-serve percentage) when you are playing competitive and with your normal speeds of the serve! Playing them much softer will give the opponent the opportunity to hit winners on his return. Nothing is gained from keeping track of those statistics."

14—STRATEGY AND TACTICS

This chapter of the book is about how to play the game by outthinking your opponent during match play. Although you can make a game plan ahead of time, the actual playing of points is more a form of instinctive play and reflexes. You have to deal with patterns, shot choices, tactical situations, and adjustments to the style of play of your opponent. Most of the time, the rallies of advanced players are at a tempo level where automated responses and recognition of tactical situations take priority over deliberate thinking. In between the points, games, and sets, a player has more time to think about strategy and different tactics. It takes a lot of mental discipline for a player to train his or her brain to be committed to the strategy and stay the course. Errors in shots or being outplayed by the opponent can discourage a player and force them to lose track of their plan and patience. The result is usually a change in strategy and tactics that might take the player out of their comfort zone.

The Difference between Strategy and Tactic

Strategy is an overall plan to use your own strengths to attack and exploit your opponent's weaknesses while preventing them to attack your weaknesses.

Tactic is the method of execution of a plan. An example of a strategy is to attack the weaker side of the opponent. This can be executed with several different tactics:

> **Tactic A—** Play long rallies to the weakness of the opponent. This will increase the pressure on the weakness of the opponent through consistency of the rally.

Tactic B—Use your stronger stroke against the weaker stroke of the opponent. The pace and pressure of the stronger stroke will apply physical and mental pressure on the opponent.

Tactic C—Serve and return to the opponent's weaker side. This will immediately apply pressure to the opponent to take advantage and initiative in the rally.

Tactic D—Play the ball with topspin or slice. This will keep the ball out of the comfort level of the opponent and apply more pressure to hit the ball correctly with direction and depth.

Tactic E—Play out wide to the stronger side of the opponent to open up the weaker side. This will increase the pressure on the weakness of the opponent.

As you can see demonstrated with the examples above, the strategy forms the concept of the plan, while the tactics contain the detailed execution plans of the strategy. There are many tactics available for each strategy, and players need to be made aware of the many possibilities to combat their opponents. Besides the tactical aspects, players can combat their opponents with technical, physical, and mental capabilities. Some players are very talented with their technical capabilities, and others might be more physically and mentally gifted or a combination thereof. Whatever their strengths might be, in today's game, advanced players need to be well-rounded to be successful.

I used to coach this eighteen-year-old girl in Amsterdam at the academy where I was the director and head coach. I first met her when she was just sixteen, and she was not so easy to coach. She was very stubborn, and it took me a long time to gain her trust. She had just turned pro (130 WTA) and was doing really well at the challenger level, beating a young girl called Martina Hingis in the final. It was that time of year when we had the international league tennis at Popeye Gold Star. Besides the top players in Holland, there were always a few international players on the team. The final matches were to be played at our home club, and there were about two thousand spectators out that day to watch the matches. She was to play her match against the top player in the Netherlands at that time (30 WTA).

I was discussing the strategy with her and told her that I knew how to play against this girl. I said, "The trick is to play high topspin balls to her forehand since she hits those really late, and it will cause a problem for her."

She replied, "No, I cannot do that."

"Why not?" I asked.

"That will look terrible with all these spectators here," she replied.

"Do you want to win?" I asked.

"Yes, but not like that. I just can't do it!"

So she went out and played the first set, and I had to watch her quickly lose (2–6) in the first set. She sat down on the changeover and said, "OK, what do you want me to do?"

"I want you to play high topspin to her forehand."

So she went out and played the high balls to her forehand and won the next two sets. We ended up winning the team championships for the third time in a row! This was a great lesson for her and a big win for her personally. You don't always have to win pretty, and you can't worry about what the spectators might think of your game! Do what is necessary to win the match. After finishing her pro career, she became a coach in Amsterdam and is still coaching there today. I wonder if she remembers this story.

Tennis and the Art of War

In reading the old Chinese text of Sun Tzu on *The Art of War*, you would realize very quickly the similarities between waging war on a battlefield and the battle of players in a tennis match. Let's examine some of the most famous phrases and see how they can work for you in your match.

"To know your enemy, you must become your enemy." You have to imagine you are the enemy. What would you do if you were the opponent? You must know his strengths and weaknesses to be able to avoid his strengths and to exploit his weaknesses. Most often, the best strategies to use against your opponent are the ones that you dislike being used against yourself.

"Strategy without tactics is the slowest route to victory. Tactics without a strategy is the noise before defeat." Without a good plan, you will most likely fail to succeed and struggle to win a match. Always prepare before the match and have a game plan. Make an analysis of the strengths and weaknesses of your opponent and also know your own. This way you can devise a strategy with several tactical plans that provide you an advantage (serve, return, baseline, attack, and defense plans).

"Opportunities multiply as they are seized." When you see your opportunities, try to act on them with boldness and confidence. When you take advantage of the opportunities, more opportunities will arise in your favor. When you are hesitant and tentative, your opponent will notice and take advantage of the situation.

"All warfare is based on deception." The most talented players seem to have a knack at camouflaging their strokes and strategies and always have their opponent off-balance—not only with their strokes but also in how they approach the game mentally. Keeping your opponent off-balance mentally will keep them from performing at their best.

It took me a while before I realized how to use strategies and tactics for my own game. One of the most profound things I learned about strategies and tactics was to figure out what I hated the most from my opponents and to turn those tactics against them. I would practice the solutions to the problems until I perfected them one at a time. I would not introduce them into my game until I became comfortable with the execution. Start making a list of things for yourself and write down the solution to the strategies of your opponents. This method definitely worked for me, and I know it will work for you as well!

Tactical Fundamentals

The basic strategies and tactics are the fundamental concepts and requirements that are needed to execute a chosen plan. These tactical fundamentals are listed below in order of importance:

1. Consistency
2. Depth
3. Direction
4. Spin
5. Power
6. Tempo

The tactical fundamentals are the same as the technical teaching order. The order of teaching tactical subjects is therefore connected to the technical development of the players. These tactical fundamentals alone provide many subjects for practice and point play for advanced players.

Consistency

This is the first tactic every player should use, at any level, as a game plan to combat an opponent. Consistency is the first element to break down when a player becomes nervous. In playing longer rallies, the pressure builds up, and mistakes are more likely to happen. Consistency is a weapon that can be used by every player. Every player has a shot tolerance to when they (on average) start missing balls. With each level you play, this is an important number you have to figure out. It could be as simple as playing one more ball than your opponent! But there are other aspects that influence consistency and can increase the shot tolerances:

- **Play more crosscourt than down the line**

  By playing more crosscourt, you can make your opponent move more and have more margin for error versus playing down the line. You can imagine that when you play down the line, it is easier to miss the ball wide, especially when changing direction from a crosscourt shot. The margins are smaller down the line, so make sure to choose larger target areas when changing direction down the line. Playing crosscourt makes your opponent run more than playing down the line. If 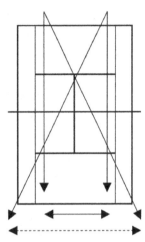 you look at the diagram, you can see the difference you need to cover in court in running from single line to single line versus running from double line to double line. Note—For every yard you have to run wide, you also have to run back. So every yard wide is double the distance you have to cover!

- **Use spin and slice to control the trajectory better**

  The use of spin and slice on your strokes can change the trajectory over the net and change the speed and depth of the targets. The spin can assist in playing higher over the net and create a larger margin over the net. At the same time, it can be used to make the ball dip down shorter in the court when the speed of the ball increases. The slice is a great shot to slow the ball down and also to create a low ball after the bounce so the opponent has to hit the ball out of their strike zone. Spin and slice both apply pressure on the opponent.

- **Use bigger targets**

  Use larger margins with your targets when directing the ball around the court. Especially in starting the point, this is a wise strategy. Not only is using the middle of the court a good strategy to start the point for consistency, it also decreases the angles the opponent can use to strike. You will see experienced players do this all the time in starting points and also in the first few games in matches. This method increases confidence in the strokes by warming up your coordination and timing to then dictate play as the rally evolves.

- **Shot choices**

  The choices you make have a great influence on your consistency. Knowing in an instance what direction, trajectory, and spin to use takes time to learn. You can't learn how to execute your choices without knowing the various options that give you the highest chance of dictating or neutralizing your opponent. A good example is to know how to play when you have an open court in choosing a big target and hitting firmly and with commitment to that corner. Another example is how to neutralize your opponent when you are in trouble by playing to the middle of the court with more spin and height over the net.

- **Other factors**

  There also other factors that can contribute to consistency. One of those factors is the physical and mental condition of the player. Tennis matches can last very long and can be in some extreme weather conditions that tax the player's ability to perform. Being in top physical shape gives you the ability to outlast your opponent and stay in the rally longer. Patience and a calm demeanor give you the ability to think clearly on your shot choices by not going for winners in bad tactical positions. Use the proper targets to keep the opponent off-balance and in a neutralizing position. This mental attitude saves energy with efficiency of play. Focus during the points gives players the ability to keep the initiative to execute with purpose. The timing of the split step is a highly underrated skill that provides the ability to start moving on time to the direction of the ball, reach more balls in the corners, and change direction of movement. This will create more time to set up and prepare the strokes and increase the balance during play. Flexibility and agility of footwork provide the ability to move with ease around the court to reach more balls in difficult situations and to recover with urgency to the tactical position of the next shot. Intensity and readiness provide a player the ability to start the point each time with the proper match speeds. Too often, you can find players getting tired or losing focus and standing up out of the ready position and playing with less intensity and purpose and slowing down. Keeping your thoughts on strategy and intensity is the key to success.

Depth (Change of Depth)

This tactical fundamental can be used as an offensive, defensive, and neutralizing weapon. When used appropriately, it is possible to force mistakes from your opponent and also accomplish four important factors in defending yourself. It provides you with extra time with a longer ball flight. It assists you in covering the court more easily, with the opponent having fewer angles available. It often generates short balls from the opponent with the opportunity to attack and use the wider angles against

Depth and Angles

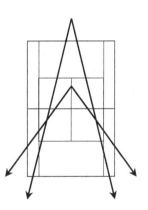

them. And finally, better depth generates opportunities to move the general position of a player closer to the baseline. This is a good position for defense, offense, or neutralizing play. Depth can also be used by changing the length of the trajectory to move the opponent forward and backward. Some players move well from side to side but don't handle the short and deep ball situations very well.

Direction (Change of Direction)

The accuracy of direction is a powerful weapon and tactical skill. This can be performed by returning the ball in the same direction or by changing the direction. Changing the direction of the ball requires more skill because of the adjustments needed for the contact points, trajectory, and racket angle at contact with the ball. Understanding when and when not to make direction changes takes experience and practice. Advanced players rely heavily on the ability to control the direction in order to maintain consistency in the rallies.

Spin

The rotation of the ball will influence the trajectory and bounce of the ball. Rotations are useful to control the ball flight and increasing consistency and speed of rally. Players are able to hit the ball harder and higher over the net with the use of topspin. The topspin will also increase the speed and height of the ball after the bounce, increasing the pressure on the opponent. With slice strokes, it is possible to slow the ball down and keep the ball below the net and decrease the chance of winners from the opponent. Sidespin, or combinations thereof, is a common rotation with the service action and controls the trajectory and bounce of the ball. These rotations are a valuable tool for advanced players to increase consistency, speed, and ball flight before and after the bounce. This makes it a powerful weapon to pressure the opponent and to attack their weaknesses.

Power

This component can be measured by the speed alone or by the speed in combination with the rotation of the ball (also named heavy ball). It is possible to use power to the strokes by speeding up the ball to outpace the opponent. In this case, the speed of the ball will be faster than the opponent can run and/or react to the ball. However, power can also be used by combining speed with spin or slice to maintain the control of the ball. Players will experience the pressure from unpredictable ball bounces. Nadal is a good example of a player who uses this component extremely well. Players have to make split-second decisions on how to handle each situation (speed, spin, bounce) separately.

Tempo

Speeding up or slowing down the tempo of play will disrupt the rhythm of the opponent. This powerful weapon is used by many advanced and top players and is also the most difficult tactical skill to master. Tempo is determined by the timing of the strike of the ball. This can be achieved by taking the ball earlier or later after the bounce and, in some cases, even in the air before the bounce of the ball (volley and volley drive). The tempo change will pressure the opponent to feel rushed (speed up) or lose rhythm (slow down) in their play. Opponents will be pressured into making many adjustments that will often lead to confusion and more errors.

The Basic Strategy

All good players follow a basic plan to play points and compete in tournaments. This basic plan should be founded on very simple principles to construct a point and apply pressure on the weakness of the opponent. Especially when players don't have so much power yet (younger players), this basic strategy is an important game plan for their tactical development. The basic strategy is as follows:

1. Know the strengths and weaknesses of your opponent
2. Keep a high first-serve percentage (70 percent or higher)
3. Hit the return to the middle, preferably to the weakness
4. Play the second ball after serve and return to the weakness
5. Play aggressively to the open court and then attack the weakness again
6. Knowledge of percentage play will influence your game strategy

1. Exploiting the weaknesses and strengths of players and opponents requires reading these well and recognizing them. Scouting your opponent in other matches will give you valuable information on their strengths and weaknesses and style of play. It takes focus and experience to learn these skills in order to make a basic plan for a strategy and tactics. (Practice scouting players by looking at matches

together with your coach and discussing styles of play, strengths and weaknesses, strategies and tactics, patterns, shot choices, etc.)

2. The first-serve percentage should be high in consistency and aimed at the weaker side to apply pressure. Ideally, the serve percentage will be 7 out of 10 or above in order to set up the second shot. This will also assist the server in avoiding double faults and take the pressure off, especially on crucial points in the game. (You can practice this by setting up target areas and counting how many you can make out of ten serves or tracking some of your matches and looking at the serve percentage.)

3. The return should be close to the middle (preferably on the weaker side) and deep in the court to increase the consistency and pressure on the opponent. Big targets on the return will also relieve pressure on the return player and prevent unforced errors early in the rally. It will also decrease the angles on the second shot from the opponent and prevent them to attack you right away. (Practice returns to target areas in point play and what shots to expect next.)

4. Players should be looking to position themselves quickly after the serve or return to hit their best strokes on their second shot. Ideally, this should be targeted to the weakness of the opponent to keep applying pressure. Many times, the less-experienced players are not ready after the first shot and end up playing a defensive shot on their second exchange. Maintaining controlled pressure is the ultimate goal to keep the opponent in a neutral or defensive position, with less opportunity to strike back. It is important to practice this second ball situation in order to read the trajectory and establish a routine for the different options. (This type of practice can be executed with the coach feeding you a certain return to improve the next shot. As you make improvements, it is possible to mix them up and play out the point.)

5. At the start of the match and each point, rallies should be initiated to big targets of the court before venturing out closer to the lines. However, as soon as the player is more comfortable and pressure is established on the weaker side, the open court should be used to make the opponent run and then apply pressure back to the weaker side. This method will keep the opponent in a neutral or defensive style of play and not allow them

Martin van Daalen

to attack you as often. Pay attention next time you see the top players start matches and watch how they construct points, what targets they use, and what their shot choices are in the rally. (Practice the patterns of seeking the weaker side first and then open court and back to weaker side and vice versa. Play out the point.)

6. The knowledge of basic percentage play will influence your way of playing in match play. Some examples of percentage play in match play are the following:

- The person who wins the first set wins about 70 percent of all matches. Knowing this stat should increase the focus on the preparation and intensity at the start of the match and first set. The tactic here is to take initiative early and deliver the first punch and diminish the opponent's options to play freely.
- The person who wins the first set and is up a break in the second has 85 percent chance of winning the match. Many players tend to slow down in the second set and lose intensity in their play. The tactic is to win the first set and to get an early break in the second. This puts tremendous pressure on the opponent.
- Keeping the focus and intensity on certain points in the game and set can help you win much easier (first point of the game, 30–15 and 30–30 points, game points, the first three games of the set, the seventh game of the set, how to take initiative in tiebreaks, and closing out sets and matches).

These simple rules in competition are used on a daily basis by the best players in the world, and it would serve you well to follow these tactics as well. Having a method and a game plan will always increase your chances of success. I have taught these rules to many students in the past, and all of them have dramatically increased their consistency and results. After learning the basic strategies, you can make the next step by learning the patterns of play, improving and applying different shot choices, learning to master different styles of play, and working on weapon development of your strokes. The possibilities in learning new strategies and tactics are limitless, but learning the basics and a method to apply them will always help you improve your confidence in your game and have more fun in competition.

Percentage Play

Understanding percentage play will help you win matches much easier or can even assist you in beating stronger players without the knowledge or skills. Percentage play is not only the knowledge of the percentages, it is also about the execution of strategy. Below are the most important tactical factors of percentage play:

- score percentages
- serve and return percentages
- patterns of play
- shot choices with trajectories and targets

Knowing how to execute tactically and mentally in all these circumstances will improve the chances to win matches. Focusing on strategy and tactic reduces the emotions that might arise during execution. Below is a list of average percentage situations that might affect the outcome of the game, set, tiebreak, or match.

Winning the first set	-70 percent chance of winning the match
First set win and a break in second	-85 percent chance of winning the match
Winning first point in the game	-60 percent chance of winning the game
Winning first two points	-70 percent chance of winning the game
Winning 30–15 or 30–30 point	-75 percent chance of winning the game
Being up a break in the set	-75 percent chance of winning the set
Being up a break in tiebreak	-70 percent chance of winning the tiebreak

These average numbers are not defining if you will indeed win or lose, but they do give you a good indication what gives most players, percentage wise, the best chance of success. If you study these percentages well, you are able to make some very definite conclusions. Taking initiative to lead is obviously an important tactic. It applies pressure on the opponent and reduces their ability to play freely without nerves. This will be visible when they play more conservatively or do the opposite when they panic and play overly riskily. As a player and a coach, it should be clear that preparation becomes much more important and that the energy and focus should be on the first set and on getting an early break in the second set. This requires the player's intensity to be as high as possible in the beginning of each segment of the games, sets, and tiebreaks.

Serve and return percentages could vary due to the level of the players, gender of the players, the surface, and even the weather conditions. Below are some examples of average percentages and how to improve them:

First-serve percentage should ideally be at 70 percent; however, even some advanced players are between 40–60 percent. If players knew that their points won on first serve most often relates to their win percentage, they would pay more attention to this detail. For example, many times, the player that has a 40 percent first-serve percentage also wins 40 percent of the points and subsequently loses the serve game. (On the men's side in pro tennis, this can vary if the player has a good second serve.) The reason for this is that the opponent experiences far less pressure and will also start to take more chances on first *and* second-serve returns. In general, most players hit first serve returns neutrally or defensively; whereas on the second serve, they play more aggressively. This is even more visible on the women's side, with the serve speeds being lower on second serves. Knowing this trend should make the strategy even more clear in making sure that first-serve percentage generally should be higher for women (80 percent). There are many clay court specialists who also have a very high first-serve percentage (80–85 percent) since there is less chance of scoring directly with a slower surface speed. The opposite is true with big servers (pro players). They can score so much easier with their first serve that sometimes their percentages drop to 60 percent or even a bit lower. There is an easy way to practice the first-serve percentage—by counting how many shots are made out of ten tries. This drill can be made even more difficult by dividing the service box into three target areas (backhand, body, forehand) to improve the direction.

Second-serve percentages should be at 100 percent in giving yourself at least a chance to win the point. Every second serve you don't hit in the service box gives you 0 percent chance of winning that point. At least getting it in the service box gives you a minimum of 50 percent chance of winning the point. The better you are able to apply pressure with this shot, the more the winning percentage will increase. So you can imagine what can happen if you are able to neutralize or put your opponent on the defense. This is possible by targeting the weaker shot and/or by using speed, spin, and angles. Practicing the second serve should be a priority for every player. Winning second-serve points is more difficult, with the serve being neutralizing in nature and players being more aggressive on second-serve returns. Most top players are defined by the quality of their second serve. (Pete Sampras was an exceptional serve player who sometimes hit two first serves when his confidence was high or when he was leading in the serve game).

The return has become a weapon over the past decade with the improvements in string and equipment. So much so that many players forget the first objective in hitting returns: getting the ball in the court! Watching professional tennis can be confusing for juniors or advanced players trying to reach a higher level. You often will remember the flashy returns with outright winners, forgetting the score in the game, the quality of the serve, and the skills of the player. However, top players know when to play high-percentage shots when it is needed. No matter what return is played, consistency should be a high priority in order to increase the chances and pressure. The beginning of the match should be a clear strategy by playing the middle of the court (preferably to the weaker side). This neutralizes the serve and also limits the angles of the opponent to strike on their second shot. The second-serve return can be a different strategy, with variable targets, as long as the quality and consistency of the return is maintained. Players should become proficient in their return shot choices. Adjustments and risk management are skills that will greatly influence the execution of the return. In order to apply pressure and break an opponent, a certain amount of controlled aggression is necessary. A quality server has more options to be more aggressive in the return games. The priorities of the return should be as follows:

1. Always try to get the return in the court (consistency)
2. Play the return back in the middle of the court (especially during first serve)
3. Play the return to the weaker side (make opponent feel uncomfortable)
4. Attack weaker serves with aggressive returns (especially when up in points)
5. Return to stronger side to attack open court / weaker side (as a surprise option)

Patterns of play will affect the percentage points won in the rallies. Players have to understand the pressure and opportunities they face and make the appropriate decisions. This can vary from playing to the middle of the court when under pressure or playing crosscourt to move the opponent. When the opponent is out of position, it can be also be considered a percentage play to go down the line, as long as you maintain a margin for error by playing bigger targets. All these patterns should be decided by situational strategies and tactics, considering the risk management and shot choices. They can also be used to create a higher percentage play by setting up patterns that suit your game and involve your best strokes and strongest weapons.

The shot choices and targets are the last aspects of percentage play in decision-making. Experience in competition and match play will enhance the decision-making of better shot choices under various tactical circumstances. These shot choices should be made to the tactical status (offense, neutral, defense), the type and amount of speed and spin, in combination with the trajectory and targets on the court. There are several times during the match that shot choices and targets should be adjusted with starting a match or set or by gaining the momentum and in finishing the games, sets, and matches properly. The experience will teach players to start conservatively with the shot choices and targets at the beginning of the match and reset to this strategy in the following sets. (This does not mean that players have to slow down. On the contrary, they should keep the intensity as high as consistency permits.) As players settle into the match, they can venture out more to the sidelines. The most difficult topic to learn is the targeting and the margin for error to keep the consistency as high as possible. It is all a matter of practice and experience.

Styles of Play

There are several different styles of play when playing the game. They represent a personal method and structure in executing the points during play. Here are some of the different styles of play:

- aggressive baseline player
- the all-court player
- the defensive player
- serve-and-volley player
- the counterpuncher

Many players have not just one style but a mix or combination of the styles above. The style of a player is determined by the method and consistency of the reproduction of the strokes and patterns. Every player eventually chooses a certain style of play they feel comfortable with. A style of play has to mature over time. It is not something that is often found in beginner tennis players. They either have an aggressive, neutral, or defensive style of play. It is the task of the coach to assist players in finding a style that suits their strokes and skills in order to be successful and make them feel comfortable during play.

- **The Aggressive Baseliner**

  This player tries to dominate from the baseline with aggressive baseline strokes in order to get the opponent off-balance. They move the opponent around the court using the speed, spin, and angles of the ball. They play aggressively in every way: physical, mental, technical, and tactical. The player is quick to move around the court and has a first-strike mentality. The qualifications to become an aggressive baseliner are (1) aggressive nature of play, (2) mental and physical strength, (3) speed in arms and legs, and (4) first-strike mentality.

  Training

  The coach will try to assist this player by teaching the basics of the third-ball strategy, open-court strategy, and mid-court strategy. The third-ball strategy is the tactical and technical execution on how to play the ball after the return from the opponent. This first-strike strategy is based on taking advantage of the return by taking time away from the opponent and applying pressure. The open-court strategy is the tactic and execution in keeping the opponent running to draw errors and to not allow them to apply pressure on you. Note—Once this open-court pattern is established, you will have an opportunity to play behind a player and wrong-foot the opponent.

- **The All-Court Player**

  This player tries to mix up baseline and net play in order to disrupt the rhythm of the opponent. The all-court player is comfortable at the baseline as well as playing serve and volley or approaching the net. A player can mix up spin and slice and accelerate at any time. The footwork needs to be very adaptable to the situations in playing either offensive or defensive tennis. The qualifications of an all-court player are (1) technically developed in all strokes, (2) good footwork in offensive and defensive situations, (3) good strategic and tactical insight, and (4) creative and adaptable mind-set.

Training
The coach will stimulate this creative player in learning all the different strokes and footwork in feeling comfortable all over the court. The player will have to spend time practicing offensive and defensive situations and also practicing serve and volley and approaching the net. The coach has to be very supportive and instill patience since the development of an all-court player takes more time to develop.

- **The Defensive Player**

  This player plays very consistently and tries to run down and return as many balls as possible in order to draw mistakes from their opponent. Often, these players will try to slow down the rallies by playing higher over the net and adding spin. The defensive player has very good footwork and relies most on their speed to track down every ball. They can play topspin as well as slice on their ground strokes. They have a high first-serve percentage and focus on consistency. The qualifications for this player are (1) well-developed ground strokes with topspin and slice for great consistency, (2) high speed on their footwork, (3) excellent stamina, and (4) high mental endurance.

  ### Training
  The coach will support this player by practicing consistency in the execution of the defensive ground strokes. As the player becomes more proficient, the coach can add more topspin and slice. Footwork and fitness are key elements to play this game style. Practice matches are focused on playing defensive and neutralizing patterns.

- **The Serve-and-Volley Player**

  This player seeks to go forward behind the serve and volley the ball in order to apply pressure by taking time away from the opponent. The serve-and-volley player has an aggressive playing style and likes to play fast points. The player has strong legs and great balance and likes to use the volley and speed of the footwork to dominate the opponent. The first and second serve are key elements in supporting this style of play. Most often, the player will have the same aggressive nature in the return games and try to seek the net position. The qualifications for this particular player are (1) good serve and volley skills, (2) fast and agile footwork, (3) aggressive ground strokes to force a short return, and (4) aggressive nature in playing the game.

Training
The coach will assist in the practice of the serve and volley techniques and aggressive ground strokes. This style of play takes a lot of time to develop and is not suitable for beginners. It is possible to practice a lot of approach games to hone the skills later in their development.

- **The Counterpuncher**
  This style of play is for players who like targets to pass the player at the net or to lure them into certain positions and then accelerate. The counterpuncher has fast and agile footwork and is handy and crafty in creating shots to maneuver the opponent. The qualifications for this player are (1) fast and agile footwork, (2) good topspin and slice ground strokes, (3) creative mentality, and (4) good touch.

Training
The coach will try to create practice sessions where the player has to either defend at the baseline or create a passing shot or lob over the opponent.

As juniors progress to intermediate or advanced players, it is important for coaches to introduce all styles of play over time. This will give students an opportunity to make an informed decision on the style of play that suits them best. A coach can assist in this by pointing out the strengths of each individual player to fit a certain game style.

Serena Williams

Martin van Daalen

Tactical Status

The tactical status of strokes is determined by the style of play and the specific tactical situation of the player. The style of a player can greatly influence the character of play. A serve-and-volley player will most often play offensive tennis and will even have that same mind-set with the return games. A defensive player will rarely take an offensive position and will use neutralizing and defensive strokes to bait the opponent to make errors. There are three options available with the tactical status of play, and these can vary during the course of a rally:

- **Offense**

  The player seeks the initiative by applying pressure on the opponent with forceful shots, tactical situations, tactical positioning of the body, and/or the tempo of play. Players will seek to continually pressure the opponent to defensive positions on the court until they can hit a winner or force the opponent to make errors. Dictating the points with continuous pressure is not easy to do and is a skill and tennis art form.

- **Defense**

  The player will apply pressure on the opponent by playing deeper in the court to reduce the offensive capabilities of the opponent, slowing down the speed of the ball with rotation of the ball (topspin, slice, sidespin), playing the ball higher or lower out of the strike zone of the opponent, and reducing the offensive angles of attack for the opponent. The player seeks to win the point with consistency and/or the buildup of mental and physical pressure during the point.

- **Neutralizing**

  This mode of play is the most complicated tactical status in preventing the opponent to play offensive strokes. There are several different ways to neutralize a player. Unlike the defensive play, the neutralizing strokes can be speedup strokes and also slowdown strokes to neutralize the opponent. To successfully execute a neutralizing shot, a player has to understand when to accelerate or slow down the speed of the ball in combination with the trajectory of the ball, the type of rotation, and the amount of rotation. As the word indicates, neutralizing an opponent means that a player has to seek patterns, strokes, and tactical situations that provide the opponent with little or no opportunities to attack.

Practice
- Alternate defensive and offensive strategies by having a player play back to the middle of the court, while the other player must try to move the opponent around the court by hitting to the corners. This will create many situations that train the trajectory and spin (topspin and slice) of the ball.
- One player covers the whole court against the opponent covering only one side of the court with that stroke (alternate sides for forehand and backhand side). This will train players to not only hit to the outside lines of the court but to also use all targets on that side. The opponent will learn how to neutralize the situation with spin and slice strokes and also gain more defensive skills.
- Feed a wide ball to a player on the other side, starting on the opposite sideline. The player has to run across the baseline to recover the ball and find different tactical solutions according to the position and difficulty of the shot and play out the point. This can be practiced with different types of feeds and different targets to play on the return. The feed will determine if the player has a defensive or neutralizing shot choice. Start by teaching the high defensive topspin return in the middle of the court before giving players a choice. This will provide a basis to work from and will train the footwork first in setting up properly in a balanced way. On a wide backhand, it is possible to train the slice backhand to the weaker side of the opponent.

- Do the same exercise as above but start in the middle of the court with an inside-out forehand. Teach the topspin forehand first to apply pressure on the high backhand of the opponent. This drill not only trains both strokes but also illustrates how to neutralize the opponent with a high backhand. If the inside-out forehand is struck too flat, it provides the opponent opportunities for a winner down the line.

- Feed balls to the player on the opposite side with the objective of hitting approach shots and playing out the point against another player. This exercise can be executed by hitting the approach shots down the line at first. As this game is mastered, it is possible to include crosscourt approaches. This will increase the difficulty for players to pass the net rusher.

- Playing either topspin or slice will provide players with a greater understanding on how to manipulate the opponent with a certain spin. It teaches the pros and cons in using these particular strokes. It also teaches players how to use them in order to apply pressure on the opponent (topspin to topspin, slice to slice, topspin to slice).

- Serve and volley games are an excellent way to practice the different tactical statuses and to find solutions to each situation. By starting with returns to prechosen targets, it is possible to set up a great practice routine with a starting pattern and an open end by playing out the point whatever way you want.

Shot Choice

During the course of a point, game, set, and a match, a player will often have to switch gears and adjust to the tactical situation by making a choice on the different available shot options. Players have to decide on how aggressive the shot needs to be, what the trajectory and speed of the ball should be, and what rotation to use. These individual tactical shots are named shot choices. They are determined by several different factors:

- **The technical and physical capabilities of the player**

  Players are only able to make good shot choices when executing shots within their own technical and physical capabilities. The moment they try to force the situation (pressing), they will lose control of the ball. It will cause them to muscle the shots within their reach (unforced errors) or try for too much risk when pushed in the corners of the court (forced errors).

Practice

A good way to practice these situations is to play baseline points with the emphasis on consistency of the rally. This will ensure that players focus on staying within their own capabilities without forcing the situation. The length of the rally will tax both players and eventually cause one of the players to lose patience and pull the trigger. This is an excellent time to explain the parameters of their capabilities and how to avoid taking too much risk.

- **The tactical capabilities and experience of the player and the opponent**

  As players mature and gain more experience on how to use strategies and tactics, they are better equipped in making sound tactical decisions to the shot choices during the rallies. In combating an opponent, the tactical experience of both players plays a large role in the shot choices and the eventual outcome of the points and, eventually, the match.

Practice

By playing different levels of players, it is possible to show the experience and skill level of each competitor. Playing different levels requires discipline in the execution of strategies and tactics against both levels of players. Make it clear how it is possible to win and lose against both with good and bad shot choices (think of when players play a weaker opponent and play sloppy).

Each level requires a different strategy, and there is no shortcut to experience.

- **The mental discipline of a player to focus on the strategy, tactic, or pattern**

  The discipline of the shot choices determines the consistency of a player to execute a chosen strategy, tactic, or pattern. When players stray from their chosen strategy, the shot choices become erratic and unreliable. This particular phenomenon is clearly visible when players make sudden last-second decisions in their shot choices. Usually the technique will break down with errors in consistency and direction.

Practice

It is fairly easy to lose focus of your strategy or tactics during a match. Shot choices become erratic. It is usually the score in the match or a distraction of thought that makes players lose focus, with a replacement of the original thoughts. When this happens, keep asking the player about the strategy and tactics during a break in the action and remind them to focus on strategy and tactics alone.

- **The tactical status, situation, and positioning on the court**

  These three factors play a large role with the shot choices of a player. It will influence the trajectory of the ball with direction, height, speed, and spin. For example, the farther a player is positioned behind the baseline, the more height the ball flight should have over the net to create a deep neutralizing ball for the opponent. By adding topspin, it is possible to make the ball bounce up higher and push the opponent even farther back behind the baseline or force them to take more risk by hitting the ball on the rise.

Practice

Teaching the different shot choices in these three situations is possible by starting the rally with a feed and playing out the same point repeatedly. This method will enhance the tactical knowledge and situational strokes of a player.

- **The score in the game, set, or match**

The score will always determine the amount of risk involved with shot choices. When players are leading in score they will produce different shot choices than when they are trailing in score. When leading, it is possible to hit the ball harder and earlier (tempo) to larger targets. This increases the pressure on the opponent without taking excessive risk. Another method is to start moving the opponent around the court by hitting slightly closer to the lines and not letting up on the pressure. When trailing in score, players usually play more conservatively by aiming for larger targets and by playing higher over the net with spin. In some cases they panic and go for overly risky shots and make quick errors.

Practice

Changing the score in the game and/or set will require the player to think of different methods to play tactically when up or down in score.

- **Intangibles: surface, weather, etc.**

The surface and weather situations have a direct impact on the shot choices. Playing on different surfaces like clay courts, indoor surfaces, grass courts, or outdoor hard courts will directly influence the style of play and therefore dictate the shot choices. Playing on clay courts and grass courts can be very demanding on the footwork, with the possibility of sliding. This requires players to adjust shot choices that fit the style of play of that particular surface. The weather can also play a role with windy conditions and influence play. The temperature is a factor when cold weather affects the bounce (low) of the ball, while extreme warm weather affects a player's stamina in a match.

Practice

Playing on different surfaces will enhance the experience of a player with adjustments in strategies and tactics, different styles of play, and different types of footwork. The various weather conditions are an excellent time to coach players in adjusting to the conditions and becoming mentally tough. Make sure to use these conditions to instruct the players with strategic and tactical information.

Tactical Situations

Every exchange of strokes is developed from a specific tactical situation. These tactical situations are specific to the position of both players on the court and the type of strokes that need to be executed from that position. The situations can develop at the beginning of the rally with the serve and return; during the middle of the rally in baseline play, net play, and approaching the net; or at the end of the rally with playing against the net player. The five basic tactical situations are these:

- serve and return
- baseline play
- approaching the net
- net play
- playing against the net player

Roger Federer

Martin van Daalen

The Serve

These tactical situations represent the start of every rally from both players. The tactical situations of the serve and return are quite different even though they start the rally for both players. The serve has always been the most offensive weapon of advanced players and has dominated the game for decades. Not only does it have the possibility to win the point outright with an ace, but it can also apply tremendous pressure on the opponent to force them in a defensive position. Besides being a first strike weapon to win the point outright, the serve can be used to set up a pattern and to put the opponent in a defensive position. Some of the tactical situations of the serve are the following:

1. **Serving out wide** will pull the opponent off the court, leaving the whole court open to attack. This tactic will only work well when the server is committed to the target area and the execution of the serve. A tentative serve will have the opposite effect—with the returner possibly attacking the serve and putting the server in a defensive position. The third-ball situation (the ball after the return) needs to be practiced frequently to create a rhythm and automation to the responses from the return. After the serve out wide, the server has to recognize the trajectory of the return to take up position behind the ball early and also judge the recovery speed of the opponent. The footwork recovery will indicate to the server where to aim the third ball. If the return player recovers slowly, the server should play to the open court. If the return player recovers fast, the server can wrong-foot the opponent by playing behind them in the opposite direction of the recovery or have the return player overrun the ball by playing through the middle of the court. Serving out wide to either side has various tactical advantages and can be executed for various reasons:

   • to pull the opponent out of position
   • to attack the weaker return of the opponent

- to open up the weaker side of the opponent by serving to the opposite side
- to open the whole court to attack the footwork of the opponent
- to force a weak return from the opponent to attack
- to force a specific return from the opponent to your strength

2. **Serving through the middle** of the court has one very specific advantage above the other service options. The net is lowest in the middle of the court! The server has a higher percentage chance of hitting this target with more speed. Whenever players are struggling with the first-serve percentage, they should be choosing this target through the middle more often for consistency and to build confidence. There will be a higher percentage chance to ace the opponent through the middle of the court. The tactical reasons for using the target through the middle of the court are these:

- higher percentage serve
- first strike opportunity is higher (ace)
- to pull the opponent out of position
- to force a weak return
- to attack the weaker return of the opponent
- to open up the weaker side of the opponent by serving to opposite side
- to force a specific return from the opponent as part of a pattern

3. **Serving at the body** is often an overlooked service option and is least trained by players and coaches. It is a very important strategy to keep the opponent off-balance. Judging the depth and speed of the ball is hindered with objects traveling straight at the body. Your eyes need a slightly sideway view in order to make proper judgment of trajectory and speed. It makes perfect sense to make use of this optical problem as a tactical solution. There are several different options the server can use to make it even more difficult to judge the return:

A. The flat serve will jam the ball inside the body, leaving the opponent little time to move out of the way to hit the return. The server should be prepared for a short return to take advantage of the court position.

B. The slice serve should start outside the body and slide inside the hips to jam the opponent's stroke. The return player will misjudge the direction or try to move around the ball the wrong way and only create more problems.

A. The kick serve should be aimed just outside the body to kick back high and inside the body. The player will often move around to hit the ball, only to see the ball come back inside the body and jam the movement and return motion.

Players and coaches need to be much more aware of this powerful tactic in keeping the opponent off-balance not only from a tactical and technical perspective but also from a mental perspective, with a surprise attack they did not expect and/or by taking them out of their comfort zone. These are tactical reasons for using body serves:

- high percentage target option
- surprise strategy
- to force a weak or short return from the opponent
- to use at a critical score in the game
- with tactical knowledge that the opponent handles these badly
- with the serve and volley to force a weak return and easy volley
- is used often as a service option in doubles, with net player "poaching"

4. **Serve and volley** is a lost art in today's tennis. The speed of the game has made this standard strategy from the past almost obsolete. With the return becoming one of the most improved strokes in the tennis game, it has become a far less used strategy in attacking the

opponent. Only in doubles is it still prominent as a basic strategy, but some adjustments are made there as well. Nowadays, the serve and volley strategy is used as a surprise tactic or to take advantage of a high return. There are three basic serve options: wide serve, body serve, and middle serve (or T serve). These can be advanced by using different types of spin: flat serve, slice serve, topslice serve, reverse serve, and kick serve. The options on the return are a high return or low return with three direction possibilities: down the line, middle, and crosscourt. These high and low returns will give six different scenarios for the volley player to consider. These scenarios can double in possibilities, taking the depth and angle of the volley into consideration. So you can imagine the many different situations a serve-and-volley player has in executing this game style. The serve and volley tactic is used for the following:

- to surprise the opponent
- to attack high and weak returns
- to pressure the return of the opponent
- as a prominent strategy in doubles
- to pressure the footwork of the opponent
- to shorten the rally
- to use at a certain tactical score in the game

Rotation Options of the Serve and Tactical Applications

Advanced players often use the rotation or spin of the ball to control the trajectory before and after the bounce of the ball. The spin can be used for various reasons. The topspin makes the trajectory of the ball dip down and jump higher after the bounce with an increased forward speed. It can be used to create more angles to the ball by playing it wide and shorter in the service box. The side spin or slice make the trajectory of the ball curve sideways. The bounce stays lower and creates a skid action to the ball that makes it speed up after the bounce. It can be used to make the ball curve away from the opponent or turn into their body. Combination of rotations, like the kick serve, creates a side spin and topspin to the ball that makes the ball curve and bounce in the opposite direction of the curve after contact with the ground. It is mostly used to pull the opponent even farther out of position, with the extreme deviation of the ball from the service box, and/or to play it high to the backhand side to complicate the return. Below are some of the examples with their applications:

Flat serve -to attack the opponent with the speed of the ball on the first serve

Slice serve -to move the opponent out of position or as a body shot

Topspin serve -to attack with high bouncing balls to weaken the return

Topslice serve -used as a second serve to control the trajectory/consistency

Kick serve -to move opponents out of position with high bouncing balls above the shoulders

Reverse serve -to surprise and curve the ball with a reversed slice

As you can see, there are many different service options with a variety of spins and tactical applications. Mixing them up is difficult, but it is also very effective in giving the opponent little chance to get used to your serve. The best servers can surprise the opponent and keep them constantly guessing what serve you will use. It keeps them in a defensive position and gives you more opportunities on the second shots.

The Mental Attitude When Serving

The key is to stay relaxed and don't force the situation. You will be a better server if you are using controlled aggression in your tactical approach. Stay calm but always be alert under pressure and be ready to play the next shots after the serve with a plan.

The Return

The return is one of the strokes that has benefitted from the new developments in racket and string technology. Players are able to hit the return much more aggressively to neutralize their opponent. In many cases, playing the return deep in the court to the weaker side of the opponent will force them to play off their back foot with a defensive shot and enable the player to take initiative in the rally. There are basic strategies and objectives of the return to keep in mind. You can see them in order of importance below.

Objectives and Tactics of the Return

1. **Get the ball back in play**
   The first objective of the serve should be to get the ball back in play no matter what. It increases the consistency of the return and applies pressure on the opponent when they have to play for every point and is not getting any free points with you missing the return. You should always provide the opponent with an opportunity to make an error before making one yourself. By using a reasonable margin over the net and a high-percentage target in the middle of the court, the consistency of the return will improve, and it will always give you a chance at playing for the point.

2. **Play the ball deep in the court**
   Depth on the return is important for many different reasons, but most of all, it creates time to recover for the next ball and less opportunity for the opponent to attack right away on the next ball. Most often, a deep return will push the opponent well back beyond the baseline or force them to take the ball on the rise as a high-risk shot. It can also force them to play off their back foot, which can lead to a short and/or weak ball in the court. The farther the opponent is pushed back behind the baseline, the less chance there is to attack the next ball with pace or angle. A longer flight

path creates time for the player to recover back in the court to take initiative with the next ball. Deep returns create opportunities and advantages in the tactical situations.

3. **Play to the weaker side of the opponent**

    In returning the ball from the server, a player should always try to aim the ball at the weaker side of the opponent. This not only creates pressure on this particular stroke but also has a mental impact on the opponent. They are already uncomfortable with that stroke, and now they are made aware of your knowledge, which will only further increase the pressure. Once the pressure and patterns have been established, it will be possible to change up the direction of the return to surprise the opponent and to keep them off guard. One important note with this is, do not change the direction of the return if you see the opponent struggling. Never change a winning strategy until they adapt and improve the situation and force you to change.

4. **Attack the return on weaker serves**

    Whenever the server is slowing down or produces a weaker serve, the returner should take advantage of the situation and seek initiative in the rally. This will either result in an outright winner or a weak response from the opponent. It is not always necessary to aim for the sidelines in this case; sometimes hitting straight back at the opponent can produce an error or a weak response to take the initiative in the rally.

The return of the serve can be directed to different tactical targets on the court. These direction possibilities depend heavily on the overall strategy and the tactical objective of the return combined with the targets, speed, and spin of the serve. The player has to decide, based mostly on experience, what the best shot choice is for each return situation. The overall strategy of the return needs to be adjusted to the overall strategy of the match. If the overall strategy of the match is to be offensive, you don't want to be defensive in return games. There are three tactical objectives with the return:

1. **Offensive Return**

The player will try to attack the return to hit an outright winner or to force the opponent into making an error or to force them into a defensive position. These are tactics of the offensive return:

- Move forward into the court to take the ball on the rise. This will take time away from the opponent and pressure them to hit the ball very quickly after the service action is completed. This time constraint often causes errors in response because of shortened reaction times.
- Hit the return hard and deep straight into the opponent's direction. The opponent will just be finishing the follow-through and recovery of the service action and will be pressured to move backward or take the ball early on the rise. There are also fewer angles for the service player to attack with the follow-up shot.
- The return is hit right away to a corner to force the opponent into a defensive position. This return will stretch the service player out wide and pressure the footwork and reflexes of the opponent. Ideally, you want to hit this return to the weaker side of the baseline strokes, but sometimes you can surprise the opponent by hitting this particular return to their strength.

2. **Neutralizing Return**

The player will try to neutralize the service action with depth, trajectory, and spin to minimize the opportunities for the server to attack. In some cases, speed is added as well to surprise the opponent. The objective is to prevent opponents from hitting attacking strokes. The tactics of these neutralizing returns are as follows:

- The depth of the return is the most important characteristic in neutralizing the opponent. It pushes the opponent farther back in the court and minimizes the chance for attacking strokes. The longer ball flight provides the player with more time to recover and set up for the next ball.

- The higher trajectory of the ball over the net can assist in neutralizing the return by creating a longer ball flight and a higher bounce of the ball to push the opponent farther back behind the baseline. Pressure is created not only by the trajectory of the ball but also mentally by testing the patience of opponents.

- The spin can play a factor in neutralizing the return with topspin or slice. With topspin, it is possible to play the ball higher over the net and still keep the ball in play. It also provides the option to slow the ball down by adding more spin and controlling the recovery time with a longer ball flight. The slice minimizes the chance of attack with a low and slow trajectory of the ball. In both cases, opponents are forced to move back or take a high-risk shot on the rise.

- Speed can be used with the return to neutralize the opponent in two different ways. It can be used with the position on the court by stepping in and taking the ball earlier on the rise. This will often cause the server to play a neutral ball back as response. The other option is by playing straight at the body. The opponent's movement and time to react will be restricted, and they will often opt to play a more neutralizing ball as response.

3. **Defensive Return**

The player will try to ward off well-placed, hard-hit, and difficult spins of the serves by returning the ball as often as possible. This will apply pressure on the opponent to hit the ball harder and closer to the lines with more spin. The tactics of these defensive returns are as follows:

- The position of the return player can be adjusted to gain more time to react to the target, speed, and spin of the serve. By moving farther back behind the baseline, the player has more time to react and move to recover the ball. The anticipation, the distance to the ball, and the speed of movement become important factors to the execution of this tactic of the defensive return.

- The consistency of the defensive return is the most important factor in forcing the opponent to play each return and not receive any free points off the return. Factors like speed, direction, spin, and trajectory can assist the defensive return but are of lesser priority.

- The direction of the return can minimize the response angles of the server. By playing crosscourt returns or straight back into the direction of the opponent, the player can play high-percentage shots and influence the attack angle for the following shot while making the recovery of the return less complicated.

- The trajectory of the return can be adjusted in height over the net to provide the player with more time to recover for the next ball after the return. The higher the ball is hit over the net, the more spin and less speed needs to be applied. The higher trajectory creates more depth to the ball and forces the opponent to move farther back behind the baseline and will test the patience of the opponent (mental pressure).

- The spin of the ball can influence the return to become more defensive. The spin will affect the ball to bounce higher with topspin and lower with slice and also make the ball flight somewhat slower. Both returns will force the opponent to hit the ball outside the normal strike zone and give the player more time to recover from the service action.

Baseline Play

The tactical situation of baseline play is the most common in today's tennis matches. With the players hitting the ball harder and deeper, it has become ever more difficult to approach the net. The objectives in baseline play are to outmaneuver and apply pressure to the opponent. In order to accomplish this task, the tactical situation during the rally demands that the player adjusts to the style of the play with offensive, defensive, or neutralizing strokes. The tactical status of the strokes, the patterns of play, and the shot choices determine the outcome of each individual point.

Effective Baseline Play

For baseline play to be effective, the tactical status of play needs to be coordinated with the shot choice of the strokes. The intention of a player to be offensive, defensive, or neutralizing will depend on the position of the opponent and the tactical situation. Players have to react to the strokes of the opponent and find the appropriate tactical response. These tactical responses can vary depending on the overall score in the match, set, or game and the mind-set of the player. The shot choice can affect the tactical status and vice versa. Having the wrong frame of mind (mental attitude) can also affect a player's shot choice. Being upset, frustrated, or emotional can lead a player to the wrong tactical decision and result in the wrong shot choice. The tactical status of play and the shot choices are determined by the following factors:

- **The positions of both players on the court**
  The tactical position of both players has the greatest influence on the tactical status and shot choice—not only the position from side to side along the baseline but also the position in the depth of the court. For example, if a player is out of position on the baseline, the opponent can pressure them by hitting to open court. If the opponent recovers slowly, hit behind them. But when they recover faster, make them overrun the ball by hitting more up the middle. If the player is too far behind the baseline, the opponent might hit a drop shot. If the player is caught inside the baseline, there are openings to play behind them (short to long). Adjustments of the shot choices can be made with direction, speed, net clearance, and spin of the ball.

- **The speed, angle, trajectory, and spin of the ball**
  The judgments of the aspects and characteristics of the ball will greatly influence the shot choice of the player. Trial and error and experience over time improves the player's recognition of these aspects and will increase the consistency of baseline rallies. Players need to make quick calculations and use risk management with their shot choices to improve ball control during the rallies.

- **The distance to the ball in relation to the movement of the player**

  Improvements in the judgment of the characteristics of the ball and movement make it possible to measure the risk of the possible shot choices. The speed, flexibility, change of direction, recovery, and balance of the footwork become important factors to quickly and comfortably cover the distances to the contact point with the ball. Fluidity of movement will calm the eyes in tracking the trajectory, speed, and spin of the ball and coordinate it all with the movement and the swing speed of the racket to make an informative decision on the tactical status and resulting shot choice.

- **The strengths and weaknesses of the opponent**

  The knowledge of the strengths and weaknesses of the opponent is very valuable information for constructing a strategy or game plan. They provide you with a means of using different tactics to avoid their strengths and exploit their weaknesses during the baseline rallies. This information should not just be restricted to the technical factors but also include the tactical, physical, and mental weaknesses and strengths. This will enable you to make an overall and complete game plan by using all methods available to combat your opponent.

- **Pattern recognition**

  The recognition of certain patterns in the exchanges of the rallies occurs over time, when players remember how certain points are constructed. There is no shortcut to this buildup of memory (experience). Time and playing matches will increase the learning curve in gathering information for future matches. Coaches can stimulate this learning curve by teaching easy patterns as soon as the players start playing points. It will show them early on the importance of patterns to outsmart their opponent. Another method is to teach the tactical applications and patterns while teaching the technical part of the strokes. This game approach to teaching develops the tactical skills at a faster pace and increases the experience of the player. Playing with experienced players will teach students some hard lessons on what and what not to do much quicker. Having a mentor to teach the finer art of playing matches can be very instrumental to the development of the tactical and mental aspects of the game.

- **Situational changes in the rally**
  There are several different times in the rally that the tactical status, tactical situation, and shot choice might change. A good example is the beginning of the rally with serve and return. With the dominance and offensive tactical status of the serve, the server might commence the rally offensively but might be forced to play a neutralizing or defensive response with a good return. During the rally, the pressure can build up through consistency or initiatives from a player who changes the responses of the opponent. These will affect the tactical status, the tactical situations, and shot choices of both players. The end of the rally can be a combination of buildup of pressure, consistency, stamina, and impatience of a player for the rally to come to an end. Players who don't adjust their playing style well throughout the rally will make more unforced errors.

- **Tactical shot choice options**
  Not all shot choices are available in each tactical situation. Players have to make a quick risk assessment of the tactical options and shot choices. Some might not be practical from a technical, physical, or mental perspective under those tactical circumstances. Players have to learn to play within their capability and not venture out too often with risky shotmaking by forcing the situation (pressing). As they become more proficient, players will have more tactical, technical, and physical skills that will influence their mental attitude and shot-choice options. Finding the proper shot choice for each tactical situation is the ultimate goal to improve your tactical game.

- **The score in the match, set, or game**

  The choices of tactical status, tactical situations, and shot choices can dramatically change with the score in the match, set, game, or even during the point. Sometimes the score can be a stimulus to play more offensively when the player is feeling confident. Other times, the score can be a hindrance, with the player feeling much more pressure from being behind but sometimes also from being ahead in score. The pressure leads to more tentative play with neutralizing or defensive styles of play. When ahead in score, it is possible to play with more initiative and offensive game styles. Players will feel more liberated to take slightly more risk in shot choices in pressure situations. When down in score, most players will either play too riskily by playing outside their capabilities or play too neutralizing or defensively. In fact, players should learn to play with less emotion and become more practical by focusing on the proper strategies and tactics and committing to their execution. You might not win the match, set, game, or point; but you can play the right way and eventually improve your game over time.

All these factors above have an influence on how the rally develops over time. Using the proper tactics leads to a design or pattern of play to outmaneuver the opponent to draw a mistake or to eventually make a winner.

Patterns of Play

The construction of points in baseline play is organized by a sequence of strokes that follow a certain design on the court. The designs, or patterns of play, should be coordinated according to the capabilities of both players with their strengths and weaknesses in mind in order to outplay the opponent in each point. The patterns of play can be organized in an offensive, defensive, or neutralizing way. It is also possible that it changes during the rally and that players adjust to the pressure provided by the opponent. Patterns of play are not only for baseline play, but they do always start out that way because of the serve and return. They can be found in all tactical situations in the tennis game. The baseline patterns are set up for both players by the quality of the serve and return with speed, trajectory, and spin or slice of the ball. These two strokes are the start to the baseline pattern and can open up the court or can neutralize the opponent. The response to the serve will determine the buildup of the rally to a predetermined strategy.

Every player should have a plan (strategy) on how they want to play against their opponent. This plan should be designed to expose the weaknesses of the opponent with the use of your favorite patterns of play. Each player should have four to five favorite patterns of play that he or she can use in combating most players he or she encounters in competition. In many cases, players design these patterns of play instinctively as they play competition, but they can also be taught when players show less strategic insight themselves. Sometimes players can be stimulated to improve their strokes more when they have a purpose of why and where they need to play their next stroke. Later on in this chapter, we will have a closer look at all the basic strategies and the patterns of play to execute them.

How to Dominate with Your Forehand

The forehand is one of the strokes you can use to dominate your opponent. It can be developed as a very strong weapon to attack or hit winners from any corner of the court. There are some very good examples of dominant forehands on the pro tour, with Rafael Nadal (see picture) being the most prominent. He not only has speed and spin in the stroke production but also possesses the quickness in the legs to run around his backhand and set up on time to hit the ball with purpose. Without this forehand, it would be very difficult for him to dominate his opponents like he does. Running around the backhand gives you many advantages in opening the court, applying pressure, hitting winners, and camouflaging the strokes to wrong-foot your opponent.

Six Steps to Develop a Dominant Forehand

1. **Consistency**

   Before you can develop any weapon, you have to obtain consistency on this particular stroke. No stroke can be called a weapon if you cannot rely on the execution. You have to train the forehand by practicing longer rallies and testing your skills under pressure in point play. You can start by improving the accuracy of your forehand in crosscourt, longline, and inside-out drills. Try to only use your forehand even though the ball goes in the direction of the backhand. This will train your ability to read the trajectory and react accordingly. After you are satisfied that the consistency has improved, you can introduce drills to change direction to better your footwork.

2. **Footwork**

   In order to cover both sides of the court with your forehand, you have to be quick and agile. It takes great footwork to run around your backhand and set up your feet to step in and strike the ball on time and still cover the open court with a running forehand when necessary. You can do this with on-court drills and off-court footwork training. The on-court drills can include feeding drills and life-ball situations. By feeding the ball to both corners, players can get adjusted to running around the backhand and hitting running forehands and developing a rhythm with the footwork. Life-ball situations are best executed with two-on-one drills using only your forehand. By playing to different targets (two players), you can practice your footwork speed and setup in combination with the accuracy of your strokes. Off-court physical training should be a combination of weight training, speed training, movement training, and plyometrics to enhance your footwork and agility.

3. **Train runaround shots and running forehands**

   You should only run around your backhand to use your forehand when you are able to hit a running forehand. By running around the backhand, it will leave the forehand side wide open for the opponent to strike; and most likely, they will take advantage of this. The more confidence you acquire in covering the court with your running forehand, the easier it becomes to use your runaround forehand. Once you master both shots comfortably, you will have less fear of running around the backhand and leaving the court open. You might even choose to position yourself slightly on the backhand side to use your forehand more often.

4. **Power and spin**
   The speed and spin of the ball play a large role in developing your forehand. The racket head speed creates both speed and spin of the ball. The racket angle at impact with the ball and the swing angle through impact determine the speed, spin, and trajectory of the ball. These can all be applied to outmaneuver the opponent. The speed of a ball can beat the opponent's running speed in many situations, whereas the spin can create a heavy ball or an angle shot to pull your opponent out of position. The trajectory of the ball is important to speed up or slow down the pace and/or play outside the strike zone and comfort level of the opponent.

5. **Strategy**
   By running around the backhand, you are able to use the power of your forehand to the weaker side of the opponent to open up the angles of the court and to keep the opponent off-balance and on the run at all times. Keeping your opponent off-balance and on the run makes them hit shots with very little or no time to set up with their feet. This will cause them to play defensively and make more unforced errors. Knowing the strengths and weaknesses of your opponent will assist you in your strategy and the timing of your attack. It will make you the dominant player on the court.

6. **Camouflage**
   As you become more proficient in the execution of your strokes, footwork, and strategy, it is possible to camouflage your intent. By setting up the same way as if you are hitting the ball inside out, it

is still very easy to change direction and hit the ball down the line (inside in). Your opponent will have a hard time reading your intent. The longer you are able to hold your position just before the strike, the more you can hide your intent and camouflage your shots. It will increase the effectiveness of your forehand even more.

Following these six steps in progression will develop your forehand into a powerful and dominant weapon for your future game.

The Slice Backhand

The slice backhand is the most versatile of all the strokes played in the tennis game. It can be used for many different purposes in playing against your opponent. You can use it to slow the ball down or speed it up or to return a wide or low ball. But you can also use it to play a lob over the opponent, to return a difficult spin serve, to approach the net, or even to play a drop shot. All these tactical situations require an excellent technique and control of the stroke. There are several technical variations in hitting the slice backhand that create the desired effect to the trajectory, slice rotation, depth, and speed of the ball:

1. **A Low Tempo Slice Backhand**

   This slice backhand starts with a higher backswing to generate more underspin. Most players use a continental or even continental forehand grip to open the racket angle. The swing path is downward and forward. The longer follow-through is pulled underneath the ball with the racket face being flat at the end of the stroke. The amount of underspin makes the ball float through the air and slows it down. After the bounce, it will skid through or sit up, depending on the height over the net. This type of slice can be used for the following tactical situations:

- **A defensive wide ball**. This is a very common shot choice for intermediate and advanced players to neutralize the power and pressure from the opponent. Especially for players with single-handed backhands, the slice backhand can be a great defensive stroke to slow down the tempo and to reduce the attack possibility. The important tactical aspects are to play a slower slice over the net to reduce the speed of play and to place the ball closer to the middle to eliminate the angles from the opponent.

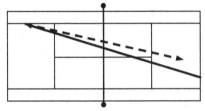

- **A defensive low and/or short ball**. This situation requires the player to stabilize the pressure by returning the ball back low so the opponent cannot easily attack. The slice will keep the ball below the level of the net and prevent the opponent from attacking with much force. The trajectory of the return will be just above the net level and not hit too hard.

- **A defensive deep slice backhand**. With the ball hard and deep in the court and staying low after the bounce, it is important to have a good answer to this situation. The slice backhand absorbs the speed of the ball by sliding the racket underneath the ball to keep the trajectory slightly higher and deeper to limit the chance of attack on the return.

2. **A High Tempo Slice Backhand**
   - This stroke requires a compact backswing and a swing angle that moves more through the ball. Most players use a continental backhand grip in order to hit the ball with more force out in front of the body (backhand grip is also possible in some cases). The length of the backswing depends on the speed of the oncoming ball and the speed you want to add. The backswing is slightly lower to keep the swing angle just above the line with the ball. This will keep the ball lower over the net. The speed

and the swing angle will cause the ball to skid and accelerate after the bounce of the ball. This type of slice is used in the following tactical situations:

- **To attack a high bouncing baseline shot** downward with a penetrating slice backhand. The weight transfer will provide a lot of energy to the ball to make it bounce low and aggressively. The height of the bounce of the ball dictates the use of a slice backhand to keep the trajectory low, decrease the attack possibilities, and pressure the opponent.

- **To attack a low ball with an approach shot.** This surprise tactic increases the pressure on the opponent by giving them less time to react and set up for the passing shot. The short ball is taken quite aggressively with a slice backhand that accelerates the tempo of play and keeps the trajectory low over the net and makes the ball skid and stay low after the bounce of the ball. Starting slightly above the ball and extending forward increases the speed and amount of slice of the stroke to apply pressure on the opponent.

- **To attack the return**. This can be a slice backhand return or a chip and charge. This strategy neutralizes the first-serve return or increases the pressure on the opponent's second serve by attacking it and following it into the net position. The stroke has a short backswing and a compact follow-through to keep the timing less complicated.

3. **To Change the Tempo, Trajectory, and Depth of the Slice Backhand**

These particular slice backhands are the touch shots of the slice backhand strokes. It adjusts the flight path of the ball with speed and elevation of the ball. The backswing is shorter to adjust to the speed of the oncoming ball, but the follow-through can be longer to control the depth and elevation. Most players use a continental forehand or backhand to execute these shots. These slice backhands are mostly used for the following tactical situations:

- **The drop shot.** The execution is easier performed on the backhand side after hitting a slice backhand on the previous shot. The stroke can then be camouflaged with an identical preparation. The backswing is short, but the follow-through can be longer to provide touch to the length of the stroke and amount of backspin to limit the forward movement after the bounce. The drop shot is most effective when hit inside the baseline, with the opponent far behind the baseline in a defensive position. This tactical position and distance will make it difficult to reach the short ball behind the net.

- **The defensive lob.** The backswing is compact with the racket angle open to allow the racket to slide underneath the ball. The follow-through is upward and longer to ensure the height of the ball and flight path over the opponent. The lob is most effective when the opponent is too close to the net, and this makes it easy to pass over their head.

- **A short-angle passing shot.** With the opponent attacking the net position and playing the ball outside your range to hit a topspin passing shot, you might have to resort to a short crosscourt slice backhand. The ball is placed crosscourt and low over the net in the service box in order to pass the opponent before they can reach it.

After showing all the possibilities of the slice backhand, you can understand how many tactical applications exist and that it takes dedication, practice, and great skills to execute them. However, it will be a great asset to your game to practice these strokes to enhance your tactical competence. I am sure you will enjoy your newfound weapons once you try them.

Novak Djokovic

Martin van Daalen

Approaching the Net

Advancing to the net is the next progression in applying pressure on the opponent. By approaching the net, the pressure on the opponent will be increased on many different levels. First of all, the reaction time will be shortened with less time to set up for the strokes. This not only applies physical pressure on footwork and reflexes but also applies mental pressure by having to make quicker decisions. Most often, the decision to come forward is on a short ball by finishing off the point or to pressure the opponent into a defensive position to volley the ball at the net. By transitioning to the net, the angles and target areas are significantly decreased, and players will be pressured to take more risky shots (passing, lob, and others). Let's examine the different types of approaches to the net:

- **Short ball situation**
  The ball falls short in the court and is easily taken advantage of by quickly closing in and approaching the net. According to the positions of both players, the approach can be hit to the open court or hit behind the opponent or straight at them to confuse them and reduce the angles of the passing shots. The decisions of the direction, depth, spin, and speed of the ball depend largely on the positioning of the player. If the ball is struck closer to the sideline, the options are reduced to down the line and straight at the opponent. If the ball is struck closer to the middle of the court, more options are available, and execution will depend largely on the positioning and footwork speed of the opponent.

- **Cutting off the angle**
  This tactical situation is usually established after a crosscourt rally by cutting off the angle, taking the ball early on the rise, and hitting the ball down the line. It is a classical method that is often used by advanced and professional players to not only surprise the opponent with a tempo change but also move in with an approach shot. This

approach tactic applies even more pressure on the opponent by taking away time for them to set up for the passing shots.

- **Drive volley and swing volley**
  In high trajectory exchanges over the net, it is possible to sneak in and take the net position unexpectedly without the opponent noticing. With high trajectories over the net, the opponent is looking up at the ball instead of forward. This provides players the opportunity to move in and take the ball out of the air. This can be executed with a drive volley (slight slice or flat) or with a swing volley (topspin with a follow-through). The type of stroke used depends largely on the height of the ball, the position on the court, and the purpose of the shot selection.

- **Following in after a high ball**
  With playing high topspin balls over the net, it is possible to take advantage of the time of the ball flight to approach the net. The moment a ball falls relatively short, the player can spin it high and deep to the weaker side of the opponent and run into the court to take position at the net. Even though they can see you coming, there is not much they can do about it with the higher arc and bounce of the ball. It causes a very difficult high bouncing ball, and the opponent has to wait and back up to hit the passing shot from a defensive position.

- **Serve and volley**
  The server applies pressure with the placement, speed, and spin of the serve and follows behind with a volley at the net. The object of this tactical situation is to apply constant pressure on the opponent's return by pressuring the opponent to hit into much smaller target areas with less reaction time. A high-quality service action will often produce a weaker return, resulting in an easy volley. Serve-and-volley players need to train the many different situations resulting from the service directions and responses from the return player in order to execute this tactical situation with consistency.

- **Return**

  Whenever players are returning weaker serves, they can take advantage of the court position by stepping inside the court and approaching the net after the return. The return approach can be executed with slice or topspin strokes. The slice approach, often called chip and charge, is often used on higher bouncing balls and in doubles play. The topspin returns are used on lower bouncing balls and as a first strike weapon to put the opponent on the defensive. The objective is to the get the opponent out of position and make them reach for the ball or jam them inside their body by hitting through the middle of the court to the weaker side. This method provides fewer angles to pass at the net. The approach of the return is often used against less-experienced net players to pressure them.

- **Lob**

  When opponents are attacking the net, the lob can be used to approach the net and reverse the tactical position. With a well-executed lob, players can take advantage of the defensive position of the opponent while running down the ball and moving in behind the lob to finish the ball at the net. The defensive lob (slice) works well against the wind. The offensive lob (topspin) is preferable with its rotation speeding up the ball after the bounce, making it more difficult for the opponent to retrieve and/or to play a passing shot.

- **Attacking the net player**

  Besides attacking the net player with the lob, it is possible to dip the ball low at the feet of the opponent with a slice or topspin stroke. Dipping the ball low over the net is possible both out of a defensive position or an offensive position. This will make the volley player play up and/or short in the court to approach the net position. You can then attack the net player with a passing shot or by going straight at the net player when there are fewer angles available to pass.

- **Drop shot**

  The purpose of a short ball behind the net is to apply pressure on the opponent, not to provide your opponent with a net position. So follow your drop shot into the net and take advantage of your opponent having to retrieve the ball and hit it upward to clear the net. Often, players will stay at the baseline after the drop shot, only to see the opponent retrieve the ball and reverse the tactical situation by taking the net position. Players are then forced to hit a passing shot from a defensive position instead of finishing off the volley at the net in an offensive position.

Approach Direction and Positioning

The tactical options of directing the ball to certain targets on the court coincide with the positioning of the player to cover the net. In other words, the player's shot and target selection influence the positioning at the net. The approach direction and positioning depend on a number of tactical aspects:

1. **Approach Direction**

   - *The positioning of both players* on the court plays an important role in deciding the direction of the approach. If the opponent is totally off the court, the approach will be played to the open court. If the opponent is in the middle of the court, the approach will often go to the weaker side. These options depend largely on the position of the approach player. With the approach in the middle of the court, all options are open. With the approach from the sideline, the player has to choose either down the line or to the middle of the court.

   - *The angle of attack* is important in order to pressure the opponent and at the same time be able to cover the response possibilities of the opponent. Angles are a possibility, but in some cases, the best approach is straight at the opponent to avoid opening the court for passing shots and pressure the opponent into an unforced error.

- **Sh***ot selections* can vary with the distance of the approach to the net, the type of shots the opponent dislikes, and the consistency of the player's approach. It is also possible to speed up or slow down the ball or change the height (slice or topspin) of the approach to decrease the passing possibilities.

- *Tactical response options* can vary due to the likely shot selections and capabilities of the opponent. The tactical experience and knowledge of the opponent plays a large role in the different options.

2. Positioning

- *The target selection* of the approach will determine the net position of the approach player. The player will follow the direction where the approach is targeted.

- The *angle of approach* will determine the net position. The more angles are played on the approach, the more the net player has to cover the outside of the court.

- *Net coverage* is determined by the direction of the approach. It is not necessary to cover the entire net. Choose a section of the net behind the direction of the approach and cover it well. Prioritize down the line above crosscourt!

Tempo and Shot Selection

The speed of play and the shot selection are very much connected in order to maintain control and consistency during execution of the strategy. The speed and force used with the strokes and the contact points used after the bounce can increase or decrease the degree of difficulty in the execution of the stroke. By increasing the speed of the stroke and the ball, more errors are possible without adjusting the margin of error (target areas). The same goes for taking balls earlier after the bounce. The shot selection is a tactical decision that needs to be gauged by both these factors in combination with the speed, angle, and rotation of the oncoming ball. It also makes a big difference if you make a tempo change that is forced upon you rather than make the choice to take the ball earlier on the rise yourself. Let me illustrate the difference.

Shot Selection 1

Player A has just served the ball, and player B returns the ball hard and deep right in front of the feet of the server. Player A has just finished the follow-through and is in the process of recovering behind the baseline. Player A has no time to back up and is forced to take the ball on the rise. To avoid an error, player A returns the ball with a spin deep through the middle of the court to neutralize the opponent. This tactic will give player A some time to recover without opening the angles of the court and a chance to play the point. In this particular situation, player A chooses a high-percentage shot.

Shot Selection 2

Player A and player B are in a crosscourt rally when player B plays the ball short in the court. In this situation, player A can step forward into the court and take the ball early on the rise to change direction by hitting the ball deep down the line. Player B not only will be pressured by the change of direction but the change in tempo will also give player B even less time to run down the shot to return the ball. In this situation, player A is taking the initiative by hitting the ball to a smaller target area. Note—Be aware that in this particular situation, the focus should be to hit the ball close to the baseline, not necessarily close to the sideline (large target).

Martin van Daalen

Camouflage and Redirection

As players become more proficient and confident with the execution of their shots, they are able to camouflage their shots and/or redirect the opponent by concealing the direction of the stroke. This is particularly important with passing shots, when opponents are approaching the net often, or when passing the net player in retrieving drop shots. Camouflage can be used a lot in the serve. The rotation of the shoulders and the positioning of the feet can hide the intentions of the direction. Players that master this well have a huge advantage in service games. The camouflage of the shots can be trained and executed the following ways:

1. **Positioning of the stance**
   Placing the feet in a semi-open or open stance will accommodate the player to play either way and to camouflage the direction of the ball with the timing of the contact point. It will become much more difficult for the opponent to read the intentional direction of the ball, with the stance of the feet being the same for either direction.

2. **Execution consistency**
   By retaining the same execution technique for each direction and using the timing to change direction, the opponent will not be able to read the intentions of the player. Especially with the positioning of the feet, the backswing and the recovery are important in this case since they are telltale signs for the opponent to deduct a direction. With the serve, the toss would be a telltale sign of the direction of the ball.

3. **Shoulder rotation and racket head speed**
   In keeping the speed on the rotation of the shoulders and the racket head, it is much more difficult to determine the direction of the ball coming out of the strings. The swing speed camouflages the direction of the ball and adds speed and spin to the ball. This only increases the degree of difficulty for the opponent.

4. **Ball contact**

It is possible to strike the ball with various contact points and rotations. Adding spin to the ball makes the racket head cover the ball and creates a camouflaging effect. Adding sidespin to the ball increases this effect even more. Good examples of this are the various service actions and the passing shots.

5. **Recovery**

Most players don't realize how much the opponent can read out of the recovery footwork of a player. Most often, a player will recover differently from a crosscourt stroke than from a down-the-line shot. In order to camouflage or conceal this as much as possible, players have to apply the same recovery footwork.

Redirection

The redirection of the opponent is more complicated and takes extensive training and experimentation of the players to master it well. It is different from camouflaging in the sense that it is a deliberate movement before the ball is struck to make the opponent believe that the ball will be struck to a certain direction. This can be executed in a very obvious manner or by purposely waiting to strike the ball and have the opponent commit to a (running) direction. Redirection can be trained and executed the following ways:

1. **Positioning of the feet**

The stance of the feet is not only useful to camouflage the direction but can also be used on purpose to redirect the opponent. By making sure to exaggerate the stance in a certain direction, it is possible to redirect the opponent in making them believe the ball is going in a certain direction and then changing the direction of the ball. This particular tactic is often used in putting away short ball situations. The player will fake one direction with the feet and strike the ball in the opposite direction.

2. **Movement before the strike**

A movement to redirect the opponent before the strike can be executed with the body and/or the racket. Executing this with the body is very difficult, but with the racket head, it is slightly easier. This shot is often used in executing the drop shot or a passing shot after retrieving a drop shot. The racket head is purposely held in a certain direction and changed to another direction at the last instant.

3. **Timing the strike**

Whenever a player is in full control of the rally and has extra time to finish the point, it can be an advantage to hold the strike an instant longer to see what direction the opponent is running to and wait till he commits to this direction. This particular technique takes some practice in knowing how long to hold the strike without endangering the contact point and consistency of the stroke.

Net Play

This particular part of the tactical situations in singles and doubles play is the execution of the strokes in closer proximity to the net. For singles play, this means all the playing situations after the approach shots. For doubles play, it means all the playing situations after the serve and volley and after the partner is already in the net position. Net play takes plenty of practice to execute well, and there are quite a variety of shots available. These can range from high and low volleys to overheads, half volleys, and drop volleys.

Differences between High and Low Volleys

Even with the same direction of the return, the height of the return determines the tactical options of the volley. For example, with two identical direction returns down the line, the high return will give the volley player a lot of options to speed up the volley deep crosscourt or down the line against the recovery direction of the opponent. A low return down the line will open up the angle short; crosscourt for a possible winner volley. In doubles play, there are more possibilities—with low volleys played mostly shorter crosscourt, away from the net player (unless the net player tries to poach, in which case a volley down the line opens up), while high returns will be punished by going straight to the feet or hips of the opponent at the net.

Options with a High Volley	Technical Tips
1. Put away volley cross or down the line	Aim for big target
2. Angle volley	Sidespin
3. At the net player in doubles	Aim for hips or feet

Options with a Low Volley	Technical Tips
1. Play short cross	Get low with the knees
2. Play a drop volley	Open racket face, soft hands
3. Play down the line in doubles	When net player poaches early

In playing either low or high volley, players have to learn how to keep a margin for error in order to apply pressure on the opponent and to force good passing shots.

Roger Federer

Overhead or Smash

The overhead is the shot that is supposed to finish the point at the net if the ball is hit up high over the head of a player. It is very similar in motion to the serve without tossing the ball. There are three types of overhead that need to be considered:

1. The regular overhead (with both feet on the ground)
2. The jump overhead (when the lob is hit higher)
3. The backhand overhead (when hit over the backhand side)

All three require some training and have specific technical and tactical implications. The recognition of the trajectory is crucial to make the proper shot choice. In some cases, it can be advantageous to *not* let the ball bounce before hitting the overhead. Think of a high lob that falls short to the net or a shorter lob in windy conditions. Players can use a regular overhead after the ball has bounced.

1. **The regular overhead**
   This is the easiest to learn since it is so similar to the service motion. The backswing is abbreviated with an early preparation of the racket in a striking position behind the body. The balance arm can be used as an aiming device in tracking the ball till contact. If the trajectory of the ball is lower, this is the most reliable and stable stroke to use to finish the point. Most players will tend to fold the upper body down instead of stretching out and extending during the follow-through. The posture needs to be maintained throughout the stroke for a solid contact and powerful overhead. If the ball bounces lower than expected, extend your front leg for a wider stance and bend both legs to adjust to the proper height.

2. **The jump overhead**
   This is more difficult to learn but can be a valuable tool in difficult lob situations. It requires the player not only to shuffle back quickly but also to make a scissor kick in the air. The back foot makes the

jump and kicks up high to maintain the balance in the air. The arms are instrumental here in assisting with the jump. With a rhythmic swing, you lower them together and raise them above the shoulders to assist the upward jump. The legs exchange place with the front leg catching the body as it descends back down on the ground. The timing of this motion needs to be practiced in order to hit this stroke with any kind of balance and placement. Start with little jumps and master the timing before attempting more difficult situations. Even if the ball drifts over the backhand shoulder, this stroke can be used very effectively as long as the player is fast enough to get in position.

3. **The backhand overhead**

   This is technically the most difficult stroke to master. It requires an understanding of when and how to use it in being out of position or out of time to run around to hit a regular overhead. The keys to a good backhand overhead are the use of the legs and the flexibility of the elbow and wrist. The knees are bent before impact to provide an upward force of the arm and racket head. The elbow and wrist have to be held loose in order to create the racket head speed through the ball. The timing of this specialty shot is crucial to the trajectory and placement. It is a stroke that needs some practice before players understand how to use it technically and tactically.

The targeting can be affected by the situation and pressure of the moment. It is prudent to choose a large target area and to hit the ball with determination. There is no need to be heroic in these situations. It is good to remember that the pressure is really on the opponent who has to return the overhead. There are four target areas to consider when hitting:

A.   A large target area in the open court
B.   A large target area on the weaker side of the opponent (example: backhand)
C.   Behind the opponent if he or she is running to a certain corner
D.   Through the middle of the court if you are not certain where to go

The **mental approach** of the overhead has to be clear and direct. The purpose of this stroke is to finish the point. The worst thing you can do is think that the rally is over and you don't need to focus any more. That is exactly when mistakes creep in. It is not uncommon for players of any level to have this frame of mind and then struggle to make the next overhead. The pressure will build up from the memory of the previous missed overhead. So keep your focus, hit the finishing stroke with determination to a big target, and don't relax until the point is over. This way, you will avoid many problems.

Half Volley

This stroke is actually not a volley at all. The ball is not struck in the air but right after the bounce. The name is definitely misleading. In high-level tennis, it is a commonly used stroke to redirect the power from the opponent and to speed up the tempo. It can be used to hit the ball on the rise when it is too late to back up at the baseline or to pick up the ball when transitioning to the net. The stroke is shorter in execution, and the racket angle needs to be adjusted to a more closed position to control the trajectory. A half volley will accelerate the speed of the ball with the energy still being high right after the bounce. In transition to the net, it is a very important stroke to keep the rally alive when a stroke is hit to the feet of the net player and it is too late to get the racket under the ball. The tactical approach should be to hit these strokes to big targets for a larger margin of error. In transition to the net, you can choose the middle of the court or the weaker side of the opponent. In the case you are pulled wide, try to keep the ball in front of you by going down the line. This will make it easier to take the net position with less distance to travel.

Drop Volley

Playing the volley short behind the net can be a great way to outplay the opponent. The drop volley is executed by absorbing the pace of the ball with less grip pressure and a negative or reverse motion of the racket head as the ball hits the string. It is possible to dissipate the energy of the ball in the string by letting the ball push back the racket head at contact. The other factor in playing the drop or stop volley is to add slice spin to the ball by opening the racket face at contact. The backspin will limit the forward motion of the ball and lower the bounce of the ball. This will make it more difficult for the opponent to retrieve the ball and can enhance the performance of the drop volley. The placement of the drop shot depends on the position of both players on the court. It can be easier to execute the drop volley at an angle. It provides the player with more margins for error and limits the forward motion of the ball toward the opponent. However, it can open the court for a passing shot if the opponent is able to reach the ball. In general, you can use the following tactical method: hit the drop volley crosscourt whenever the opponent is positioned on the same side of the court as yourself. Hit the drop volley down the line when the opponent is on the other side of the court as yourself. You will greatly enhance your performance of the drop volley by not trying to hit too close to the sidelines or too close behind the net. You do not receive extra points for playing fancy shots, and it will hurt your confidence when opportunities are missed.

Movement

The movement at the net has to be efficient and quick in order to keep up with the speed of the game. Being closer to the net reduces the reaction time and execution of the strokes greatly. This is why movement at the net becomes crucial in order to set up on time. The timing of the split step is one of the most important factors to improve movement and balance. Even when observing top players, you might catch them reacting too late because the timing of the split step was incorrect. The split step provides a balance point to move in any direction with the feet being in a wider and stronger position. The recovery action of a player at the net is very similar to the baseline but again has to be much faster. Being aware of the urgency when you can close out points in a final action is the key to better movement and being more successful at the net.

Anticipation and Risk Management with the Serve and Volley

Even though there are many variables and possibilities with the serve and volley, it is possible to choose the high-percentage plays by the direction of the serve. A serve-and-volley player can anticipate the most common responses of the opponent's returns by reading the preparation of the opponent. The setup of the feet and backswing of the opponent can show the direction they intend to hit the ball to. The contact points with the ball and the racket angle will also be a clear indication of the trajectory of the ball. The risk management lies in covering the high-percentage return options at the net. Going by the target direction of the serve, a player should cover the following areas at the net:

Serve wide   - cover the net from the side to the middle net strap
Serve to the body   - cover the middle of the net
Serve to the middle   - cover the net from the side to the middle net strap

Having a plan of where to move and what part of the net to cover will enhance your chances of setting up on time and hitting a good volley. There could always be surprise situations, but it is best to cover the obvious choices first. Being prepared for the most obvious choices will improve the speed and reflexes of the actions and will improve confidence. Having a few choices instead of all possible choices makes it easier to focus and speeds up the reaction time and execution of the action.

Playing against the Net Player

There are several instances when you need to apply techniques and tactics to combat players at the net. Playing against the net player can be a difficult task if you are not used to these situations or when they happen by surprise. It can be very helpful to train players how to deal with these situations so they have an appropriate reply. The following are different situations in playing against a net player:

1. After a serve and volley
2. After an approach by the opponent
3. After a drop shot
4. After a lob and the opponent moving in
5. After a return approach from the opponent
6. In doubles play

There are several strategies and tactics possible in playing against a net player. These tactics are the following:

• passing the net player crosscourt or down the line
• playing straight at the net player and jamming them with a body shot
• playing a lob over the net player
• preparing a pass with a low dipping shot at the feet and passing on the next shot

These four options are possible against all six situations of playing against a net player (see the six different situations above). By training for all these situations and the four options, it is possible to give an advanced player many ways to combat the opponent at the net.

Weapon Development

Every good player has several weapons at their disposal when playing matches. On the men's side, it is usually the serve and the forehand. On the women's side, it is usually the baseline strokes and returns of second serves. Of course, these are general trends that are visible on the pro tour, but there are many individual weapons that players might have, and they are not limited to just strokes. Their weapons could be physical (with speed and stamina) or strategic or mental in the way they play points and matches. In developing junior players, we need to help them develop their weapons that fit their style of play. Trying to develop weapons outside one's style of play can be disastrous for the development of a player. Players have to feel comfortable with the style and also show some ability to develop this into a weapon. This process can be started when players mature physically, and the first signs of this become visible in practices and matches. In learning these weapons, juniors sometimes try to use these weapons all the time. This can lead to many unforced errors when not building the rally first and waiting for the correct time to use their weapon (shot choice). Weapon development is part of the advanced tactical skills needed to become a national or international player.

How Points Are Played

There are three type of points played in tennis. They are all played with a different purpose, and it is good to recognize them so you can react with the proper attitude and strategy. The three types of points are as follows:

1. Short rallies (ace, winner return, one-two   one to three shots combination)
2. Medium rallies (buildup of pattern to   three to six shots accelerate and strike)
3. Long rallies (consistency, endurance, patience,   plus six shots and placement)

1. **Short rallies**

   Short rallies, or first strike rallies, are designed to use speed and power to get the opponent out of position and to strike early with surprise. This type of rallies only become available once players develop more strength, which comes with age, and develop the weapons needed to execute this strategy. Hitting winners with the serve (ace) and the return can be one of those weapons. The one-two strike is a very common rally in advanced and pro tennis. The player tries to get the opponent out of position and then strike right away to the open court or hit behind to wrong-foot the opponent. Beside the ace and return winner, an example of this rally is a wide serve and taking the next ball early to hit the winner to the open court. A variation of this would be to wait till the opponent starts running and then close in to hit behind the player. The timing of the strike is the key to the success of both tactical situations. The same can be executed with the return. Taking the ball early on the return is the key to success.

2. **Medium rallies**

   Medium rallies, or pattern rallies, are designed to build up the rally with medium pace and directional control to then accelerate with surprise within the rally. Hitting big targets with initiative is important to maintain consistency and control over the rally. The acceleration or tempo change will create the opening to eventually win the point or force the opponent to make an error. Unlike the short rallies, where it is more about winners, this method is won by applying steady pressure in the rally combined with a tempo change.

3. **Long rallies**

   Long rallies are designed to test the opponent's consistency, patience, and stamina in the rally by outlasting the opponent. These exchanges can be quite long and force players to use their footwork, willpower, and endurance to overcome the pressure of the moment. With juniors, these rallies can look quite different with high trajectories over the net. The objective with this age is just to keep the ball in play and apply mental pressure. Even though the intensity is not very high, these rallies are still exhausting to the player—not because of the movement or intensity, but more because of the mental stress. Players are forced to abandon their regular way of play and become frustrated in not being able to hit a winner or to pressure the opponent. With advanced players, the intensity and rallies are very tiring as well but in a more physical and tactical way. However, the aftereffect in losing these rallies does influence the mental state of a player. Every match has long rallies. Losing a few of them is not crucial to the outcome of the match; however, they can influence the strategy of your opponent if they see they are becoming successful in winning more of these rallies. It is your job to recognize this and to make sure you continue to win these rallies as well. This will convince your opponent that you cannot be beaten this way, and they will adjust their strategy since this one takes too much energy from them as well. Only winning makes pursuing this strategy worth it.

How to Win Points

It is important to understand how points are won and lost. With inexperienced players, most points are won by errors of the opponent since the players are not good enough to hit outright winning shots yet. As players progress and become more accomplished, they learn how to accelerate the ball to a speed that is not retrievable anymore. Advanced players are able to hit more outright winners and/or create forced errors from the opponent. However, this process can also bring along some unforced errors as well. The ways to win points are the following:

- winners
- forced and unforced errors from the opponent

1. **Winners**
   These points are won without the opponent having a chance to touch the ball or barely touching it (think of the serve). It is important to learn the mental commitment and shot choice needed to produce these shots with consistency and confidence.

2. **Forced and Unforced Errors**

Consistency in your ground strokes is one of the most important factors to build confidence for your game. Players will try to eliminate errors as much as possible to increase consistency. In playing different opponents, however, errors can be affected by the playing style and pressure applied by the opponent. There are two types of errors:

1. *Forced errors.* They are errors that can occur with increased pressure from the opponent. The direction of the ball, the pace and spin of the ball, and the patterns of play can force the player into compromising positions. The contact points of the strokes and the balance of the body can be adversely affected when you can barely reach the ball. This will often result in poor control of the ball and a forced error.

2. *Unforced errors.* They are errors that occur without an apparent reason. The player is not pressured in off-balance strokes or increased speed or spin from the ball. The unforced errors result from improperly executed strokes or misjudgment of the timing.

To produce a quality match, unforced errors should be kept to a minimum during matches. However, there are some elements that can influence the amount of unforced errors—the style of play, the physical and mental state of a player, the surface it is played on, and the conditions of the match.

- **The style of play**
  The specific way the player plays the game can be of great influence on the amount of unforced errors. A serve-and-volley player will make more unforced errors than a counterpuncher but will also create more winners than a counterpuncher. In baseline play, the same goes for an aggressive-style and offensive-style player with more unforced errors than a defensive-style player. Coaches, players, and parents need to be very aware

of these facts when coaching or playing the game. For players to improve their game, the amount of unforced errors has to decrease. This is only possible by committing to the game style, becoming more disciplined in the execution of the game style, and practicing consistency during point play.

- **Tactical targets**
  Choosing the proper targets not only can improve the overall strategy and execution of the tactics but can also provide less unforced errors. Players have to make a quick risk assessment in order to choose the proper shot selection and target selection. By using sufficient net clearance and bigger targets, farther from the sidelines, players will produce less unforced errors. Some examples of tactical targeting are these:

  1. Errors in timing produce more late-struck balls than struck-too-early balls. With this in mind, playing crosscourt strokes will produce less unforced errors than down the line.

  2. There are many instances when the court produces a different bounce than anticipated. In these situations, players need to train themselves to produce a recovery shot with higher net clearance, preferably deep and in the middle of the court.

  3. Whenever pushed in a defensive position behind the baseline or in the corners of the court, players have to choose targets with depth and closer to the middle court. This will reduce the unforced errors and reduce the angles of attack from the opponent.

- **Physical components**
  The fitness level of a tennis player is of great influence to the number of unforced errors. Fatigue can cause footwork and strokes to fail in its proper execution. It can also negatively

affect the coordination and result in timing errors with the contact points of the strokes. Fatigue will eventually affect the brain functions, resulting in poor decision of strategies, tactics, and shot selections. All these factors will cause more unforced errors during play.

- **Mental components**
  The mental conditioning of players will affect the strategy, the tactical decision-making, and the shot selection. During play, players could experience many different emotions—ranging from elation, serenity, frustration, aggressiveness, anger, desperation, and surrender. Keeping all these emotions in check and finding the serenity or stillness during play is the ultimate goal. All the other emotions will cause the player to lose focus and force them to many more unforced errors. This is never an easy task, but players have to understand how to train their emotions under every circumstance, just like their other skills.

- **The surface**
  The tennis game is played on many surfaces and demands tactical and shot-selection adjustments to reduce the unforced errors. Hard courts demand the least adjustments with the bounces of the ball being more regular and relatively reliable. Grass courts and clay courts can be much more demanding with irregular bounces with speed and spin changes. Players have to always be alert to make constant adjustments in trajectories, direction of the ball, target selection, and rotations of the ball. Preparation of footwork and strokes will reduce the number of unforced errors on any surface. Over time, it is possible to improve the racket head skills in order to make reflex adjustments and improve overall consistency under the most difficult circumstances.

- **The weather**
  The weather conditions can play havoc on the consistency of a player and greatly influence the number of unforced errors. Wind,

rain, and cold or warm weather conditions can all play a factor in making adjustments in tactical solutions and shot selections. They also have an impact on the psychological state of mind, and players need to be mentally prepared for these situations by adapting to each specific weather condition. The mental and tactical flexibility of the player will determine how successful he or she will be in each situation to reduce unforced errors.

Most Common Types of Unforced Errors

I have mentioned above some of the circumstances when unforced errors can occur, but there are several types of unforced errors that players make in executing points. I have selected a few types of unforced errors and different ways how to fix them. Examine them carefully:

- **Technical errors**
  These types of errors are related to the execution of the strokes. A breakdown in the execution can occur randomly and can also have a specific cause. Not every stroke is going to be executed perfectly every time, and technical errors can creep in over time. Every player should strive to execute the strokes as perfectly as possible, but they should also accept a certain amount of unforced errors during the course of a match. Some of the technical errors can occur from a weakness in the stroke or the lack of sufficient training. Most of the technical errors, however, have a specific cause that is related to a combination of different factors (confidence, judgment, fatigue).

  Solution
  Work on your technique of the stroke. The timing of the ball and rhythm of the stroke are important to the confidence of a player. The consistency of the execution of the stroke under pressure should be the ultimate goal, so slow things down at first before gradually increasing to match speeds. Keep testing each of the components separately during point play to see if they will hold up before moving

on to the next component. If a breakdown occurs along the way, then take a step back and practice it again till consistency and confidence during point play are restored. Even though the execution of the strokes needs to be consistent, small technical adjustments will always need to be made due to unforeseen circumstances. Think of the slightly different bounces of the ball or the different rotation of the ball—especially as the speed, tempo, and spin increases. Those adjustments can only be made after the bounce of the ball and demand a lot from the player's skills and talent. To be truly consistent, players have to train these adjustments on a daily basis to become automated functions. Training on clay courts can help this development as the bounces are less predictable. With progress in levels of play, the mental and physical components obviously play a larger role in the consistency and commitment of a player to execute the strokes correctly. This is evident in the examples of some of the top players you see on the pro circuit today.

- **Strategic and tactical errors**

  Strategic
  These unforced errors can occur by having the wrong strategy (overall game plan) and playing into the strengths of the opponent instead of their weaknesses. Playing against a strong baseline player from the baseline will play into his strength and provide the opponent with more opportunities to apply pressure. It is a very common for players to force the strokes too much in that situation, resulting in unforced errors.

  Solution
  Try to expand your knowledge of the different playing styles and how to execute them. Training for the different styles not only will help you recognize the playing style but will also expand your knowledge on how to play against them and how to cut down on the unforced errors. A good preparation requires an analysis of the opponent's strengths and weaknesses to properly devise a game

plan. If plan A does not work as intended, don't be afraid to go to your backup plan B. If you are winning majority of the important points (game, set, and break points) and not committing too many unforced errors, don't change your game plan. If not, then you can consider changing it. A good strategy is not by how you start the match, but by how you finish the match.

Tactical

These unforced errors can occur from choosing the wrong combination of strokes, patterns of play, or shot choices. An example of a bad combination of strokes is pressuring the opponent from the baseline, being in an offensive position, and trying to play a drop shot from the baseline. Not only will this often lead to errors, but it will also give the opponent the opportunity to run down the ball and reverse the pressure, with the offensive player now having to hit a passing shot.

Solution

Whenever in an offensive position, try to open the court or wrong-foot the opponent and keep attacking them relentlessly. Do not let the opponent off the hook and do not allow them to reverse the pressure back on you. Drop shots are only a good solution when well inside the baseline with the opponent well behind the baseline or to use it as an answer to a drop shot from the opponent. This is even more evident on a clay surface where it is more difficult to change direction.

Patterns of play are important in pressuring the opponent to play a designed pattern of strokes that suits your strengths and exploits their weaknesses. Most often, players will make the mistake of staying in a crosscourt rally that targets their weaker side; but eventually, the opponent will take advantage of this.

Solution

The simplest one to construct is changing the direction of the ball down the line to force the opponent to play to your strength. The opponent can choose to play a higher-risk shot, back down the line, but this can possibly open the court for you to attack.

Shot choices are tactical decisions made by the players in executing the shot under a tactical situation. The most common mistake in shot choices is the trajectory of the ball on wide crosscourt balls. The trajectory is often too low and without added spin to control the ball flight. The opponent can take advantage of this situation by taking the ball on the rise and hitting a winner down the line.

Solution

Learn to control this situation by hitting the ball higher and deeper over the net with topspin. This will neutralize the opponent who has to wait for the ball to bounce or risk hitting a low percentage shot on the rise. Crosscourt or through the middle of the court is the high-percentage solution. Playing the ball high down the line to the backhand is a riskier solution.

- **Physical errors**

  Fatigue is the number 1 cause of unforced physical errors. The length of the points, games, or matches will influence how much energy is used and affect the endurance of a player. Players need to be well trained and mentally prepared to play physical matches.

Solution

Being in great shape will prevent you from committing too many unforced errors of a physical nature. Be aware that this is a specific tennis conditioning that needs to be trained on the court as well as off the court. Players can do most of the physical training during practice by simply running for every ball. I know it sounds easy, but I am sure that if you actually start paying attention to it, you will find that you often stop running for balls and/or don't continue running when a situation seems hopeless. You will end up doing the same in matches and not be used to those extreme situations when it really counts. Other aspects that affect the endurance and the unforced physical errors are as follows:

The playing surfaces. Playing on clay courts, hard courts, or grass courts will make a difference to the endurance of the player. The same goes for playing on outdoor or indoor courts. With indoor play and grass courts, the points are usually much shorter and training of endurance will shift to agility, flexibility, reflexes, balance, and speed of movement. The sliding and changing of direction on clay courts is much more demanding due to the balance and footwork corrections. With matches lasting longer on clay, it takes more power and endurance to execute the balance and recovery footwork than on a hard court or indoor court. So the unforced physical errors are reliant on the ability of a player in shifting the focus to the appropriate physical components required for the specific surfaces. The ability to do this well will eliminate many unforced errors.

The efficiency of the player. Learning to play the game aggressively with the least amount of energy is an important key to successfully compete at a high level. The efficiency of the player will determine the endurance in long matches and might make a huge difference in critical points at the end of a match. The key to efficient play is learning to relax the muscles in the backswing and follow-through of the strokes, recovering properly on every stroke, moving efficiently and cutting of the angles, and timing the split steps properly. This will all prevent players from wasting their energy over the course of a long match and eliminate many unforced errors.

The weather condition. Playing in different weather conditions is common in tournament play. Extreme warm weather can wear a player down, but it is also the cold and the windy weather that influences the endurance of a player. Players have to learn how to prepare properly for each event. Training endurance in these conditions is an important preparation that leads to experiencing how to handle these situations. The weather conditions can also affect the mental endurance of a player.

- **Mental errors**
These types of errors occur when the players feel pressure. This pressure is brought on by the opponent and the player themselves. Nevertheless, whenever players feel this, they have an opportunity to deal with it any certain way. Some players feel this pressure when leading in score, some more when behind in score, and others feel this pressure when the score is close and it can go either way. As the pressure builds, most players start deviating from their strategies and have trouble thinking clearly about what to do. This causes indecision and confusion that undermine the confidence in the strategy and execution of the strokes. It is at this precise time during play that most unforced mental errors occur.

The following are pressures that lead to unforced mental errors:

1. Physical fatigue leads to mental fatigue over the course of a long point or match.
2. A tactical situation can pressure the player to wrong shot choices.
3. The score distracts and affects the player to lose focus on the strategy.
4. An incident on the court can lead to a loss of focus and feeling anger.
5. The crowd can affect a player to lose focus and lose confidence.
6. The player forces the situation (pressing), resulting in overhitting.

Tactical Priorities

Just like the technical progression of learning, there is also a tactical progression of learning—a methodology of teaching tactics in a certain order according to a priority of play. This methodology follows a logical order of priorities from easy to more difficult and from standard strategy to combinations of tactics. I like to call this the tactical progression or tactical priorities. Here is the order in priority:

1. **Consistency of Execution**
   This aspect runs like a thread through every aspect of the game. The consistency of strokes and movements produces a basic strategy for every match. Whatever the strategy might be, the consistency of the execution remains the most important factor to become successful in a competition. Every player strives for consistency.

2. **Depth of the Ball**
   The second priority should be the depth of the strokes in the court. Even when playing in the middle of the court, when the ball is hit close to the baseline, the opponents have to move back or make a riskier shot by taking the ball on the rise. Depth reduces the attack angles on the court and gives players more time to recover. The deep balls often produce a short ball, with possibilities to attack.

3. **Direction**
   After the first two priorities are established, the direction of the ball can be introduced to the mix of tactics. Directing the balls to the corners of the court will increase the pressure on the opponent's strokes, footwork, and stamina. Playing more crosscourt will force the opponent to run more distance than playing down the line since the ball is directed outside the sideline. Changing the direction from a crosscourt rally to hitting down the line can catch the opponent off guard in hitting a defensive shot. The decision to change direction down the line should only be made when the opponent is out of position and having a shorter and easier shot.

4. Spin (Rotation)

By adding rotation to the ball, it is possible to influence the trajectory of the ball and increase the consistency of the rally. The spin and slice rotations of the ball increase the pressure on the opponent by the irregularity of the bounce of the ball and the height of the bounce. By keeping the ball out of the comfort striking zone (between hips and shoulders), the pressure on the execution of the strokes will be increased. Changing the depth of the strokes, in combination with changing direction (short or long) and topspin, will further increase the pressure by pulling the opponent forward and then placing the ball behind them.

5. Power (Speed)

Increasing the pace of the ball can be the next tactic by pressuring the footwork of the opponent. More speed should only be added to the ball when it is within the control capabilities of the player to maintain the execution of the priorities above. The speed of the ball takes time away from the opponent to react to tactical situations and increases the pressure on the consistency and the physical endurance of the opponent. Knowing your own physical endurance level in comparison with the opponent's endurance level can be an important factor to consider before applying this tactic as part of your strategy.

6. Tempo

This last tactical priority is the tempo of play by taking the ball earlier or later after the bounce of the ball. The timing of the ball will be affected by taking the ball on the rise or by moving back and playing the ball somewhat higher over the net. Slowing down the tempo can be just as much effective as speeding it up. The difference is the time availability to strike the ball. Some players like to play faster, whereas others don't like the slower and higher-bouncing balls. The change of the tempo can also be used as a tactic in pressuring the timing skills.

Players should use these tactics according to their own capabilities. We have all seen the inexperienced players trying to hit too hard in copying the better players. In doing so, they are skipping over the first four tactical priorities and jumping directly to the use of power in their game. With the use of too much power, they are also affecting their own control capability with the reduced coordination and fine tuning of the strokes.

Crucial Points in a Match

Make no mistake, every point in a match can be crucial, but there are certain points that have a mental effect on a player's state of mind. Knowing these points in a match is not enough. The intent of how the point is played at that time becomes important. Being aware that the opponent also might know the importance of these points in the match can influence the strategy and outcome of the point. Some of these points in a match are as follows:

- **Important points in a game**
  When playing points in a game, you need to pay attention to the first point of the game, points that can lead to game point, and game points itself. Players who often win the first point of the game are usually initiative takers in the game. They are competitive and tactical players who fully understand the mental consequence this might have on their opponent. The middle part of the game contains the points that can lead to game point and are important for both players. Some examples of these scores are 30–0, 0–30, 30–30, 15–30, and 30–15. If the leading player wins the next point, it will be game point. If the player that was behind wins the point, it could bring the score closer or even. At 30, both players have a chance to move ahead. Playing these particular points well by setting up the patterns and shot choices will increase the pressure on the opponent to make mistakes. The game points should preferably be won without giving the opponent a chance to come back. Keep the strategy, focus, and intensity to avoid casual shots or unforced errors.

- **Important points in a set**
  When playing games in a set, there are some tactical points to consider. *The first three games* in each set are different in the way they are played. There is no rest period in play, and especially in the following sets, this can lead to loss of focus and a break of serve. Creating a break of serve on the opponent can increase the pressure during the entire set and limit the opponent to play freely. In the following sets, the first three games can determine the momentum entirely, depending on who is leading with the previous set(s). This makes the start of each set so important, and players should be aware of its impact on the whole match, especially players who are slow starters or those who play more casually in the following sets. Learn to play these first three games in each set with larger target choices and high intensity.

  The seventh game in each set can be a determining factor to win the set or can be a turning point in the momentum of a play. Here are some examples of these scores: 3–3, 2–4, 4–2. Players and coaches should be aware of this point in a set so they can adjust their intensity and strategy when necessary. You can imagine that persons who are aware of this momentum point in the set will have an advantage over those without this knowledge. Coaches should assist their players with this tactical information.

> Years ago, I was working at Saddlebrook and was asked by the USTA to coach a young top player (he was top 50 ATP at the time). We were at a pro event in Charlotte, and it was my first time seeing him perform in a tournament. After a few matches, I noticed how he tended to slow down when leading 4–2 in the set. After the match, I decided to talk about this subject. When I had explained the whole situation, he looked perplexedly at me and said, "I can't think about that during a match. This would be very distracting."

I smiled and answered, "Well, you can continue doing what you are doing. Just be aware that your opponents do think about this factor."

I was not sure how he was going to react since he did not seem to like my advice. We never talked about it again, but every seventh game, he picked up his intensity and won most of them after that point!

Winning the final game or tiebreak in a set can be an issue for some players. For those players who are good front-runners, these final games are usually not a problem. For players who get nervous and/or think ahead about winning or losing the set, they will usually get distracted from their strategy and freeze. This slows down the intensity and tempo of play, giving the opponent an opportunity to change the momentum in the set. Playing not to lose rather than playing to win is the frame of mind at that moment, and it needs to be reversed to be successful.

A tiebreak is a special situation where both players have an opportunity to take the advantage and win the set. Staying calm, playing point by point, keeping the intensity high, and focusing on the strategy at hand are the keys to winning the set.

- **Important points in a match**
  There are some reoccurring focus points in a match that can determine the outcome. The start of a match, with the first three games and the first set in general, can have a large impact on the eventual outcome—especially if you know that 70 percent of matches are won after winning the first set. You can imagine that knowing this fact alone can help coaches and players by helping them prepare better for matches and encouraging them to spend more time with the warm-up. The intensity and readiness to play can be improved with a longer physical warm-up, more intensity in the warm-up, and playing some points before the actual match. You can observe some pro players performing some shadow tennis (mimicking a rally

without a ball) and some sprints right before a match. They obviously understand the importance of a good start in a match.

This brings us to the next point in a match: the start of the second or following sets. After winning a set and taking the advantage of the first three games in the next set, the chances of winning the match will rise even higher than 70 percent. On the other hand, the next set can be an opportunity to change momentum for the opponent. The end of a match is much the same as the end of a set or a game. Teaching players to be good closers of matches will assist them to take advantage of opportunities. It all comes down to controlling emotions, playing with controlled aggression, and focusing on strategies and tactics. Players have to learn to develop a killer instinct to perform to their best ability. This will give them the best chance of success under stressful situation, prevent opponents to come back from behind, and close out matches whenever possible.

Constructing a Game Plan

Playing matches without a game plan is a recipe for disaster. You may observe many matches where it will be difficult to determine a specific strategy or reoccurring pattern of play. Your eyes are not deceiving you; there is no plan!

Some basic information you need to know before constructing a game plan:

- **Information about your opponent**
  You will only know how to play against your opponent when you have information of their strengths and weaknesses. Preferably, you can obtain this beforehand, but sometimes you are only able to do this during the warm-up and match. Observing the strokes will give you some insight on their capabilities, but there is much more. Look for weaknesses in handling technical, tactical, physical, and

mental aspects of the game. Some of the technical aspects are wide shots, body shots, short balls and deep balls, or high topspin or slice shots. Also take note of their good strokes so you know what to avoid. (Note—be aware that an apparent strength can also be a source of unforced errors when opponents try to hit too hard.) The physical ability is, for a large part, determined by the footwork. The mobility of players on the court, with their speed and change of direction, should also be an important factor of strengths and weaknesses. The next things to detect are the strategies, patterns of play, and tendencies of the opponent. You can only observe these during actual points and need to gather this information as soon as possible to assist you with a game plan. The mental factors only become visible when players are pushed or when they feel stressed, but they can be helpful to know how your opponent reacts under pressure. Do they stick to their game plan, or are they easily rattled and then change their tendencies?

- **Knowing your own capabilities**
  Just like knowing information about your opponent's capabilities, you need to know your own capabilities to properly execute your game plan. Knowing your own strengths and weaknesses can help you avoid the opponent from pressuring you while still applying pressure on them. By taking the initiative in a strategy, you can keep the advantage by preventing the opponent from using their strengths. An example of this would be to kick the serve to the weaker side of the opponent so they have trouble getting to your weaker backhand. You, on the other hand, could run around the backhand to take your stronger forehand back to their weaker side to keep the advantage in the rally. There are many examples like this that can be used by either side. Knowing your own game will make you more successful.

- **The court surfaces**
  The type of court surface can also determine the tactics and game plan. You can imagine how your strategy might be different on

Martin van Daalen

a grass court versus a slow red clay court. The bounce, spin, and speed of the ball will create many specific playing characteristics that may change the basic strategies and playing styles of a player. It takes time and experience to learn these differences in playing styles before players are able to execute them properly. Knowing the court surfaces and how to use them to your advantage can help you with your game style and game plan (strategy).

- **Weather conditions**

  Playing in hot and humid weather is quite different from playing in cold and windy conditions. In making your game plan, you have to take the weather conditions into consideration. Extreme heat or windy conditions can have a large impact on the style of play and shot choices of a player. Knowing how to deal with these conditions beforehand can greatly impact the outcome of a match. This is why you need a game plan that includes weather conditions.

Making a Game Plan (Strategy)

Constructing a strategy or game plan starts by taking all the four previous points into consideration. This will lead you to the following diagram:

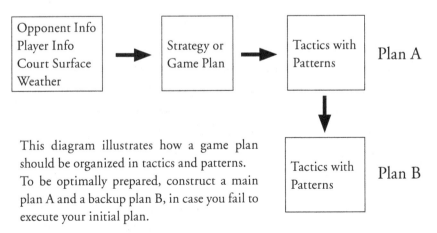

This diagram illustrates how a game plan should be organized in tactics and patterns. To be optimally prepared, construct a main plan A and a backup plan B, in case you fail to execute your initial plan.

Even though you might have your main game plan (plan A), it might not sufficiently work out as you expected or the opponent might be able to adjust to your game plan. That is why you need a backup plan (plan B) to adjust when things are not working well. The strategy is executed by various tactics and patterns. Make sure to have several different tactics and patterns to pressure the opponent with. Having just one pattern is not sufficient. Players need to find their favorite patterns that personally work for them. Finding patterns that fit the strengths of a player and that complement their game plan is the key to a successful strategy.

Fundamental Strategies and Behaviors

There are some basic strategies that can be taught to give students a better insight on how to play the game. By making them focus on the objective of the strategy, you can make it clear how a structure of a point (pattern) develops to gain the advantage. Keep it simple and organized so players understand and remember the most important patterns for their personal game. The fundamental strategies can be divided into three major categories:

1. How to start matches
2. How to play under pressure
3. How to pressure your opponents

1. How to Start Matches
The start of a match can be crucial to the momentum and the final outcome against the majority of opponents. As we stated before, when you win the first set, you, generally speaking, have a 70 percent chance of winning the entire match. So taking the initiative and knowing how to start the match is therefore even more important. The most important factors to keep in mind are the following:

- **Make sure to have an optimal warm-up.** The warm-up ensures that your body is ready to go a 100 percent from the first point on. Most inexperienced players will have less intensity in the warm-up and need four to five games to get used to the speed of play. By that time, the opponent will probably have taken control of the match and likely feel more confident than you. Preferably, you will be the one taking control of the points and games in the early stages of the match.

- **Pressure the opponent from the start.** Taking the initiative is better than waiting for the opponent to pressure you. It will have a positive effect on your demeanor in looking to pressure the opponent with offensive actions. This will keep you on your toes, with a better court position, closer to the baseline. Waiting for actions from the opponent creates a defensive position that will push you on your heels, farther back behind the baseline. Offensive play can be executed in many different ways. Being consistent is the most basic strategy to pressure the opponent, and players should keep this in mind when starting a match. Besides pressure on the opponent, it is also a great way to enhance confidence in your own game. Having a game plan makes it possible to pressure your opponent right away by playing to their weaknesses.

- **Play high-percentage tennis.** Playing with a large margin of error will reduce unforced errors and increase consistency. This means playing higher over the net, using large target areas, and not hitting it too close to the lines. In the first few games, most top players play their strokes with controlled aggression through the middle of the court. They use this method to pressure the opponent while increasing the rhythm and timing of the ball. They groove their strokes with deep shots before opening the court. As the match develops, they will venture out more closely to the sidelines, always keeping a safe margin in mind for consistency. Playing high percentage tennis also means playing a high percentage first serves and return. The speed, spin, and placement of the serve should be adjusted to pressure the opponent instead of yourself. Playing too many second serves can reverse and increase the mental pressure on the server, with the opponent hitting aggressive returns.

- **Don't be afraid to strike when the opportunity arises.** During the course of each rally, there are many instances when opportunities arise to attack the opponent or to take advantage of the court position. It is important to realize these situations clearly and accelerate the footwork and stroke to pressure the opponent with determination and confidence. Any doubt or hesitation will usually create an error or a loss of the initiative in the rally. Playing the ball to bigger targets will reduce the amount of fear of mistakes. Being determined in the execution and having a plan will reduce the amount of hesitation in shot choices.

2. **How to Play Under Pressure**
When the opponent is applying a lot of pressure during the rallies, there are several important factors to keep in mind to stay in control of the rally. These factors are as follows: the anticipation of each next stroke, the movement and positioning on the court, and the shot choices you make. Let us look at all these factors separately.

- **The anticipation of each next stroke will help you move quicker and more efficiently.** By reading the stroke of the opponent, the trajectory of the ball, and the type of shot, it is possible to time the split step and movement to the ball better with quicker reactions. This will eventually save energy in the long run by not having to make last-minute adjustments and abrupt movements.

- **The movement and positioning determine the opportunities to strike.** The split step, together with the speed and accuracy of the movement, will position the player in an advantageous position with time to spare to strike the ball in a balanced position. It provides a player more opportunities to play aggressively and offensively rather than defensively. It also provides more shot choices with a higher chance of success. The speed of recovery will set up a better position on the court for each following shot.

- **The shot choices need to be functional to the tactical positions.** Shot choices are determined by the tactical status and tactical situation of each player. The tactical status of an offensive, neutral, or defensive position affects the type of shot and the trajectory of the ball. The tactical situation (serve and return, baseline play, approaching the net, net play, and playing against the net player) of the rally decides the shot choices of each player. Choosing the correct shot at the appropriate time will enhance the opportunities to take advantage and initiative during the rally.

3. **How to Pressure Your Opponent**

In order to keep the initiative and advantage in the rallies, it is important to pressure the opponent whenever possible. Playing neutral or defensively will eventually lead to getting pressure from the opponent and having to make high-risk shot choices with a lower percentage of consistency. There are several ways to pressure the opponent without taking unnecessary high risks with the following methods:

- **Play with controlled aggression to big targets.** This will often keep you in control of the point while limiting the offensive position and opportunities of the opponent. By taking the initiative, the opponent will have to react to your actions and play neutralizing or defensive strokes instead of you reacting to your opponent. Being in control is better than being controlled and having to play high-risk tennis.

- **Play the ball with depth in the court.** The depth of the ball plays an important role in decreasing the offensive angles of the opponent and provides a player more time to set up for the next stroke. It can also produce a weaker and short return from the opponent while enhancing the tactical position with opportunities to attack.

- **Immediately and continually pressure the weaknesses of your opponent.** By not letting the opponent take initiative with their strongest weapons, you can control the pressure that is applied to you. Applying pressure to the weaker side of the opponent will also add mental pressure. This anxiety can slowly build up over time as errors increase and the opponent starts thinking about the pressure more. Finally, it can cause doubt and fear to creep in.

- **Make your opponent move more than they move you.** By keeping the opponent on the move and off-balance, you will give them less chance to pressure you. The opponent will have fewer chances to hit offensive shots and will likely be reduced to hitting neutralizing and defensive strokes. As soon as they are able to set up their feet, power will increase to the strokes and will likely lead to offensive strategies.

- **Keep the ball out of the opponent's comfort zone.** Players will have less offensive capability when the ball is struck above the shoulders or below the knees. The type and amount of rotation of the ball (topspin or slice) can enhance this effect even more. This is obviously only effective when depth is maintained to the ball.

Use the score to apply pressure. The score in the game, set, and match is an important way to maintain pressure on your opponent. That's why as a junior, it is so important to call out the score when leading. You will remind opponents of the score. By the rules, you are supposed to call the score if there is no chair umpire. It is always amazing to me when juniors do not use this rule to their advantage. Getting ahead in the game or the set increases the burden on the opponent mentally and physically and can cause them to be scared or to panic. They could change strategy by playing more cautiously or playing riskily. Either way will help you to to gain advantage.

- **Keep your momentum going.** You always want to keep staying ahead when possible. Don't do anything different when things are going your way. In fact, you should repeat whatever was working until your opponent changes his or her strategy. Keep the positive energy flowing as long as possible. When the momentum is lost for a point or two, try to regain it as quickly as possible. Keep the rhythm of the match by playing with initiative and keeping your thoughts on the current strategy. Don't let your mind wander or get distracted by the antics of your opponent. Keeping the momentum on your side is always a good strategy.

These components above give you strategies and methods of play to gain advantage over your opponents. If you are disciplined, these methods will become an automated competitive behavior, which is exactly what you want. You don't want to think about it but just do it without hesitation. These competitive attitudes and behaviors apply continual pressure on your opponents and relieve some of the pressures on yourself. Make sure to do them all the time!

Point Construction

There are several ways to construct a point. The knowledge of a basic strategy and the patterns of play and specific situational shot choices can help, but there is also some common logic to each point construction. I will illustrate in detail below how to do this with all variables.

Starting Point Situations

1. **First Serve**

   This is a serve that is struck with great force and commitment to a target that is out of reach of the opponent (or sometimes, on purpose, at the body). The objective is to create a winner or a weak or short return from the opponent. This serve will often create the following options:

   A. Offensive return

   These offensive returns are usually reflex returns where the opponent uses the speed of the serve and returns the ball with high speed and depth. In this situation, the server has two options:

   - neutralizing shot   on-the-rise shot in the middle of the court
   - defensive shot   backing up and hitting topspin (slice) high and deep

   Examples

   1. The server hits an aggressive first serve up the middle of the court. The opponent hits the return hard and deep up the middle of the court. The server has to react and recover really quickly in order to hit the ball at their feet for a half volley back up the middle of the court to neutralize the tactical situation.
   2. The server hits a first serve out wide, and the returner hits an offensive return crosscourt. The server is immediately in a tough defensive position and is forced to play a defensive topspin or slice shot to slow the ball down in order to neutralize the opponent.

   B. Neutral return

   These returns are designed to neutralize the server with direction and depth and the rotation and bounce of the ball (topspin or slice). The server is often able to take initiative or at least neutralizes the opponent on the following shot:

- offensive shot   aggressive shot for winner or to pressure opponent
- neutralizing shot   committed shot to take away initiative from opponent

Examples

1. The server hits an aggressive serve to the body and receives a neutral return in the middle of the court. The server has two options: to serve and volley in this situation (to take advantage of the confusion) or to attack the return right away after the bounce of the ball.
2. The server hits an aggressive serve to the backhand and receives a slice backhand in return. The server will attack the slice return immediately.

C. Defensive return

This return has the purpose of staying in the point at all cost under pressure. The player realizes they cannot take initiative but hopes to stay in the point in order to have a chance to later on turn the table and take initiative after neutralizing the rally. The server has to take initiative and take control:

- offensive shot   aggressive shot for winner or to take control

Example

The server hits an aggressive serve to the backhand and receives a short ball on the forehand side. The server has two options: play an aggressive shot to the strength side to open up the weaker side or to go for the weakness right away.

2. Second Serve

This serve has to be consistent and neutralizing in nature to force the opponent to play a neutral return. This is done in order to take control and initiative in the rally. The pressure of making errors (double fault) on this serve often causes players to be more conservative and tentative. The second serve will often create the following options:

A.   Offensive return

Attacking the second serve by stepping forward and hitting aggressive returns is a good way to get the initiative while at the same time increasing the pressure on the opponent's serve. This is a favorite strategy especially in women's tennis since the serve speeds are lower.

- offensive shot   aggressive winner shot or to take initiative

Example

The server hits a weak second serve to the body. The returner runs around and hits the return for a winner in either corner.

B.   Neutral return

The returner has the objective to neutralize the return by playing a topspin return deep and higher over the net. The server will not be able to hit a direct winner on the return and is forced to build the rally.

- neutralizing return   aggressive deep topspin return

Example

The server plays a heavy kick serve to the backhand in the hope to receive a weak return. The opponent hits a deep topspin return to neutralize the rally. The returner will be able to take initiative on the third ball if the server does not act immediately.

Third-Ball Situations

The third-ball situations are the tactical decisions made on the third ball, starting with the serve or with the return. So if the server hits a first or second serve, what are the tactical options on the shot after the return? Or in the case of the return player, what are the options on the shots after the serve and second shot from the server? These third-ball situations are crucial and mostly determine the outcome of the point as they set the tactical purpose and intensity level to win points. Juniors are often tentative and scared to take initiative, especially when the score is close or there are opportunities to close out a game, set, or match. Even top players can experience this phenomenon of fear creeping into their game.

This was evident in the recent Wimbledon final (2019) between Roger Federer and Novak Djokovic. In the first set tiebreak, Roger failed to play with the proper intensity and shot choices and lost the tiebreak after leading. Later on, in that same match, he had two match points and again played very tentatively, with poor and risky shot choices. This was uncharacteristic for Roger, but it was not the first time this happened to him against Novak. A few years earlier, he played against Novak twice in the US Open (2010 and 2011). On both matches, Roger had a 40–15 lead on Novak, with two match points. In 2010, he was returning; and in 2011, he was serving for the match, just like at the recent Wimbledon final. Was it a coincidence that all three finals turned out this way? Maybe, but very unlikely. All three matches were very close matches. In the first two finals, he did not necessarily "kill" himself with unforced errors, but he did not hit decisive and committed shots to put Novak in extreme defensive positions. All the rallies were constructed with neutral shot choices, waiting for Novak to make errors rather than applying the pressure and forcing his opponent to take more risk. This same situation occurred in the Wimbledon final (together with some bad shot choices from Roger), and Novak was able to win again in an epic final. The third-ball situations and decisions made at this crucial time made a large impact on the outcome of all three matches.

The decision-making on third-ball situations needs to be highly disciplined in order to be effective. There are three tactical status positions to recognize:

1. Am I in an offensive position to attack my opponent?
2. Am I in a neutral position to continue the rally?

3. Am I in a defensive position to retrieve balls?

These three questions need to be analyzed almost instinctively in order to have the proper shot choice in each situation. When playing points, it is good to discuss some of these tactical situations with your coach to make sure you are making the right decisions in each tactical status position. Mixing up the third ball options in either going for the weakness and sometimes going for the strength keeps the opponent off guard and guessing where you will attack next.

Basic Patterns

There are some basic patterns that players need to be aware of. These basic patterns will return in nearly every match and need to be trained in point play as often as possible. The basic patterns are the following:

- **The Center Pattern**
  This pattern is mainly designed to neutralize the opponent. The shots in the corners of the court are returned deep to the center or slightly to the weaker side of the opponent.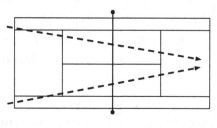
  This pattern will limit the angles to attack and is often used as a neutralizing strategy. It can even be used as a defensive strategy as long as the player is able to return the ball with depth.

- **The Open-Court Pattern**
  The purpose of this pattern is to keep the opponent on the run. This can be accomplished by serving or returning the ball wide and aiming the following strokes to the open court. This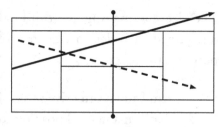

Martin van Daalen

pattern is effective with opponents who don't move well or have fewer defensive skills. Even if the ball is returned crosscourt or down the line, players should play the following ball to the open court.

- **Playing Behind the Opponent**
  This pattern is used as a variation of the open-court pattern. While starting with an open-court pattern and playing the ball from side to side, a variation can be introduced by playing the ball 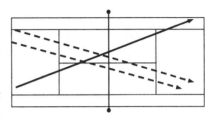 back behind the opponent. This method will often wrong-foot the opponent and cause a loss of balance and rhythm. This in turn can lead to unforced errors.

- **Opening Up Down the Line**
  After a crosscourt rally, the court can be opened up by directing the ball down the line. This pattern is often used to surprise the opponent by a sudden change of direction or a change 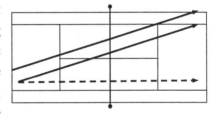 of the pattern. This change of direction needs to be organized at the appropriate time, keeping in mind the position of both players on the court and the difficulty of the stroke when changing direction.

A good rule of thumb is to not be outside the sideline when changing direction and having time to execute the ball down the line in a balanced and controlled fashion. If the player is too far outside the sideline, it will be difficult to cover the court. The targets should be well inside the sideline to reduce unnecessary errors. It requires discipline and experience to execute this stroke with consistency and confidence, but it can be very effective when executed well.

- **Playing Short and Long**

  Another pattern is to combine an angle shot with a deep shot behind the opponent. The angle shot will draw the opponent inside the court with the opportunity to create 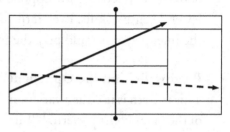 a defensive situation with deep shots behind the opponent. This pattern is also very effective against heavy topspin players (moonball players) to force them to lower the ground stroke trajectories in order to hit forceful strokes. These short angle strokes can either be performed with topspin or slice strokes. Either way, this pattern is effective against different styles of players as long as you are alert and prepared to strike.

- **The Inside-Out Pattern**

  By running around the backhand and using a powerful forehand, it is possible to pressure the opponent even more with the angles and speed of the ball. This pattern is a 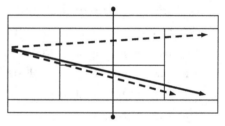 favorite shot in today's aggressive baseline game. This pressure shot will open up opportunities to either hit the ball inside out or inside in. This shot choice will largely be made by the positions of the opponent.

- **Changing the Pattern**

  It is often necessary to change a pattern when the pressure during the rally increases. This is possible in many different ways by hitting the ball in a different direction 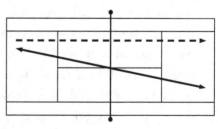 or by changing the spin or trajectory. An obvious example is a backhand-to-backhand rally that is changed by hitting up the middle or down the line. Hitting up the middle of the court would change the angle with more opportunities to hit the following ball or to run around the backhand. Hitting down the line would change the pattern with the opportunity to hit the return with a different stroke. This would also be the case by changing the spin and slice in combination with the trajectory.

Starting the Point

Starting play happens either with the serve or with the return. Having a game plan and a pattern will increase the amount of success in each point. In playing the first shot, it is important to understand the strengths and weaknesses of the opponent. In general, the forehand is the strongest and often a weapon in the arsenal of strokes. The first shot can set up a neutral or defensive stroke from the opponent and increase the chances of winning the point. With this in mind, it pays to apply pressure as soon as possible to the weakness of the opponent. Serve and return strategies can vary from men's and women's tennis at each level, so it is imperative to know when to introduce these strategies. (Example—many young inexperienced female players often serve to the forehand even though this is the stronger side.) The slice, which is naturally created on the right-handed serve, curves the ball to the forehand side of a right-handed opponent. As players progress, there is more variety and placement to the body and backhand side. On the pro side, you see a dramatic change with players attacking the return since the pace is less and in having a first strike strategy, especially in women's pro tennis.

Serving Patterns

There are several options available in opening the pattern with the different targets of the serve. The targets can give the server a large indication where the return might go, so they can plan the second

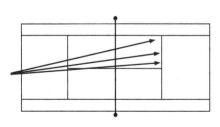

shot. The return will usually be in the opposite direction of the serve or in the middle of the court. This gives the server the option to choose for the weaker return or play the serve that will most likely provide the return they want. It also sets up the pattern to play the open court or play behind the opponent.

Return Patterns

In order to start the rally with the return, you first have to get the ball in play. With the stronger serves today, this is not always an easy task. The return player has to make quick judgments on the 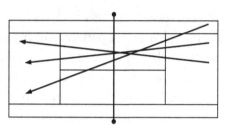 type of return, trajectory, spin, and direction to start a preferred pattern. In general, it is best, and simpler, to return to the middle of the court on first serves, especially if it is a difficult serve to return. On second serves, the player can have the option to attack other targets as long as consistency is maintained to start the rally. The second objective is to neutralize the opponent or even put them in a defensive position, if possible. Return players need to plan ahead where to hit the return so they can start the pattern that provides the most chance to pressure the opponent on the return or second shot.

It is possible that players do not only use one pattern to play a point and have a combination of patterns that follow one another in sequence.

Once you have determined the strengths and weaknesses of your opponent, you draw up a game plan to outmaneuver your opponent and you play the patterns that suit your game the most and will expose the weaknesses of your opponent. Practice and experimenting with these patterns will improve your understanding of strategy and tactics and your commitment of how to play the game.

Playing Against Different Style Players

There are several different styles of play from opponents that advanced players need to learn to play against. Below you will see some methods and patterns on how to play against these specific styles of players:

Playing Against the Moonball Player

We have all played against a moonball player at least one time in competition. Especially in juniors, this is a favorite style of play when juniors don't have the strength to hit winning shots yet. A moonball player is a defensive competitor who hopes to win points by lobbing the ball over the net with consistency and frustrating the opponent. Inexperienced players will usually hit flat and hard to make winners. The result, however, will be many unforced errors with highly risky shots. I will show you some methods on how to play against the moonball player with much more success:

Tactic 1

Be patient and exchange topspin shots until you get a short return. At this time, you can move in with an approach shot to take the net position. Most moonball players are not good at hitting forceful shots and will have trouble playing passing shots. You can also mix this method up by taking the ball out of the air when the opponent is in a defensive position. This can be executed with a volley drive or a topspin stroke.

Tactic 2

Moonball players like to position themselves deep in the court so they can use the high topspin ball more effectively. By using slice strokes slightly shorter in the court, it is virtually impossible to get under the ball to play high over the net. They will be forced to flatten the trajectory of the ball and will find themselves in an uncomfortable position inside the court. This court position is where the moonball player is vulnerable.

Tactic 3

There is another method to bring a moonball player inside the court: by playing short angle shots. This will not only bring the opponent inside the court but also position them outside the court with the whole court unprotected. They will be forced to either play an angle shot back or go for a winning shot that will flatten out the trajectory. By being alert for these options, it is possible to take advantage of this tactical situation.

Tactic 4

As players advance in strengths and capabilities, they are able to play aggressively from the baseline to force the opponent farther back behind the baseline. This gives you the opportunity to hit drop shots that they are not able to reach or puts them in a net position they are not used to. This last method should only be used by advanced players who are very confident in their ground stroke game and have the touch to execute the drop shot with consistency.

Tactic 5

Playing serve and volley is another method to force the moonball player to flatten out their strokes, starting with the return. Just using this tactic occasionally will keep the opponent guessing what shot choice to make. Once you are successful in knocking off the volley on the high returns, you will force them to take more risk and hit the ball lower over the net, which was the objective in the first place.

Martin van Daalen

Tactic 6

The return can also be used as a weapon against the moonball player, if used correctly. By stepping forward and attacking the return, it is possible to get the opponent on the defense from the start. You can either hit angles or go straight at the opponent to rush them. After backing up the opponent in a defensive position, this tactic will open up the possibility to hit a drop shot. A slice return will also be very effective to keep the ball low and reduce the height of the ball, making it easier to attack the opponent.

Playing Against the Aggressive Baseliner

The aggressive baseliner is the most common style of the modern game and the most physical style to counter. Most advanced players will have consistent ground strokes to play the game; but the footwork, stamina, tactical skills, and mental toughness of a player will make the difference in combating an aggressive baseliner. Here are some tactics you can keep in mind when playing against this style of play:

Tactic 1

Use the topspin and slice to keep the ball out of their optimal strike zone between knees and shoulder height. By using a higher topspin ball, it is possible to slow down the tempo and push the opponent farther back behind the baseline, making it more difficult to apply pressure. By using slice strokes, you can eliminate the direct scoring shots since the ball is far below the net. This tactic will neutralize the opponent until the time you are able to attack a suitable tactical position and situation.

Tactic 2

Taking the initiative is extremely important in combating the aggressive baseline player. Running the opponent around keeps them on the defensive and will limit the opportunities of taking the offensive. Having a plan to find the opponent's weakness and attacking this immediately will be crucial to stay on the offensive. As soon as this objective is achieved, keep the opponent under pressure by making them run more than yourself.

Tactic 3

The positioning on the court will assist in pushing the opponent farther back behind the baseline. By staying closer to the baseline, it is easier to dictate the opponent and find the angles and openings on the court. By using this method, it is possible to enhance the offense while limiting the opponent from seeking the offense.

Tactic 4

Occasionally playing serve and volley not only can shorten the length of the rallies but also keep the return lower over the net. This tactic can be very effective when you are leading in the game or when you have a game point. It will pressure the opponent with a surprise attack, and you might very well catch them hitting a safer high return at this point.

Playing Against an All-Court Player

This type of player is the toughest opponent to play against since they can successfully execute any style of play and feel comfortable in any position on the court. It is not so easy to find a weakness or a position on the court to exploit. The all-court player likes to play with various strategies by either building the pressure from the baseline with the objective to approach the net or playing a serve and volley or chip-and-charge-style game. Either way, their objective is to eventually take the net position when possible. With this in mind, you can devise the following tactics:

Tactic 1

This style of player is usually also a flashy player. They like to play faster and shorter rallies instead of long drawn-out rallies. Knowing this can help you by playing the opposite style with long and consistent rallies that draw errors from the opponent.

Tactic 2

The all-court player likes to take the net position to win points. Taking the initiative in the baseline rallies will assist you in taking the net position away from the opponent. By using this strategy, you will make the all-court player feel uncomfortable in only playing a defensive style of play and feeling restrictive in strategy and movement.

Tactic 3

Playing rallies with heavy topspin will not only slow down the tempo of play but also make it extremely difficult for the opponent to play an all-court style of play. The spin and bounce of the ball will limit the opponent's ability to speed up the game and attack the net position. It pins them down behind the baseline and will force them to take high-risk shots to play their style of game.

Playing Against a Counterpuncher

The counterpuncher is a very consistent defensive player who likes to draw you into making mistakes and unforced errors and strikes when you don't expect it. Their great speed and footwork enable them to recover the ball from seemingly impossible situations. As you attack the net position, they are very accomplished in passing you or playing well-placed lobs. Here are some tactics to use against the counterpuncher:

Tactic 1

The counterpuncher is used to hitting balls out of the corners of the court but is not so comfortable in playing forcefully through the court. So try to mix up your shots through the middle of the court instead and give them less angles when approaching the net by playing through the court. In many cases, the counterpuncher will overrun the shots since they are expecting them to be in the corners.

Tactic 2

By playing forceful or heavy topspin shots, you can force the counterpuncher farther behind the baseline, which opens up the opportunity to hit the drop shot on short returns. The drop shot will either be a direct winner or force the opponent into an uncomfortable position at the net. By closing in the net position after the drop shot, you can take the advantage and finish off any response coming from the opponent.

Tactic 3

You can use a strategy of serve and volley to force the opponent to play a more aggressive style of play. The direction of the serve should be either at the body or through the middle of the court to eliminate the angles to pass. The wide serves should be used to surprise the opponent and/or to keep them off-balance and guessing.

Tactic 4

When attacking this opponent, try to play the volley shorter in the court. This particular player likes to pass and use the lob, so by playing a drop volley or a shorter volley, you can reduce their chances of success. The direction of the volley should be angled away from the opponent or played against the running direction of the opponent to enlarge the distance to retrieve the balls.

Playing Against an Attacking Player

This style of player has many different ways to pressure the opponent. They can execute this style by attacking from a baseline game, by using a serve and volley game, or by using the chip-and-charge approach. The continuous onslaught of pressure in both the serve and return games can be devastating to the morale of any player. The variety of methods makes this player very difficult to combat. Here are some tactics you can use against the attacking player:

Tactic 1

Keeping the opponent away from the net position is a key component of the strategy against the attacking player. In baseline rallies, this means keeping the initiative by playing an aggressive but controlled style of play that pushes the opponent farther back behind the court. By pressuring the opponent's forward movement, you can limit their offensive capability.

Tactic 2

Whenever the attacking player approaches the net in the beginning of the match, your first strategy should be to forcefully hit right at the opponent. First of all, not only is it the easiest target of the return but it will also surprise the opponent. The net player will have to protect their body shots and will have fewer angles for the volley. Especially in the beginning of the match, it is important to establish this pattern before you reach more crucial points in the match. As the match progresses and the returns improve, you can venture out to the sides of the court or even try to pass the opponent.

Tactic 3

Against a serve-and-volley player, you can control and sometimes limit the angles and offensive capability by returning the ball crosscourt or at the feet of the net player. The net player has to slow down the pace to keep the ball in the court and will have fewer angles to attack. A low return at the feet gives the return player the opportunity to run down the volley and will enhance the passing shot chances.

Tactic 4

As the attacking player approaches the net position, you can organize the pass by dipping the ball low at the feet. This causes the net player to slow the ball down and also draws them closer to the net, making it easier to pass them or play a lob over their head. The lob should be used frequently whenever the opponent moves too close to the net position in order to keep them away from hitting easy volleys.

Tactic 5

Playing against a chip-and-charge player takes some skill, but it can also be limited and controlled with the direction and spin of the serve. Whenever the opponent applies this strategy, you should change the direction of your serve to wide and body serves. The wide serve is difficult to cover when trying to move in, and the body serve will limit a forceful approach with an uncomfortable stroke. It is also important to make sure to hit the first serve in the court to limit the offensive capabilities.

Summary

In developing your tactical skills, you should try to practice these tactics by playing against the different styles of play. As you practice these skills, you become more familiar with the appropriate responses. This, in turn, will enhance your confidence in competitive play and improve your tennis game to a higher level.

15—DOUBLES PLAY

Playing doubles requires a lot of skills from the players. With two players already in place at the net, the speed of the game increases and the target areas of the return are reduced in size and direction. With the rallies becoming shorter, the consistency and accuracy have to increase to be successful in doubles. Being creative and flexible under pressure are important intangibles to develop as a doubles player. Here are some of the most important topics for practicing doubles:

- **Positioning**
  The positioning of players in doubles is the starting position, on the court, before play has commenced. The positioning is an important signal to your partner and the opponents of possible strategies. The positions of the players in the service games are different from the return games (see picture below).

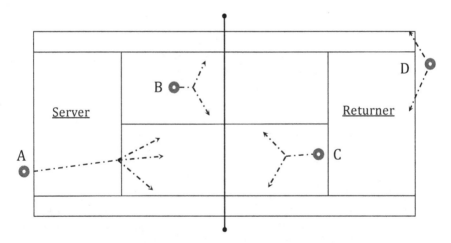

Player A serves from the middle of their side of the court. This position varies from the singles position in order to cover half of the court. The player can either stay in that position to play baseline stroke (beginning players) or move in after they serve and play the volley (intermediate and advanced players).

Bob and Mike Bryan

They have dominated in doubles.

Martin van Daalen

Player B takes the net position in the middle of the service box and moves in as the ball from the server passes by. The net player covers half the court from this position and assists the approaching player in covering the middle of the court from the return.

Player C watches the movements of player B to intercept the return. Do not make the mistake of looking back on how your partner is returning the ball; you will not be able to follow the movements of the net player B that way. Player C moves in to cover the net if player B does not try to intercept (poach) and volley the ball.

Player D returns the serve and reacts to the exchange of the rally from the players at the net. If his partner, player C, moves across to intercept the volley, player D might have to switch over to the other side to cover the court. But there are other positions possible in doubles play. They all have to do with confusing the opponents and forcing them to hit the return in a different direction than they normally do. Here are some different positions and formations:

Australian Formation

In an Australian doubles position, the server moves over more to the middle of the court while the partner, at the net, moves over to the opposite service box in front of the server. As you can see in the diagram, the server plays to the backhand side of the opponent. The strategy here is to force the return player to hit down the line. If you are used to playing cross, it is not so easy to change direction too quickly. The net player can move over to the right after the serve to apply even more pressure. If you are a right-handed player,

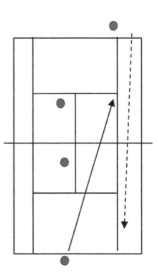

you could do it only on the odd side so that the returner plays to your forehand. You can then keep hitting down the line till you get a weak return. From there, you have many options in hitting cross in between the players or attacking the net player.

I-Formation

The I-position is more complicated. The net player bends down all the way to sit low in front of the net, close to the middle of the court. The purpose here is to force the opponent to play away from the middle. The trick, however, is that they will not know what side the net player will cover after the serve is delivered. The net player is able to mix it up, always letting the server know exactly where they are moving. This type of formation is very confusing for the return players. In the diagram, you can see the serve and return positions, the serve directions, and the movements of the server and net player. They need to communicate several things with each other concerning serve direction and movement after the serve. That way, you know what part of the court you need to cover and what you are responsible for. The server has to move in the opposite direction of the net player in order to cover both sides of the court. Here are some tactical options:

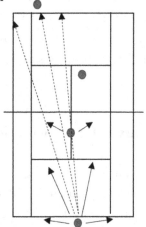

Serve Team

1. Serve over the net player to the middle of the court. The net player is already in position to get most returns hit from this position. The net player moves to the right to intercept the volley. The server has moved inside to cover the other side (see diagram).

2. Serve out wide to the outside of the court. The net player moves to the left to intercept the volley. The server moves in to cover the middle and crosscourt returns.

Return Team

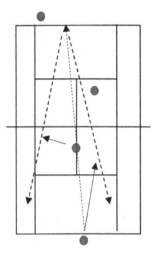

1. Return inside out in between both net players to surprise the server coming into the net on the net.
2. Return crosscourt, away from the net player, and be ready for the return volley that follows. It is important to communicate with the net player what direction you are looking at in hitting the return so your partner can react to the situation.

- **Communication**
  One of the key factors of playing better in doubles is to communicate well with your partner. By talking with your partner before each point or by using predetermined signals, you can make a game plan on how you want to play each point and to anticipate your opponent's options. Remember to discuss a strategy for the service games as well as the return games.

- **Sign Language**
  Using signs helps in doubles play to communicate much more quickly with your partner. The signs are always twofold. The first sign indicates where to serve. The second sign indicates where the net player is going to move after the serve. It is important to be committed in this method to be successful. If you hesitate, it will not work out favorably.

- **Serve for Doubles**

  When serving, practice consistency and direction to the forehand, the backhand, and most of all, the body targets. When in trouble, these are the best targets to aim for because your net partner will be able to jump in and help out. You can mark off target areas in the service box to improve the accuracy and consistency or use tape to mark an area. Practice your signs and formations together to get good communication and timing of the poaching. The position for the serve is slightly more outside so you can cover the angle shots. Movement to the net has to be well coordinated when playing serve and volley. Where to expect certain returns depends a lot on the target areas of the serve. Being aware of the angles makes it easier to anticipate the returns.

Net Partner

The net partner has an important role in covering half the court. The net partner can also assist in pressuring the return player by the movements at the net and by poaching whenever the return player is off-balance. The net player is supposed to move forward, closer to the net, after the serve and cut off any crosscourt shot within reach. If the ball passes the net player, they are supposed to move back, closer to the service line, in order to pick up any volley interception from the opponent net player. It is a constant up-and-back movement that requires very quick footwork and reactions. The opponent net player has the same movements and tasks but starts at the service line position.

As a net partner, your job is to instill in the opponent the fear that they might get hit. If you can get them to lean backward or turn around, then you have easy volleys or putaway shots. If the opponent is not scared of you, they will dominate the net position and do the exact opposite to you! They will start poaching much more and run around the net freely and make point after point. The fear of getting hit (or being passed) prevents you to do that.

Fear

Years ago, I was coaching Julie Richardson from New Zealand on the tour during the summer swing. We went to all the major WTA events and were at the grass courts in Birmingham. Her doubles partner was Anne Smith (Australian), and they were scheduled to play against Martina Navratilova and Billie Jean King. It was obviously a major task against these Grand Slam champions. They both came to me before the match, very intimidated by the opponents.

"What should we do against these two?" they asked.

"You only have one chance," I answered. "You have to neutralize Martina. Otherwise, she will dominate the net. You have to hit her early on in the match so she stops poaching."

They both looked shockingly at me. "Really, you want us to hit her?" they asked again.

"Yes, otherwise you might as well shake hands at the beginning of the match," I insisted. "I will buy the drinks if you guys are able to pull it off," I promised.

They went out there and played very aggressively. They got their chance at 3–3 in the first set. There was a lob from Billie Jean that landed short, and Julie hit the overhead right at Martina, who was standing at the service line. Martina was just able to turn around on time, and the ball hit her just below the shoulder blade in her side. She looked very shocked but took it well. Julie looked up at the stands to me and gave me a thumbs up. I smiled, realizing they had followed my advice and knowing nobody in the stands knew who I was.

They won the match 6–4, 6–3, and I had some beers waiting for them in the lounge when they came in. They learned a valuable lesson that day!

- **Return for Doubles**

  When returning, players can practice direction by using the single lines as targets. Make sure to also practice different speeds and spins so you are ready to dip the ball down when playing with a serve-and-volley player. You also have to practice when to go down the line and introduce the lob over the net player. This is specifically used on the return in doubles play. The best way to practice doubles on the practice court is to have all four players play crosscourt points since there are usually four players on a court.

  Teaching the tactics of the serve and return for doubles involves the relation between the targets and the possible returns with the actions of the players. All the targets have different possibilities. As a coach, walk your players through the different plays as they unfold so they have a better understanding on how to move and what to expect.

- **Net Play**

  Players are much more frequent at the net in doubles than singles and therefore need to practice this part of the game more often. There are two types of net play to practice for doubles play:

  1. *Playing at the net*

     This involves the role of the two players at the net and how they play their part in the doubles strategy. Running across the net and cutting off the volley, also called poaching, is an important part of practice for both players. Learning how and when to do this is the key to good net play. The timing of the movement needs to be coordinated with the serve and the return from the opponent. The net player can either communicate this action with their partner beforehand or decide at the last moment when seeing the possibility of interception.

  2. *Approaching the net*

     The player moves to the net on a short return from the opponent or behind the serve as a serve and volley. You can practice the short return by using a second serve and moving in behind the return. Learning how to time the step in when the server is tossing the ball is important so you don't give away your strategy. The serve and volley action is best practiced on second serves. Announce the target area of the serve and the return so that you can get better returns and both sides can practice their strokes and consistency. The main concept to teach for the volley is to play short crosscourt when the volley is low and to hit at the net player when the return is high. As doubles play improves, you might see the net players poach more on low volleys. This is where experience and knowledge of your opponent becomes important to surprise them with a volley down the line when they cross too early.

- **Poaching**
  The interception of the volley at the net is called poaching. This requires good anticipation and fast reflexes. As a net partner, you are standing much closer to the return player and therefore have only half the time to react to situations in comparison to the baseline partner. The fear of getting hit at the net is the largest obstacle in moving fast and with commitment. This is very evident in junior players when they start playing doubles. Players have to overcome this fear when playing tournaments. There are two types of poaches. One is planned when discussing the strategy beforehand. The second is when the net player sees a weaker shot and intercepts the return at the net. Planning the poach takes guts and commitment from both players. Reading the weaker shots comes with time but takes great urgency from the net player to accelerate the footwork to get there in time to intercept.

- **When Should I Poach and When Not**
  Playing doubles matches requires you to make much faster decisions. When you make the wrong decisions, you usually lose the point very quickly. The intensity of play is higher than singles matches, and quick actions and movements are key. You should poach in these instances:

1. When the opponent hits the return within your reach

2. When the opponent is off-balance with a return
3. When the return is struck too soft and too high
4. When you have planned it ahead and switching positions with your partner
5. When leading in score to provide more pressure

You should not poach in these instances:

1. When your partner hits a weak serve
2. When the ball is out of your reach and creates a weak volley
3. When the opponent approaches the net on the return
4. When in desperate situations or when down in score

The most important thing to learn is reading the various situations and making the appropriate response decisions. This takes time and experience and also learning not to be scared to take initiative. You will make many mistakes in the beginning, but you can't learn without them!

- **When to Lob**
  The lob in doubles play is a very strategic stroke, when executed properly at the right time. It can be used to surprise the opponent or to move them off the net when they are both approaching the net. The lob can be played defensively and hit much higher over the net or played more offensively and followed into the net to take advantage of the tactical situation. Here are some situations when the lob can be used successfully:

1. When the opponent is playing serve and volley
2. When both opponents are attacking the net
3. When the opponents are more successful at the net with volleys
4. When opponents close in too close to the net
5. When a passing shot is not an option in defensive situations
6. When you want to surprise the opponents and to mix up the tempo

The lob can be a very good weapon in doubles play when used correctly. It is wise to practice this stroke to find the appropriate height and depth consistency.

- **Playing Against the Net Players**
  This part of the game needs more practice than it usually receives. The speed of the rally exchanges increases between net player and baseline player. Teach the baseline players to keep four targets in mind: the two body targets of the opponents at the net and the ball through the middle in between the net players and the lob. The angle shots are a temptation to play, but they often result in a short drop volley winner from the opponent. Understanding these basic doubles strategies and keeping it simple and disciplined in execution is the key to results.

Basic Doubles Tips

1. Communicate with your partner before every point (serve and return). Make sure you have a clear plan on what you and your partner are doing.
2. The first two shots are most important in doubles play. Consistency of the serve and return and the shot right after set up every point.
3. The team that can maintain the highest intensity and consistency has the highest chance of success in winning matches.
4. Serve more to the body and middle of the court. The body serve is difficult to handle and will often result in a high return. The middle, or T serve, creates less angles on the return and more opportunities to intercept returns at the net.
5. Return difficult serves cross to the single line or lob over the net player. Easy serves can be dealt with by hitting hard through the middle or at the net player. Most juniors make the mistake of hitting the returns at the net player from the baseline. This can work in the beginning, when the volleys are not developed yet; but with a

better player, this can result in a volley winner. The consistency of the return is the best way to break serve and win matches.

6. In the crosscourt rallies, players should aim for the single lines to keep a margin for errors. If the balls are aimed short cross, the return should be aimed short cross as well, otherwise the net player will intercept at the net. If balls are aimed through the middle, play the balls back with less angle.

7. Don't go for the net player with shots from the baseline. The ball has to be shorter or a weak return.

8. Support your partner by taking position in the middle of the service box. Poach on off-balance shots from your opponent and on predetermined situations. Make sure to close the net when poaching to close the distance to your opponent, to have multiple options, and to make the volleys easier to put away.

9. When coming to the net, play the low volley crosscourt and the high volley at the net player. This easy rule will give you much more solid volleys and points at the net. Don't worry so much about the direction of the volley. This will only result in unforced errors and create unnecessary pressure on the volley.

10. Playing the volley softer and shorter is more effective with the opponent having to reach low and in front to hit the ball. The ball will pop up. Practice to hit volleys in between the baseline player and net player and aim overhead shots to the service line so they are more difficult to return.

11. Play the middle of the court when both players are back and when both players are at the net. This will cause confusion between the two players and make them hesitate. Unforced errors will follow.

12. Volley and aim the overhead as much as possible at the feet of the opponent. It is very difficult to return a ball that comes right at you and bounces at your feet. Even if they are somehow able to block it back, it is an easy winner on the next shot.

13. Play with controlled aggression. Keep the momentum going in your favor as you keep the pressure on until the last point. Keep the intensity high and communicate with your partner before every point.
14. In down-the-line rallies, don't be impatient and wait for the short ball before going for the net player.

16—PHYSICAL TRAINING

The physical training has become much more important in the development of advanced tennis players. Players are constantly hitting the ball harder than before, and organizers of international events have tried to slow down the surfaces to increase the rally length. The tennis game will keep evolving with the influence of television. Even the grass courts have changed at Wimbledon with the ball bouncing higher and slower. This has made the matches much longer, and endurance has become a larger factor. Nevertheless, the racket and string technology has improved the control, spin, and power of the strokes; and players are hitting the ball much more on the rise than before. This has increased the speed of the footwork and recovery and requires much physical training to improve. In order to make progress with any type of training, it is important to consider the following:

- **Have fun**
  The more fun you have when exercising, the better your workouts are. The workouts will become much more efficient and intense. Hard work will come easy while time seems to fly by. Cross-training is an excellent way to make the workout a fun experience. Working out together as a group or with another player can be a great stimulant to enjoyment for everyone in trying to become better athletes and tennis players.

- **Do not follow a set routine**
  By changing up the routine, you can keep the workout fun and interesting. There will be less chances of becoming bored or complacent and losing interest to improve. Learn to exercise in a way that suits you. Plan your workouts carefully to ensure that you cover all the physical aspects of the tennis game: cardio (endurance), coordination, weight training (strength), movement training (footwork, speed, and balance), plyometrics (speed and acceleration), and stretching (flexibility). Changing the routine confuses the muscle fibers and keeps them improving at a faster rate.

- **Ensure good form**

  No matter what sort of exercise you are doing, ensure that you do it with good form. This not only reduces the chance of injury but also instills the discipline needed to perform the technique of the tennis strokes. Great tennis players seem to hit each stroke with almost identical techniques. Keeping good form in the execution of the strokes will provide consistency in playing points and hold up much more in pressure situations. By concentrating on your posture, balance, intensity, and breathing, you are always aware of what your body is doing. Do not switch off at any time.

- **Exercise regularly**

  Make sure to have a set time to work out during the week. This will ensure you maintain all the workouts that week or month to improve your game. With a schedule, you can set the amount of time, the physical aspects you want to train, and the type of training you want to use to achieve your goals. Do not skip any workouts. It takes much longer to get back into a routine again, and fitness levels drop very quickly.

- **Breathe right**

  Breathe in through your nose and out through your mouth in the same rhythm of the exercise. This helps you control your breathing with the intensity of your workout and prevents you from training beyond your capacity. When in recovery mode, try to breathe using your diaphragm (this type of breathing is visible when the abdomen expands). It will expand the lungs and relax the body more quickly.

- **Set goals and challenge yourself with a plan**

  Becoming more fit is a process of good planning. In order to go faster, go farther, train longer, and lift heavier, you have to come up with a good schedule to improve. Setting realistic goals within a certain time frame will assist you to constantly progress to a higher level. Making a monthly or weekly plan will keep you on track and prevent you from getting stuck in the same old routine.

- **Ensure a good balance between exercise and rest**

  Training hard requires you to get your rest as well. A good balance between the amount of training and sufficient rest ensures that you can improve at a faster rate. There will also be less chance of overtraining. Having a good schedule with variety of training and rest at the appropriate times will stimulate the nerve system and muscles to recover more easily. Having an off-season with active rest can be very refreshing for the mind and makes you want to get back to competing.

The physical training of tennis players is very diverse since the skills of a tennis player are multifaceted. The footwork is very specific and involves not only endurance in the length of the matches but also involves speed, strength, coordination, and flexibility with the many sprints, change of direction, and recovery footwork. The strokes will rely heavily on the coordination with the timing of the ball; and strength, flexibility, and balance play a role in the quality of the execution. The style of play will influence these aspects as well. The makeup of each tennis player is unique in the amounts of these components. You can compare it with slices of a pie (see graph on the right).

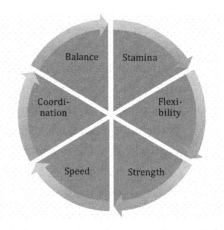

Some players will rely more on their stamina, whereas others might use their strength and speed. One of the most important components in the tennis game is the coordination of the strokes and footwork to synchronize the contact point. This is what we call the timing of the ball. The physical components of a tennis player are as follows:

- endurance (stamina)
- strength
- flexibility

- coordination
- speed and agility
- balance
- reflexes

Endurance (or stamina) comes into play when matches start lasting longer than one hour. Since the best out of three set matches can sometimes last up to three hours or more, it becomes more important to train this component well. The training of endurance for advanced tennis players needs to be diverse and specific in order to train all the muscle groups used in the movements and strokes during match play. This can be performed on-court with continuous life-ball drills but should also be supported with off-court training. The intensity of the rallies in advanced tennis is much higher, and the physical training should be performed accordingly. There are many different ways to train the endurance of tennis players. Here are some methods commonly used for advanced tennis players to improve endurance:

- Using continuous life-ball drills will lengthen the rallies as if no mistakes are made. The lengthening of the rallies will put much more pressure on the stamina of a player since there is no break in the rally. The coach keeps feeding in the next ball as soon as a mistake is made to continue the pattern. Players have to react to the speed, direction, and spin of the feed and continue longer with the same drill.

- By lengthening the time of the practice, it is possible to improve the endurance. This can be achieved by lengthening the practice unit time or by adding a second practice in the day. (As the practice time is increased, it is necessary to also increase the number of breaks and the break time to maintain quality and intensity.) As long as a decent quality is maintained during practice, it can be beneficial for the enhancement of endurance. Make sure to shorten the practice sessions again when the quality is not maintained in the execution of the drill.

- There are many factors that can help to improve endurance, and some of these can come from the way players train off-court. Having a sensible off-court training program with weight training, running and movement program, and a stretching or yoga program can be very beneficial and stimulating. All these will improve the endurance by improving the muscle structure in their own specific way. Knowing how much you need to do is the key so that it helps you improve rather than tire you to the point that improvements stall. Watch for telltale signs of the body language in players to know how much workload they can take. The mix of exercise is also important to keep players mentally fresh and keen to learn and improve.

- Adopting a running and movement program will greatly improve the stamina of a player. The endurance of the muscles will improve over time, and the movement will become more efficient during point and match play. Running is an excellent way to improve rhythm and focus and also, indirectly, will have an effect on the mental toughness and confidence of a player (see running and movement programs).

Coordination is the most important physical component in synchronizing the strokes and footwork together. It involves the flexing and extending of the muscles to move the body in a smooth and timely fashion. The coordination needed to strike the ball with the racket at the correct impact point is called timing. Proper coordination and timing control not only the correct contact points but also the direction, spin, and trajectories of the ball. The other physical components have an influence on the quality, consistency, and endurance of the coordination. In long matches, you can imagine that the strength and stamina will affect the coordination and performance of a tennis player. Note—When practicing with excessive power, the coordination will be negatively affected. Testing players has proven that with around 60 percent of the maximum power, the coordination of the strokes will decrease (see technique instruction). Knowing this fact is very important for the improvement of coordination. There are two ways to look at this: either improve coordination by using less than 60 percent of the maximum power or try to improve the strength so that the maximum power is at a higher level. Therefore, the coordination can be trained the following ways:

- Practice long rallies while using a medium pace and focusing solely on the contact points of the ball. Improving the timing will relax the muscles even more and will improve the coordination with less use of strength.

- While maintaining good timing, slowly increase the pace of the ball over time. As the maximum power over 60 percent is reached, gradually increase the pace until the coordination breaks down. Keep going back and forth in increasing and decreasing the pace of the ball while maintaining quality of coordination. This will lift the level of coordination by using consistency and timing.

- By introducing strength training, it is possible to raise the maximum power level and indirectly improve the coordination by increasing the strength. This will increase the point where the coordination decreases or breaks down.

Strength is the force or power available in the muscles to execute the strokes and footwork in the tennis game. The flexing and extending of the muscles in the movement and strokes is created with a certain power and speed. It takes time to develop strength in any tennis player, and well-defined improvements are usually made in increments of six months. With tennis being a repetitive sport and the matches lasting quite long, the strength in a player is defined by endurance as well. The strength of a player can be improved on and off the court. Here are some examples of strength training:

- The drills on court can be adjusted to simulate strength training by speeding up the footwork and the strokes. By playing two-on-one drills, players will feel the urgency to speed up the motions of the strokes and footwork in order to keep up with the timing of the ball. Especially with players in the net position, the reaction time will be cut in half and stresses the muscles to a much higher level.

- A weight-training program in the gym is highly recommended to improve the strength of all the basic muscle groups. There are many good weight-training programs for tennis players, but try to use free weights, bands, or multidirectional machines as much as possible to enhance the balance in the joints while working out.

- A plyometrics program will enhance the explosive strength of a player. These skips and jumps can be performed using benches or ladders to increase the intensity and speed of the acceleration and deceleration of the footwork.

Speed and agility are defined by how fast the movement is performed within a certain time frame. With a tennis court having the same constant dimension, it is possible to train the players to cover specific distances. Speed is made up of several components that determine how fast a player can move. They can be trained separately or in combination with one another. Some players may not be able to attain a high quality in every type of speed, but they can all be trained to a certain degree. The different types of speed are as follows:

1. *Velocity of movement* is the speed of a player in running from point A to point B. This particular speed is easily tested by timing the running speed on and off the court. The common distances on a track or grass field are easily trained and tested.

2. *Quickness of action* refers to how fast the body parts move during the hitting phase with the ball (fast body action). This speed

is measurable by the racket head speed and how fast the player hits the ball from baseline to baseline.

3. *Change of direction (agility)* is the speed of deceleration and acceleration of a player in changing direction. This can be measured in the time it takes to run a course where players have slowed down the movement and turn and run in a different direction. A good example is the spider run (see movement training).

Flexibility is defined by the range of motion in the joints in combination with the elasticity of the muscles and ligaments. This range of motion in the joints is different for every player, but it can be improved over time. It is a component that needs to be trained on a regular basis to maintain a fluidity of motion. Good flexibility comes with some added benefits to a tennis player. It provides less friction in the joints and therefore less effort in performing a motion. With good flexibility, the strokes have more efficiency and endurance. It can also be very beneficial to the speed of movement and racket head speed. By increasing and maintaining the range of motion in the joints, players will have a high level of flexibility with less chance of injuries. The methods of improvement are these:

1. A stretching program before and after practice sessions can assist in improving the flexibility. A combination of a dynamic (in motion) warm-up routine and static stretches will help to maintain the range of motion before the start of the practice and prevent injuries. Stretching (static) after practice (cooldown) will ensure a relaxation in the muscles and help to maintain the range of motion.

2. Weight training can serve as a stretching program, if performed properly. The dynamic action and range of motion of the weight training will stretch the muscles, ligaments, and tendons (see weight training).

3. Yoga is an excellent way to improve and maintain the flexibility, range of motion, and balance in the joints. I used to do yoga

myself when I was still playing competitively and experienced many benefits from this type of training. It helped me in stretched-out situations, in the corner of the court, to recover while maintaining my balance.

Balance is part of every stroke in tennis and provides the stability in motion. Without balance, it would be very hard to coordinate strokes and footwork to hit the ball with any kind of smooth action. It is a necessity to uphold the balance before, during, and after the stroke in order to maintain control of the ball. If any of these three components is out of sync, it will immediately have a negative result in the execution of the stroke and movement. Coaches should look for these signs during practices and matches since they often indicate a problem that needs attention. It could be the balance of the stroke itself or it could be a deeper-lying technical, physical, or even a mental issue. These are the methods of improvement:

- The two-on-one drills will increase the speed of movement and recovery and will stress the balance of the stroke even more. It is also possible for the coach to take one side of the net position to speed up the rallies.

- Balance drills are easily trained by using movement drills that simulate the strokes in motion. By training the action with the racket, players are able to pay attention to the balance of the body throughout the motion.

Reflexes are the automated speed actions that are performed as a reaction to an action from the opponent. The speed of the reflexes is part natural talent and part training. They can be trained by decreasing the distance and time for players to react to the ball and taking appropriate actions in shot choices. Over time, these will become muscle memory and, ultimately, reflex actions. Some method drills are as follows:

- playing two-on-one drills at the net and at the baseline
- practicing reflex volleys with both players at the net
- practicing return on first serves from the opponent

Strength Training

Strength training has become an essential element of tennis fitness for junior and pro players. Formerly, coaches believed that resistance exercises only added unnecessary bulk to an athlete, hindering their ability to execute their strokes. With the modern-day technology of rackets and strings, the ball speeds have increased, making the movement and endurance even more important. Here is where the benefits of strength training are enormous. However, sport-specific resistance training, like in the tennis sport, requires a more refined approach than simply lifting heavy weights to complete exhaustion. A physiological analysis of the game will confirm that most players require explosive power, muscular endurance, maximal strength, or some combination of all three in order to excel.

Elements of Strength Training for Tennis Players

There are several elements of strength training to consider when training advanced tennis players. These elements are the following:

- **Maximum Strength**
  The maximum strength is the highest level of power an athlete can generate. This is trained by using maximum weight possible with very few repetitions (three to five reps). For tennis players, this particular form of training is less valuable on a regular basis but can be used in a training program to increase strength. The greater an athlete's basic maximum strength is, the more it can be converted into sport-specific strength endurance or explosive power. Maximum strength training can improve exercise efficiency and endurance performance over time.

- **Explosive Power**
  The tennis sport requires rapid movements that demand a high, explosive power output that is generated with plyometric training.

An athlete can be exceptionally strong but still lack the ability to contract the muscle groups quickly enough. Plyometrics can be employed to convert maximal strength into explosive power. The training consists of rapid movements that demand maximum strength over a short period of time. A good example is jumping on and off an elevated bench. The muscles are quickly accelerated and extended when jumping on the bench and quickly decelerated and flexed when jumping off the bench (five to ten reps).

- **Strength Endurance**
  Explosive power is not always the predominant goal of strength training. You only have to watch the developments on the professional tour to realize how much the strength endurance has become a major factor in the tennis sport (especially for men at Grand Slam events, where it is the best of five sets). A higher starting level of maximum strength can influence the strength to be maintained for a prolonged period of time. Strength endurance can be developed through circuit training or with the use of low weights and high repetitions (fifteen to twenty reps).

- **Periodization**
  The method of periodization is key to sport-specific strength training. It is important to divide the training plan into phases or periods, each with a specific purpose in mind to allow the specific strength training to peak at the right times while minimizing the risk of overtraining. This also makes it possible to work more diligently on the specific strength training in parts. It is not possible to work at maximum capacity week in and week out without the chance of overtraining. Having a good plan that regulates the different types of training and the intensity is the key here. Periodization permits athletes to progress indefinitely through variations in intensity and volume to promote performance enhancements for as long as possible.

Weight-Training Program

With younger kids, it is important to understand where they are in their development before attempting to start a weight-training program. This is why it is difficult to train them as a group when they are in the growing phase since they are all at a different stage of development. Individualizing the programs is the key here unless they are at the same level. As players mature, it is possible to start a more serious weight-training program, but there are still several ground rules to consider:

1. Use your own body weight as much as possible.
2. When using weights, use free weights (not machines) with many reps (fifteen to twenty).
3. Make use of rubber bands and/or light medicine ball for resistance training.
4. Train both the sides (extension and flexion) to properly stabilize the muscles.
5. Train the muscle groups every other day: arms, legs, chest, and back.
6. Keep a record of your training with intensity, weight, and reps.

As players reach the puberty stage, they are able to adopt a much more serious weight-training program. Below is a simple program for junior tennis players:

Exercise	Muscles	Sets × Reps
squats or lunges	hip and thigh	3 × 15
bench press (dumbbell or barbell)	chest	3 × 15
seated row or lat pulldown	upper back	3 × 15
RDL or leg curl	hamstrings	3 × 15
shoulder front/lateral raise	shoulders	3 × 12 (front raise ×6; lateral raise ×6)
biceps curls	biceps	2 × 15

Martin van Daalen

triceps extension	triceps	2 × 15
core (abdominal and lower back)		3–5 different exercises; total reps = about 100
shoulder rehab		1–2 × 15

Make sure to use the proper weights that make the amount of reps and execution of the exercise possible. I have witnessed many juniors either starting too early with heavy weight training or using improper weights that distort the technique and execution of the exercise. These training situations can lead to burnout and injuries that are limiting to their progress. In some cases, they can become permanent injuries.

As players advance, it is possible to slowly increase the weights as long as technique and reps are maintained. There are some things to watch out for while players are learning to train with weights. Below are some technical points to monitor while players are performing the exercises:

- Breathing — make sure that students are breathing properly while performing the exercises. Students need to learn to breathe out during the heaviest part of the exercise so they stay in control of the motion.

- Exercise speed — train the extension of the muscle three times faster than the flexion. This is done with a counting method. The slower action during this motion increases power more efficiently.

- Balanced approach - train the muscles that are used less during tennis more. Think of the back muscles, hamstrings, and rotator cuff. This method will balance the muscle groups around the joints and is a prevention against injuries.

Plyometric Training

This type of training is designed to build power into explosive speed and agility. This is achieved by firing the fast-twitch fibers in the muscle by flexing and extending the muscles as fast as possible. Low-impact jumps are slowly increased to high-impact jumps with increasing heights. The intensity in a tennis match varies with the level of play. However, advanced players have a high intensity of explosive movement in each rally for about six to ten seconds. This intensity is even higher for pro players with the ever-increasing tempo of play. Training the explosive power and speed can be accomplished with plyometric training. Some of the exercises of a plyometric program are listed below:

- Fast footwork training—the use of a rope ladder on the ground, movement drills with the use of one or more balls, and reaction drills with a reaction ball
- Lower body plyometrics—jump training (squat jumps, box jumps, lateral jumps, split squat jumps, tuck jumps, lateral push-offs, bounding, hurdle jumps, depth jumps)
- Upper body plyometrics—overhead throws, sideway throws, over back toss, slams, explosive start throws, squat throws, single-arm overhead throws, plyo push-ups

This type of training needs to be done progressively by starting out with lower intensity and impact before moving up to higher intensity and impact. The technique of the bounce and/or jumps needs to be monitored to ensure students are performing the exercises properly in order to prevent injuries. All these plyometric exercises are designed to create more explosive power in the lower and upper body. This form of training has become a valuable tool to develop the speed and agility in tennis players. Many top players have this form of training as part of their fitness routine, and they often use it to warm up before they go out to hit balls.

Movement and Speed Training

The movement and speed training of tennis players is one of the most important parts of the fitness routine, but it is often overlooked. Weight training alone, although very important to improve power, will not make you a better mover on the court. The weight training is the basis to prevent injuries and to improve speed of movement of the legs, the hips, the trunk area, the shoulders, and the arms (preferably in that order). Players need to use the power from the ground up (kinetic chain) to produce power rather than try to muscle with the shoulders and the arms. This is why movement and speed training is so important—the speed training to get to an area on time to hit the ball and the movement training to set up, recover, and change direction with ease. There are a few factors that will positively influence the movement and speed training for tennis:

- make the movement and speed training exercises tennis specific
- time the players to monitor and stimulate progression
- use the racket as much as possible

There are some tennis-specific movements and speed tests you can perform to provide feedback to students. This feedback is important for students to gauge improvements. It will not only provide a continuous stimulating effect for players to keep improving but will also give them goals to work for. Goals will set a target to work toward, and testing the tennis-specific exercises regularly shows the progressions made over time. Some of the tennis-specific movements and speed tests are listed below:

- **Spider run**
  This movement drill mimics the movement of tennis players during points. The students start in the middle of the baseline and run as fast as possible to the five points in the corners that connect the sidelines and the middle of the service line. By using opposite feet in changing direction in the corners, you can practice the recovery footwork during rallies. It is possible

to time this movement and speed test but be aware of the results on different surfaces (clay versus hard). This test represents the level of play of a competitor very closely.

- **Twenty-yard dash**
  This is a straightforward sprint from behind the baseline to the service line on the other side of the net. This test is to see the maximum speed a player can reach. The type of surface will have little effect on the results of this test.

- **Service box movement**
  By standing in the middle of the service box, you can test the foot speed of the side steps and oversteps by touching the middle line and the sideline of the service box with the top of the racket. The player is to do this as many times as possible within thirty seconds.

- **Sideline movement**
  A. The speed of the side steps can be tested by making side steps over the singles and doubles line. This speed drill starts with the feet in between both lines. Count the amount of times you can cross past the lines in thirty seconds. Try to keep the feet in a wider position while doing this drill. Use a racket while doing this test.

  B. You can perform the same drill as above by moving forward and backward over the singles and doubles sideline. Use a racket in hand while performing the test.

  C. You can test speed endurance with the eleven-line drill. Students have to touch the sidelines of the court eleven times as fast as possible. This test will give you a quick look at where the players are with their fitness level in general. The test does have different results when performed on clay or hard courts. Use a racket in hand.

- **One-mile run**
  This test is best performed on a track when doing some running training. It will give you a very clear picture of the endurance level of a player. Especially for more serious tennis players, this test can be a valuable tool to show the necessity of a running program to increase the endurance level.

Advanced Boys (Average)

	12–14	14–16	16–18	18–23
Spider run (sec.)	16.85–15.50	15.60–14.50	14.60–13.80	14.15–13.35
Twenty-yard dash (sec.)	3.40–3.15	3.30–2.95	3.05–2.85	2.95–2.65
Service box (30 sec.)	25–28	26–30	28–32	30–35
Side A (30 sec.)	26–29	28–32	29–33	31–35
Side B (30 sec.)	27–30	29–33	30–34	32–36
Side C (sec.)	34.0–31.0	32.0–30.0	30.0–28.0	29.0–27.0
One-mile run (min. and sec.)	6.00–5.15	5.30–4.50	4.50–4.20	4.30–4.10

Advanced Girls (Average)

	12–14	14-16	16-18	18-23
Spider run (sec.)	16.95–15.65	15.85–14.65	14.95–13.95	14.30–13.85
Twenty-yard dash (sec.)	3.50–3.20	3.35–3.00	3.15–2.95	3.05–2.85
Service box (30 sec.)	25–28	26–29	27–30	29–33
Side A (30 sec.)	26–29	27–31	28–32	30–34
Side B (30 sec.)	27–30	28–32	29–33	31–35
Side C (sec.)	34.0–31.0	32.0–30.0	31.0–29.0	30.0–28.0
One-mile run (min. and sec.)	6.10–5.45	5.30–5.00	5.10–4.40	4.50–4.30

All the results above are measured and performed by elite top juniors and professional players. They should be seen as a goal to work toward if you are not accomplished yet with the movements. These results are from life measurements in the field and should be tested on a hard court to have a baseline for comparison. By training and testing on a regular basis, you will get immediate feedback for your performance. Timing yourself as often as possible and using a racket in hand make the training of the movement all the more realistic and will mimic competitive play.

Running Program

Advanced tennis players will benefit from incorporating a running program in their fitness routine. Tennis has become an increasingly faster sport where movement is key to the success of competitive tennis players. You can observe the top players and notice the difference in speed and movement. They all have made great strides in their speed and movement with a running program. A track is a great place to train since most tracks have the same dimensions. Tennis players should train mostly two-hundred-yard- and four-hundred-yard distances and time them continuously. The rest time in between can be as long as it takes to run that distance. Eventually you can bring the rest time down to twenty-five seconds (the same rest time when playing points). Below is a chart with some test results.

Advanced Boys (Average)

	12–14	14–16	16–18	18–23
20 m (sec.)	3.40–3.15	3.30–2.95	3.05–2.85	2.95–2.65
50 m (sec.)	7.50–6.70	7.00–6.00	6.30–5.40	5.52–5.05
100 m (sec.)	14.2–12.5	12.7–11.0	12.0–10.8	11.0–10.4
200 m (sec.)	29.0–24.5	25.0–22.9	23.2–21.5	21.9–19.5
400 m (sec.)	58–53	56–51	54–48	51–47
1 mile (min.)	6.10–5.45	5.30–5.00	5.10–4.40	4.50–4.05
3 mile (min.)	14.45–13.45	13.50–13.20	13.40–12.50	13.20–12.40

Martin van Daalen

Advanced Girls (Average)

	12–14	14–16	16–18	18–23
20 m (sec.)	3.50–3.20	3.35–3.00	3.15–2.95	3.05–2.85
50 m (sec.)	7.64–6.80	7.15–6.20	6.50–5.80	5.68–5.13
100 m (sec.)	14.8–12.8	13.2–11.4	12.4–11.2	11.5–10.8
200 m (sec.)	29.5–24.9	25.5–23.4	23.7–22.0	22.4–19.9
400 m (sec.)	59–54	57–52	55–49	52–48
1 mile (min.)	6.30–5.30	5.40–5.20	5.30–4.50	5.10–4.20
3 mile (min.)	15.00–14.15	14.30–13.50	14.00–13.10	13.30–12.50

Keeping Track of Results

By tracking the results over time, you can observe the progress of the movement and running program of each individual player. Below I will show you an example (spider run) as shown in a graph. It is clearly visible how much this player has improved.

Flexibility Training

The elasticity in the muscles and joints of an athlete will have a large effect on the performance and execution of the movements. In general terms, *flexibility* has been defined as "the range of motion from a joint and its surrounding muscles during a passive movement." *Passive*, in this context, simply means "no active muscle involvement is required to hold the stretch." Instead, gravity or a partner provides the force for the stretch. A better flexibility will improve the speed of recovery of the footwork movement and enhances the release of the racket head to speed up the ball and/or to provide spin. Especially when in difficult positions (think low shots up front or wide shots outside the court), it is easier to recover from those positions when the flexibility is optimal. Some players are gifted with natural flexibility, but it is also possible to train this physical aspect. There are several different types of flexibility training:

- **Dynamic flexibility training**

  This type of stretching is the ability to perform dynamic movements within the full range of motion of the joint. Common examples are low squat steps or high kicks of the foot to shoulder level. The dynamic flexibility is generally more sport-specific than other forms of stretching.

- **Static active flexibility training**

  This type refers to the ability to stretch an antagonist muscle using only the tension in the agonist muscle. An example is holding one leg out in front of you as high as possible. The hamstring (antagonist) is being stretched while the quadriceps and hip flexors (agonists) are holding the leg up.

- **Static passive flexibility training**

  This is the ability to hold a stretch using body weight or some other external force. Using the example above, hold your leg out in front of you and rest it on a chair. The quadriceps are not holding the leg up in this extended position.

After extensive studies with top athletes, they have concluded that it is better to use dynamic stretching rather than static stretching for a warm-up. The static stretching can actually have a detrimental effect on the performance and may offer no protection against injuries, although there is no conclusive evidence on this method.

There are definite benefits from stretching when increasing the joint range of motion. The performance may be enhanced, and the risk of injury will be reduced. The rationale behind this is that there is less friction in the joint and that a limb can move with a larger range of motion before an injury occurs.

Yoga can be a great form of flexibility training for tennis players. With all the combination of stretching exercises and the focus that is required to perform the execution, it is an excellent way to increase the range of motion, strengthen the muscles, and prevent injuries. It also will increase the focus on the movement and flexibility.

Diet for Advanced Players

In order to play highly competitive tennis, it is necessary to fuel the body properly. You can compare the diet of a competitive player with the fuel of a race car. You would always make sure to have the best fuel to make the car run fast and last as long as possible. The same goes for an advanced tennis player. What you eat makes a difference to your performance on the court.

Eating a balanced diet is obviously important to maintain all levels of nutrients, vitamins, and minerals for the body to function properly. But there are certain food groups that are healthier than others and improve the energy needed for practices and matches. You can find some more information on this in my first book, *Teaching Tennis Volume 1*.

The Influence of Diet on Competitive Play

A proper diet can have a big influence on the performance of a player. It can affect the endurance and energy level of a player and also influence the function and performance of the body in general. Over time, a proper diet can also affect weight and efficiency of athletes through a better weight-to-energy output ratio. Here are some diet aspects that can enhance competitive play:

- **Have a balanced diet**
  A balanced diet will help you maintain all the levels of nutrients, vitamins, and minerals you need to perform on a daily basis and stay healthy over time. A good ratio of carbohydrates, protein, and fat can be found in whole grains, meat, fish, vegetables, fruit, nuts, milk, etc. It is important to choose food groups that contain many vitamins and minerals that are easily digestible. Having excessive amounts of one

or two of these food groups or limiting one food group can have a negative effect on the performance. Every person is different, and it can be helpful to find what ratio works well for him or her.

- **Use a relatively low-fat diet**
  Although every competitive player needs some fat in their diet, having too much fat can make them feel sluggish and slows down their performance. Much fats also have an important role in providing other beneficial nutrients. An example is omega-3 oil in fish. However, by limiting the intake of fats, you can maintain or decrease the overall weight of the athlete and influence the performance of their speed and endurance indirectly. You can imagine how much faster a tennis player will be able to move and change direction with ten pounds less weight to carry around. Also think how this might help endurance with playing a three- or four-hour match.

- **Eat more vegetables and fruits**
  These types of foods not only have a high level of fiber but also contain high levels of vitamins and minerals. They are an excellent source of antioxidants that protect the cells in the body, stimulate the digestive system, and maintain a healthy and energetic lifestyle. They are also very useful as snacks when you feel hungry. Try to eat more vegetables and fruits in your diet whenever possible.

- **Use less sugar to maintain glucose balance**
  By not adding extra sugar in the diet, you can prevent a spike in the glucose levels. Maintaining a balance in the glucose levels is important for a consistent energy level when performing in practices and matches. There are many natural foods available that already have sugars in them. (Note—many processed foods have added sugars in them.) If extra sugar is added, it will often produce a temporary increase (spike) in energy levels, followed by a decrease (crash) in energy levels. To avoid these drastic changes in energy levels, it is better to not add extra sugar and get used to absorbing

the sugars from the nutrients. Natural products have already plenty of sugars in them without the need to add extra sugars.

- **Eat more frequently but with smaller portions**
  Smaller meals are more easily and better digested than larger meals. It takes a lot of energy for the body to digest nutrients. It makes sense to eat smaller portions so that energy can be used for the performance of athletes. Smaller portions also don't make you feel full and sluggish. To keep fueling the body, it is necessary to eat more frequently, especially during long matches. Bananas have been a popular snack during matches and usually don't upset the stomach. There are many energy bars on the market today that have taken the place of this commonly used nutrient. The trick is to find the one that agrees with you and that provides the most energy through nutrient replacement.

- **Drink plenty of fluids and add sports drinks when needed**
  Competitive players need to hydrate on a regular basis during practices and matches. By keeping the body balanced and hydrated, it is easier to keep performance high. It is imperative to hydrate from the start of the match. Don't wait until you feel thirsty. Once the fluids become depleted in the body, it is very difficult to restore a proper balance. In some cases, this can lead to cramping. In long matches and during tournaments, it is advisable to use some form of sports drink that not only replenishes the fluids but also replaces the vitamins and minerals that are lost through sweating.

- **Add extra salt during extreme heat and humidity**
  You need to be prepared when playing in extreme hot and humid weather. In these conditions, players lose a lot more fluids and minerals, especially salt. By adding a little packet of extra salt to a sports drink, you can prevent excessive losses during competition and maintain performance as much as possible.

Physical training and diet play a large role in high-performance competition. If you are a recreational player, it is still a good discipline to improve general health; but for the more serious competitors, this is a crucial factor to their performance. If your goal is to make improvements, you should definitely make it a life habit.

I was always trying to help players improve their diet. Ryan Harrison (left) was one of those players who struggled eating the proper foods. Years later, I ran into him at the Eddie Herr tournament. He was eighteen and looking tall and playing on the pro tour. The first thing he mentioned to me was, "I am eating much better now, Martin." This picture was taken at the under fourteen Tennis Europe event in the Netherlands. He was only thirteen at the time and had just won both doubles and singles competitions. Afterward, we went to play the event in Paris. Ryan is still on the pro tour and currently has a ranking of 138 ATP(2019). I see Devin regularly at events as a college coach.

Ryan Harrison and Devin Britton

17—INJURIES—PREVENTION AND TREATMENT

Injuries can occur in any sport, and playing competitive tennis is no exception. In this sport, you use almost all muscles, but there can be some imbalance in using some muscle groups more than others. For example, think about how many forehands and backhands are struck using the chest muscles much more than the opposite muscle groups on the back. Without corrective weight training of the back muscles and shoulder blade muscles, it can lead to rounded shoulders and tennis arm injuries.

In playing competitive tennis and having some injuries myself, I became very interested on how to prevent them or how to treat them. I ended up taking a course for a sports therapy trainer to become more knowledgeable. I am so glad I did since it has served me well in my years of playing and coaching, in recognizing injuries early, and in knowing how to prevent them and treat them.

The tennis sport has some specific reoccurring injuries that can be prevented or treated quite easily with proper training, daily routines, and/or physical therapy. You can prevent most injuries with a good warm-up before activity. As a player, parent, or coach, you should take injuries seriously so they don't get worse. Seek professional help as soon as possible. Here are some examples of injuries and how to prevent them and treat them:

Blisters on Your Feet

These occur when there is too much friction or heat between the skin and your sock. Fluid builds up underneath the skin, and there is a possibility they will pop open. They can be very annoying while playing and can distract you from playing well or even prevent you from playing at all! If at all possible, do not break the skin. The underlying tissue will be very sensitive to the touch. They can form on the bottom of your feet or around the edges of your shoe and your ankles. New shoes especially need to be worn in and tried out first.

- **Prevention**
  Don't wear new shoes in matches; get used to them first in practice. Wear the proper shoe size so that your feet don't slide back and forth inside your shoes. You can wear double socks if your shoe size permits. In extreme heat, change your socks on the set break to keep your feet dry. If you are playing much on a hard court, the heat builds up in the sole of your shoes. You can apply a layer of aluminum foil underneath your insole. It will insulate the heat to the bottom of your feet.

- **Treatment**
  There are several types of treatment, depending on the affected area. You can alleviate the pressure from the blister by puncturing the blister on opposite sides with a sterilized needle and squeezing the fluid out. You can place a round rubber ring donut pad over the affected area, hold it in place with underwrap, and tape it to secure in place. Sometimes just using underwrap and sports tape is more comfortable and sufficient to solve the problem. After the match, sterilize the area again and use some iodine to dry the blister and keep taping the area until there is no discomfort anymore and the underlying skin tissue has grown back.

Plantar Fasciitis

This injury is one of the most common causes of heel pain. It involves inflammation of a thick band of tissue that runs across the bottom of your foot and connects your heel bone to your toes (plantar fascia). Plantar fasciitis commonly causes stabbing pain that usually occurs with your first steps in the morning. When moving more, the pain normally decreases, but it could return after long periods of standing or after rising from sitting. Plantar fasciitis is more common in runners. In addition, people who are overweight and those who wear shoes with inadequate support have an increased risk of plantar fasciitis.

- **Prevention**
  Always do a good warm-up to improve circulation and don't stress your tendons right away with sudden movements. Having the proper shoes with a sufficient soft, cushioned heel and the support from good insoles makes all the difference in preventing this injury. Having a regular stretching (yoga) and massage routine will assist in its prevention.

- **Treatment**
  Refrain from activity. This ailment needs professional help from a physiotherapist, but you need to do additional treatment yourself. Therapy consists of ultrasound, laser treatment, electrical stimulation, icing, deep tissue massage, etc. The treatment you can do yourself is the massage, which can be done by rolling a tennis ball under your feet or using a frozen bottle to roll on. Stretching your calf and heel is a routine that needs to be a regular habit after this injury occurs to prevent reinjury.

Bruised Heel

A bruised heel injury usually develops through bad footwork or bad equipment. If you run for a ball, the first part of your foot to hit the ground is your heel. Having the proper shoes with sufficient cushion in the heel will prevent this injury. Being well trained and having the proper running technique eliminates this problem. If you play a lot on hard courts or cold indoor courts in the winter, this can flare up.

- **Prevention**
  A good warm-up will prevent this specific injury with better circulation and coordination of movement.

- **Treatment**
  To ward off the pain and cushion the heel from reinjuring, use a softer insole under your heel. If it is still painful, use an ankle brace for support and some painkillers and/or anti-inflammatory Advil to help with the healing process.

Ankle Sprain

The movements on a tennis court can easily lead to twisting or spraining your ankle. It usually is a scary experience, and most think they broke their ankle at first. The ligaments around the ankle are quite strong, but it is possible to sprain (overstretch) them or tear them. If you tear a ligament, you will know right away because it is very painful and a swelling will form almost right away at the affected area.

- **Prevention**
  Ankle sprains or tears are not always preventable, unless you wear a brace all the time (not recommended). They usually happen at the beginning of the activity, with improper warm-ups, or at the end, when the muscles are getting too tired and uncoordinated.

- **Treatment**
  Make sure to ice the area for extended time to keep the swelling down. You need to compress the ankle right after to prevent further swelling. Refrain from activity till the pain subsides. You can use underwrap with sports tape or a boot to immobilize it. Renew the underwrap and tape when necessary to keep it firmly wrapped. Make sure to use tape strips instead of wrapping the role in one piece. This is to prevent the cutoff of circulation. After two or three days, start rehabilitation by slowly walking first.

Achilles Tendon Injuries

This tendon is located between the heel and the calf muscle. It is possible to strain it by overstretching. By overusing it, the tendon can inflame inside the sheath. And in the worst-case scenario, it can tear and even break all the way through. The severity will depend on the amount of pressure on the tendon, how much it has been strained, and the strength of the calf muscle.

- **Prevention**
  The injuries in this area are preventable by a good warm-up, regular stretching, and proper training. For professionals, they also add regular massages. All with the purpose of increasing flexibility, heat, and circulation.

- **Treatment**
  In the case of an Achilles tendon strain, inflammation, or tear, you have to give it rest in order to give it time to heal. In the case of a complete rupture, you will need to have it operated on. It is wise to have an x-ray or MRI to diagnose it properly. With a strain, you can ice the area. If it is inflamed, it will need professional (physiotherapist) attention and possibly some medication. The inflammation of the tendon has a longer recovery time, and it should be taken seriously. During the day, the ankle should be taped or you should wear a brace or boot to immobilize it.

Shin Splints

The symptom of this injury is a throbbing pain around the shinbone. It is caused by an inflammation of the sheath around the shinbone and it partly detaching from the shinbone. Overuse, bad footwork, or change of surface can affect this. But it can also be caused by an imbalance of the muscles. Playing a lot on hard courts and having heavy or lazy footwork is the biggest culprit in getting this injury. The constant pounding of the feet on the hard surface plays havoc on the legs.

- **Prevention**
  Stretching, warm-up, good cushioning shoes and insoles, and attention to footwork will assist in avoiding this injury. Bounce on your toes when changing direction and use smooth footwork when running.

- **Treatment**
  To heal from this inflammation, you need to rest and ice the area on the shin. Some Advil can help to reduce the inflammation. Afterward, you will need physiotherapy and exercise to avoid reinjury. Taping or using a brace to stabilize the ankle can help when starting activity again.

Calf Injuries

The calf muscle is heavily used when playing tennis and is prone to muscle strains and tears. When it does tear, you can often hear a loud pop. It is a strong but sensitive muscle. Because footwork is so crucial in this sport, injuries of the calf muscle become debilitating to play the game. With continued play, it can get worse.

- **Prevention**
  Warm-up, stretching, proper training, good shoes, and massages can help to prevent these injuries. These types of injuries are more common with players who play recreational and like the fast activity but don't usually warm up.

- **Treatment**
  Make sure you stop activity right away and ice the affected area. The muscle has to heal first before any treatment should be given. Massage therapy can speed up the recovery process, if the strain or tear is superficial. With more serious strains and tears, it is advisable to

properly rest first. With a light strain, during the competition, you can tape the muscle to compress the area and provide support.

Knee Injuries

These types of injuries are quite common in the tennis sport. The footwork and the rotational movements of the strokes cause much strain on the knees. The ligaments around the sides (ACL) and over the kneecap are the ones most affected. Injuries to the ligaments in the middle of the joint (MCL) are less common. They can tear or overstretch to the point that activity is impossible. It loosens the ligaments around the knee joint and causes instability. In some cases, surgery is necessary. The inflammation right below the kneecap (Osgood-Schlatter) is a very common injury for juniors growing up. A meniscus tear is a more intrusive injury where you damage the moon-shaped cartilage pieces in the knee joint. Surgery is usually necessary to repair or remove the meniscus.

- **Prevention**
  Strengthening the muscles and ligaments around the knee joint is key to preventing injuries in this area. Proper and regular physical training improves the flexibility and strength to support and stabilize the jumps, rotations, and push off when hitting the ball and changing directions.

- **Treatment**
  With ACL and MCL injuries, you have to rest. The ligaments need time to heal and restore their original length and flexibility. Icing can assist the healing process, followed by light exercise (in a pool is best—takes the weight off the knee joint). The inflammation can be reduced with an ultrasound and electrical stem treatment. The Osgood-Schlatter injury can be treated with icing, electrical stem treatment, and by applying some underwrap and tape around the knee, right below the kneecap. A meniscus injury is much more serious. After surgery, the knee will need lots of rehabilitation with slow exercise. When the

stability returns, you can start with weight training to strengthen the muscle groups around the knee. This is followed by a slow buildup of movement and running training. Go slow and don't try to force this process. It sometimes takes a month or two to get proper movement back and build confidence to perform as before.

When I was preparing Josh Wardell for college, he tore his meniscus while riding a bike. In surgery, they shaved off the damaged part of his meniscus. We had to wait till it was completely healed before starting his rehabilitation. The beginning was slow, and you could see the discomfort and fear of reinjury when starting out. It was just walking at first, then heel raises, followed by slow jogging, and running. We were making sure not to move on to the next exercise till he was comfortable. This went on for a month before we started on the court again. Josh completely recovered and played four years for the University of Florida in Gainesville. It was so nice to see him succeed after this serious knee injury.

Thigh or Hamstring Injuries

The thigh and hamstring muscles are responsible for most of the power delivered to the footwork. These muscles need to be trained most of all to prevent injuries to the legs and also the back. Stronger thigh and hamstring muscles means better use of the knees, resulting in less bending over and reaching for the balls. Tennis players need to learn to bend and recover with every stroke they hit. This makes playing tennis at a high level extremely physical in strength, speed, and endurance. The injuries that occur are usually hamstring or groin strain. The thigh muscles have less injuries since they are stronger.

- **Prevention**
  Proper preparation in training and before matches will usually prevent hamstring injuries. A good warm-up and regular stretching will provide circulation and flexibility. Groin injuries are more

frequent on grass, with slipping of one foot in the recovery of the corners. Adjusting the footwork on grass with little steps to slow down and more steps to speed up prevents the feet from slipping.

- **Treatment**
  Once the hamstring or groin injury has occurred, use ice on the affected area to cool it down. You can use underwrap and an elastic bandage to apply more pressure on the muscle so the injury does not get worse. Groin injuries are very hard to treat. You can use icing, but resting the tendon is usually the only remedy. If the thigh muscle is strained, use a pressure bandage, like above, to provide pressure and support to the injury. After the match, you need to ice again. No massage until the muscle is healed and pain free!

Hip Injuries

The most common injury of the hips is the hip flexor. The repetitive motion of the hip muscles decreases the range of motion over time. If preventative exercises are done on a regular basis, these will not occur. It is a small muscle, located on side of the hip, just above the thighbone. It connects the top of the thighbone with the hip.

- **Prevention**
  Stretching is the most effective way to prevent injuries on this muscle. The open stances, the long lunges, and the recovery footwork strain this muscle and reduce its range of motion over time when you don't stretch it.

- **Treatment**
  Effective treatment consists of icing, deep tissue massage, ultrasound, and electrical stem. If you continue to have trouble with this injury, seek the help of a professional. Also consider some time off until it has fully recovered. Players who did not take this injury seriously usually have chronic problems or are not playing tennis anymore.

Stomach Muscle Strain

Every tennis player experiences a stomach muscle strain at one point or another. It is a very debilitating injury since you need your stomach muscles to serve. The cause is when you arch your back too much when loading for the serve after the toss. This results in pulling forward on the stomach muscles instead of using the thigh muscles to push up and provide the hip and shoulder rotation.

- **Prevention**
  You can prevent this injury by keeping your back straight in one line, from the knees to the shoulders. The toss also is important here to not reach over the other shoulder and hit the ball in front of the body.

- **Treatment**
  To heal this muscle after it is overstretched, you need to give it some rest, some deep tissue massage, ultrasound, laser treatment, and electrical stem treatment. It is not easy to keep playing through this injury, and most of the time, you can make it worse. Some Advil can help in matches, but be careful though as it masks the pain.

Back Injuries

The back injuries are mostly caused by insufficient footwork, combined with strength and flexibility in the legs. This will result in reaching and bending over too much to get to the ball. The shots require you to turn your back during contact. If the feet don't come along and swing around and recover, the pressure will be all in the bottom vertebrae of the spine. By recovering with the feet, you relieve the pressure in the spine, resulting in less injury in the back muscles and stress fractures (herniated disk) of the disks in between the vertebrae. Overuse can also lead to nerve pain, radiating out to the legs.

- **Prevention**
  Use your knees more instead of your back. The more you bend your knees, the less trouble you will have with your back. Use a topslice serve more than a kick serve; a kick serve requires you to arch your back too much. Keep your shoulders above your feet with a straight line from knees to your shoulders. Use a proper form for your serve, with the toss in front above your hitting shoulder. Initiate the power from your knees instead of from your arm. Keep your body relaxed when loading the motion for the serve.

- **Treatment**
  A herniated disk requires immediate rest for a few months to let the disk heal. Sometimes you won't know where the pain comes from without an MRI. Work on the strength training of the legs, spine muscles, and stomach muscles. For overuse of the back muscles, you can use a back massage or electrical stem.

Shoulder Injuries

There are several specific tennis injuries with the shoulder. One common injury is the shoulder bursitis. This is the inflammation of the sac of fluid (bursa) in the shoulder, which assists with movement. The other common injury is on the rotator cuff muscles (group of small muscles near the shoulder socket). Another frequent injury is on the upper biceps tendon leading up to the shoulder. You will experience a pain radiating down from the shoulder to your biceps.

- **Prevention**
  All the shoulder injuries can be avoided with proper techniques, strength training, and stretching exercises. The use of rubber bands can be very useful. When increasing the training or workload, make sure to go slowly and increase gradually.

- **Treatment**
  All the injuries above should be treated first with icing multiple times per day. After that, you should seek professional help from a physiotherapist. For the rotator cuff injuries, you might need an MRI to see how much damage has occurred before seeking treatment. Specific exercises are needed to strengthen all the shoulder muscles, especially on the back.

Neck Sprain

Neck injuries usually occur when serving too hard or when reaching for wide shots. Cold weather is also a cause that can lead to a neck sprain. They are very debilitating as you cannot turn your head without pain. They are very uncomfortable for the player, and sometimes the players are limited in looking up when striking a serve.

- **Prevention**
  The best way to prevent this sprain is to be well trained, with a good warm-up and stretching routine. In cold weather, dress warmly and zip up the collar on your warm-up jacket. If the muscles are warm, there is less chance for injuries.

- **Treatment**
  I found that a visit to a chiropractor and a good massage after does wonders in relieving the pain and stiffness of a neck sprain. Some Advil can help during play.

Wrist Injuries

The level of injury to the wrist can vary from light to heavy. With a light injury, the pain is light and you can still play by taping it and treating it before and after the game. With a heavy injury, the pain is quite severe and you will not be able to play at all. This can be caused by overuse or by trying to hit too hard. Sometimes it can be from learning a new stroke (topspin) that requires more wrist action. However, equipment can also be a factor, like when changing rackets, string, or string tension.

- **Prevention**
  A good way to prevent wrist injuries is to increase flexibility and to do strength training for the arms and shoulders. Warm up the wrist slowly when hitting and don't try to hit too hard from the start.

- **Treatment**
  When you have the injury already, treat it by icing but try to continue the strength training of the arms and shoulders. Stretching the wrist in different directions can be painful in the beginning but will assist in the healing process. Just warm the wrist up first with a damp hot towel from the microwave and stretch slowly. Using electrical stem can keep the inflammation down. Don't start playing tennis again till you have no more pain in your wrist.

Blisters on Your Hand

The friction of the racket grip with the palm of the hand can cause blisters. Warm and humid weather can worsen that situation even more. You can toughen up your hand through practice in the same conditions. Some players have more problems with blisters than others (see Nadal and his many taped fingers). They are quite distracting when you have to play matches, especially if the skin is ruptured.

- **Prevention**
  A good method to prevent blisters is to dry your hands regularly. You can even use some sawdust or sports powder to keep your hands more dry. Try to find the right grip size that will give less friction with your hand; smaller grips tend to slip more easily in your hand. The type of overgrip used on the handle affects the grip on the racket and can prevent the grip from slipping. However, some of the grips are very abrasive, and not all skin types are suited for each overgrip.

- **Treatment**

  If the blister is already formed, you have little choice but to puncture the blister with a sterilized needle from opposite sides. Squeeze all the fluids out and sterilize the area. You can cover it with New-Skin, a product that covers the area completely and seals it off from the outside air. You can get this in strips or as a fluid in a bottle. On tour, the trainers have similar stuff but even better. It is also possible to tape certain blisters so they don't cause more damage. If the situation is really severe, you can consider wearing a golf glove and cutting the fingers off it. The glove is made from very thin leather and is extremely comfortable to use. It is a good alternative if all other options fail to work properly.

Tennis/Golf Elbow

These types of elbow injuries are the most common of all tennis injuries. It is an inflammation of the tendons attached to the elbow. They are caused by different aspects:

- The racket—if the racket is too heavy, too stiff, or has the wrong grip size, it will cause excess stress on the arm and the tendons of the elbow.
- The string—the string type and tension has to fit your strength, age, and level of play. There are several different types of string for each level, and string tension needs to be adjusted to fit the racket and the player.
- New strokes—learning advanced/new strokes can cause excess stress to the hand, wrist, arm, and tendons. Make sure the players are ready and skilled before introducing the new strokes or techniques.
- Overuse—playing too much or playing with much better players (hard hitters) can cause injuries to the hand, wrist, arm, and shoulder. Be careful what you wish for in playing above your skill level. It is easy to get hurt this way!

The elbow injuries have long recovery period, and even then, you have to go slow starting up again. Seek professional help so it doesn't get worse.

- **Prevention**
  Make sure you have the right equipment to play with. Your racket needs to fit with your size, age, and skill level concerning the weight of the racket, size of the racket, grip size, stiffness of the frame, and string tension.

When I was coaching Madison Appel at age seventeen, I had only just met her and had started working together that week. She came off a shoulder injury three months prior. I noticed during the practice how she was regularly hitting the ball late. When we sat down for a break, I nonchalantly asked if I could see her racket. (I didn't want to alert her that I thought something was wrong about her racket.) I looked it over, felt the balance, hit the string against my hand to test the tension, and tested the stiffness of the racket. "Did you just get these?" I asked.

"Yes, a few weeks ago," she acknowledged. I knew she had to play a tournament the next week, and she would never be able to change rackets that fast and get used to them. So I bit my tongue and said nothing. Madison had a light build and was not that strong at that time. Everything was wrong in the setup of her racket. It was way too heavy, and the grip size was too big. That type of racket was for men, not women, and the string was way too tight and all Luxilon—meant for strong male players. I mean, you couldn't have a worse setup for her build. She went to the tournament, and it was even worse to watch over there. She could hardly make a follow-through with the weight of the racket. Once we got back, I addressed the problem. She was shocked to hear it and said, "This is what they advised me." She switched to a light version with lighter tension strings. She almost immediately started hitting better and was able to hit the balls in front. Madison went on to play number 1 in college for four years at Indiana University. She still plays with the same racket today!

- **Treatment**
  With this particular injury, you need to seek professional help right away. The longer you wait, the worse it gets. The treatment consists of heat, ultrasound, electrical stem, massage, and specific stretches. A new type of treatment used for this injury is dry needling. This should only be performed by a physiotherapist.

Heat Exhaustion

This condition can occur when being exposed to the sun too long. The symptoms range from a hot skin to dizziness, extreme fatigue, nausea or vomiting, rapid heartbeat, mental confusion, etc. When you notice any of these symptoms, you need to take immediate action.

- **Prevention**
  Make sure to drink some cool or cold (sports) drinks. Stay in the shade or in air-conditioned rooms whenever possible. Dry yourself off when sweating a lot. Use cold towels (ice wrapped in the towel) during competition. Eat light snacks.

- **Treatment**
  Try to get inside a shaded or air-conditioned area to cool off. Remove all unnecessary clothing. Use a fan or cold towels to cool the body down and rehydrate with water or sports drink. Use an IV if you have trouble drinking with vomiting. You can use some ibuprofen as medication.

Cramping

Players can experience cramping during heavy competition. This condition occurs when the player is not properly hydrated, undertrained to the physical conditions of the match, or very anxious of the outcome of the match. The muscles contract involuntarily and prevent normal movements. It comes on instantaneously and is quite painful. Movement is heavily constricted.

- **Prevention**
  Be well conditioned physically to deal with the stamina needed in competition. Hydrate well the night before so you don't start the day with a deficit. It is difficult to catch up once you are dehydrated. Start drinking before the match. Use a sports drink with electrolytes to replace what you lose when sweating. Use cold towels when under extreme heat to cool down your body. Eat some light snacks (nutrition bar, banana, etc.) to keep the carbohydrates in your body up (it affects your hydration).

- **Treatment**
  If the cramping is very severe, use an IV to replace fluids more quickly in the bloodstream. Drink sports drinks to replenish electrolytes. Don't sit in an air-conditioned area where it is too cold after competition. It actually will cause cramping more easily. Cool down after competition by getting on a stationary bike or slow jog to keep the circulation going and to get rid of the lactic acid buildup from strenuous exercise.

Overtraining

This condition can occur when playing and training too much in combination with insufficient rest. The rest periods are crucial to recover from the strenuous exercise and the mental stress from competition. Players will start showing a lackluster performance and disinterest to work on their game.

- **Prevention**
  Make sure to always include a rest day each week, especially after training weeks or series of tournaments. Make a yearly tournament

plan and include days off, breaks, and vacations. Occasional massages can help to relax.

- **Treatment**

  Once overtrained, you have no choice but to immediately take time off from competition and training. Make sure to start up gradually again.

18—MENTAL TRAINING

Character, Process of Improvements, and Results

In general, tennis players struggle with mental aspects the most in competitive play. They can all learn the strokes and understand the basic strategic concepts, but learning how to concentrate on the various subjects and how to last for many hours in matches is not an easy task. It takes great character to deal with the stress and focus of each point and to accept many defeats before becoming successful. In today's game, the competitions, results, and rankings are all online and add to the stress of ego and sportsmanship. As a coach and parent, you need to guide your player away from the focus of results and rankings. Build their character first and make them focus on the process of improvements. Only then will you see proper results. You have to improve first before you can get results, not the other way around!

Mental training is the least trained aspect of the tennis game and is usually the last to be addressed in progressions of learning. There are many forms of mental training that can be introduced subconsciously at an early age without being intrusive to the player. They can be taught with very simple methods that eventually will create an inner strength to endure and succeed in difficult and stressful situations. It is important to create a competitive spirit from an early age to hone the mental skills with plenty of point play. This will develop the patterns of play instinctively and make them react automatically to the difficult and mental aspects of the game through competition. After a while, coaches will be able to assess the problem areas of the mental aspects and address these problems with a mental training program suited specifically for each student.

Teaching Mental Aspects

The mental aspects are the most difficult to learn or change and are usually the last topic in the learning phase. However, it is much easier to teach these aspects when kids are younger and make them part of their routines and habits. Later on, these aspects are much more difficult to learn since (bad) habits and routines are already formed and take a long time to change. There are many different mental aspects that can influence the performance of a player not only in a negative way but also in a positive way. Let me give you some common mental attitudes and illustrate how they affect the player's performance:

Player A is technically and physically accomplished in producing the strokes but struggles to stay calm and execute the chosen strategies. The low confidence and nervousness during point play does not allow them to stay calm, make clear decisions, and be committed. This mental attitude could be the result of insufficient experience and/or match play, but it could also be the result of other factors.

Low confidence or self-esteem can be caused by themselves or by others. Some players can be overly critical about their performance and don't focus on the positives of their accomplishments. The focus is usually on the mistakes made in the past rather than on how and what to do with the task at hand. Practice makes perfect is a commonly used phrase, but reality teaches us that perfection is usually unobtainable. Concentrating on the strategy of the very next point and accepting the mistakes and imperfections will cause less frustration. It will enable players to play more freely and enhance their confidence in the long run. Coaches and parents can also cause low confidence in players. Being overly critical will affect the way students feel about themselves. The criticism can be about results in practices and tournaments or how the strokes or points are performed. (In some cases, players start taking in the negative criticism from parents and coaches and adopt negative attitudes.) They will start to doubt their decision-making and become insecure and uncommitted to the strokes and strategies. The frequency, tone, and manner of communication also greatly influence the mental attitudes of the students. In order to improve confidence, it is imperative to have players focus on their goals, improvements, and accomplishments. Coaches and parents have to focus on their manner of communication with positive feedback. Their comments and instructions should be informative, noncritical, and encouraging at all times in order to enhance performance.

Player B is afraid to miss the ball and holds back on the acceleration of the strokes. This player will usually step backward as they prepare to strike the ball and end up hitting off their back foot. They also might end up breaking down in technique and/or playing defensively. This particular mental attitude is not uncommon with players, coaches, and parents trying to instill consistency in strokes. In an effort to acquire more consistency, the players will slow down their strokes and become more tentative in striking the ball. The weight transfer will become limited with players being afraid and less committed to step forward in fear of hitting the ball out. The hips, shoulders, arms, and wrist actions will become more mechanical and swing less freely. Consistency is an important factor in playing better tennis, but overstressing the issue can lead to mental issues that hinder the performance even more. Players understand clearly when they are missing balls, so it is not necessary to keep confirming their errors. A much better method is to help them understand how to improve their consistency by making changes to the chosen target areas and the trajectory and the spin of the ball. Using the weight transfer and swinging freely will only enhance this even more. Don't be too critical with results in the beginning, be encouraging, and choose small minigoals of improving consistency to enhance the player's confidence.

Player C plays tentatively when up or even in score but plays aggressively and freely when down in score. This mental attitude prevents them from playing their own game. The player clearly has their focus on the wrong aspects of the game. They focus on the score instead of their game plan and on how to build the rally. When they are down, they forget about the score and focus on their game. They might feel they have nothing to lose and play more freely. This is a focus and concentration problem. Players who are able to focus on the tactical game plan at all time will have fewer issues in getting nervous. This mental attitude can be trained by playing sets and games with different scores. It is also possible to have the player imagine (for an instant) that they are down in score instead of up in score. Teaching players to stay in the moment is the key for the long term.

Player D is a talented player who has all the strokes and physical requirements to make it to the top but has a casual and cocky attitude in playing the game. The results should be better, but the effort and mental attitude is not optimal enough to make progress. This particular mental attitude will affect many of the mental aspects. The focus and concentration will be too low to make much progress. This is also the case for the discipline, routines, and habits. They will all be at a lower level of intensity and need to improve and gain better results. If results remain low for a longer period of time, it could start eating away at their confidence, which could affect the results even worse. To improve this mental attitude, coaches have to introduce a set of reachable goals and introduce a stricter physical program. The goals will keep the player on track to improve their quality and intensity in practices and matches. Have measurable goals that are compared on a daily or weekly basis for optimal feedback. The physical program needs to be challenging to push the player to a higher level of intensity. Encouraging players to perform to their highest capability should be a daily routine for it to become a habit.

In order to know what to look for and what to train, we need to distinguish the mental aspects in detail. Some aspects are more trainable than others. The mental aspects can be divided into three groups:

A. Emotional Mental Aspects
(Trainable Aspects)
- nervousness and excitement
- fear
- pressure
- aggression control

B. Intrinsic Mental Aspects
(Inherent and Less Trainable Aspects)
- motivation and drive
- determination and willpower
- discipline
- confidence

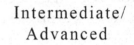

Intermediate/
Advanced

C. Reasonable Mental Aspects
(Trainable Aspects)
- concentration and focus
- discipline
- routines and habits
- problem-solving
- stress management

Although most of these mental aspects are part of the talent and character traits of each player, they can be trained to improve over time. They can be trained individually or in combination with one another. The emotional and reasonable aspects are trainable, whereas the intrinsic mental aspects are less trainable. As players progress and improve over time, it will drive them to a higher motivation and determination to stay on that path, which will ultimately lead to belief in accomplishments and having more confidence.

A. Emotional Mental Aspects

We have all witnessed how the emotions of an athlete can play a big part in the outcome of a competition, and this is no different in the game of tennis. The emotions can have a positive and negative effect on the performance. They work positively when players feel good about themselves, become excited and satisfied with their performance, and are proud about how they handle themselves in difficult situations. They can work negatively when players become too excited, get frustrated and angry, or start thinking they might lose.

Nervousness and Excitement

These two emotions go hand in hand and are important aspects to drive the development and improvement of students in practice and match play. Some nervousness is good to stimulate the energy and performance, but too much of it will hinder those just as much. Excitement is necessary to feel good about yourself or your performance. It can be a very valuable aspect to help you perform to a higher level or to push the envelope of the physical energy as long as this feeling is not too intense. When players get overexcited, it creates a nervousness that will have a negative effect on the coordination and execution of the strokes and movements. It is sometimes visible in players at the start of a match and affects the speed and quickness of the legs. It will look as if the players are moving through mud instead of their usual speed. It is important to learn the intensity level of excitement where it stimulates the energy and your performance rather than hold you back.

Practice

- Playing the proper level at tournaments can help alleviate some of the problems that arise from nervousness and excitement. As long as players are experiencing a positive experience in playing events and winning some matches, they will start to gain confidence and eventually lose some of the nervousness and gain excitement. A good gauge is a ratio of two wins versus one loss.

- Sometimes playing in a higher age group at local events or winning events at a lower level can stimulate players to overcome their nervousness and become excited about their accomplishments.
- Putting players in different circumstances with team play or doubles competition can change their attitude, emotions and anxiety level. In some cases, players become better doubles players before they become better singles players.

Fear

We all have our fears when we play tennis, but they are not always the same for each person. The fears can range from losing a match, a certain ranking, a spot on the team to fears of winning and the expectations of what that might bring. In fact, the expectations of a player are usually the underlying reasons of fear (the fear of not being able to reach your goals). Here are some examples that lead to fear:

- pressure from yourself to win or lose
- pressure from others (parents, coach, team)
- too many high expectations of success in performance or tournaments
- ego in what others think of you (other competitors, parents, coach, team)
- your confidence level in competition

Too many expectations can also lead to frustration, nervousness, and feelings of failure and embarrassment (ego can be the underlying problem to more fear). The confidence of a player is a large component of fear. In this case, players are afraid to do something wrong or afraid to confront an opponent with competitive play. The fear or failure to execute a certain stroke is visible in any player at any level. The better players are just better at hiding their emotions and have become good at replacing them with positive thoughts. A good example is when players step back from the service position whenever they don't feel comfortable with their thoughts. They gather themselves and replace the negative with positive thoughts.

Practice

- Alleviate the expectations and fear of failure of players by letting them play with both weaker and stronger opponents. It will give players a more realistic view where they are with their development. Expectations will become more realistic over time.
- Playing longer rallies in point play will improve the confidence and consistency of players. This will eventually lessen the fear of missing balls in rallies.
- Whenever you see a player hesitate to execute, teach them to go back and replace the negative thought with a positive one.
- Teach players what they are able to control and what they cannot. This eliminates many factors that players might worry about and makes them focus on the things they can control.
- One of the best ways to get rid of fear in competition is to create a fun goal or a challenge that will make players forget about their fear and focus on the challenge.

I had a young student who was scared about the opponent calling off the score as soon as he got close to winning. The opponent would say "Three more shots" as he neared the end of the set.

"What can I do in this situation?" he asked me.

"I would use it against him," I replied. "But I would call out something that would not make sense, like thirteen more shots."

He liked that idea and tried it when he was in the first set tiebreak. The opponent looked very surprised, paused, and then hit a double fault!

My student won that match and was beaming from ear to ear when he came off the court. I had exchanged his fear with a fun and challenging idea.

Pressure

Everyone feels a certain level of pressure during a match. The pressure can come from many different directions. It can be the style of play of the opponent, the importance of the match or tournament, or the score in the match. But it can also be outside pressure from expectations of other people, like your parents or coaches or media. This aspect of emotion can work in your favor when you are able to control the level of pressure, but it can definitely be disastrous when the pressure becomes overwhelming. The key here is to control the amount of pressure so that you can still perform to the best of your ability. This is only possible when the priorities are clear and the focus is on the strategy rather than on external factors. Players have to learn to block out things that can have a negative effect on their performance, replace negative thoughts with positive ones whenever possible, and not worry about factors they cannot control. These skills take time to learn, but you can slowly introduce them along the way.

Practice

- Practice playing points with different game and set scores. The simulated situation of adding pressure will train players to become less sensitive to the score and to focus on the next point (present) rather than on points played in the past or the future.
- Practice playing points that can only be won by winning two or three in a row. This added pressure in point play practices the control of pressure by focusing on the strategy and consistency rather than the pressure of the situation.
- Add pressure to situations by choosing certain points in the game to win. The first point of the game, gaining a game point at 30–0 or 30–15, and winning a game point outright can add pressure in match play. Practice will eventually change the feeling of pressure to a feeling of a challenge.

During an international league match in Amsterdam, I had one top player (60 WTA) who was struggling with her nerves. She sat down during the changeover and said to me, "Martin, I am so nervous today, and I don't know why."

The match was very close, and winning it would seal the win. So I was not surprised she was nervous. To win, I needed her to relax as soon as possible. My response was, "OK, on the next return, hit the ball as hard as you can into the back fence." She looked at me a little shocked. "Just trust me and just do it," I encouraged her.

She went out there, looked back at me with a little smile on her face, and smacked the return past the opponent and into the back fence. The opponent looked very shocked and surprised as well. After that, she relaxed and started playing much better. She sat down on the next changeover, and I said, "Sometimes you have to invest in one shot to get rid of some of your nerves." She went on to win the match and also the league championship! She had a nice career in pro tennis and went on to be a TV commentator for Eurosport and Dutch TV.

Aggression Control

In playing an advanced level of play, each player needs a certain amount of aggression to perform at his or her best ability. The amount of aggression can be a tricky thing if it is not controlled adequately. Some players might become too aggressive. This could cause them to change their strategy and go for risky shots close to the lines. It could also change their technique in muscling the ball and losing control and consistency. The aggression can turn into anger that will affect both the strategy and technique in a negative way. Using too much aggression will also deplete the player's energy very quickly and heavily affect the efficiency and endurance. Learning to control the level of aggression is the key to dominating the points while maintaining endurance, fluidity, and efficiency.

Practice

- One player plays offensive tennis and can use the whole court, whereas the other player can only play back to the center part of the court. The key here is to keep the aggression control to the point where it is possible to play with consistency and fluidity while maintaining efficiency.
- This same drill can be executed as above by playing back to one side of the court. The smaller target on one side adds pressure in running down shots and making the proper shot choice. The other player has pressure of controlling the aggression by playing forcefully to controlled targets that still hold a good level of consistency.
- Playing points with a limitation that one player has to play the approach shot within five shots. Players are forced to play with controlled aggression to open the court for an approach shot.

B.   Intrinsic Mental Aspects

These intrinsic or inherent mental aspects exist in each player, although they might not be at the same level or intensity. This does not mean that it cannot develop over time. As players progress from a prepubescent stage to advanced player, they can pick up a passion for the game that can propel them to much higher achievements than are thought possible. It is an advantage if these aspects are already at a higher level when starting the game rather than developing them later. But it is no surprise to see very timid and shy young players develop into great competitors at a later stage. It does take more time, but their achievements often surpass their peers and predecessors of the game. This is very visible in the tennis game by looking at young and talented achievers who win higher-level tournaments at a young age but are surpassed by late bloomers as it becomes time to turn pro in the sport.

Motivation and Drive

The inspiration, enthusiasm, and impulse to play tennis at a higher level are developed through a passion for the game. It can start with just liking the sport, but as the accomplishments start to grow, players will use their achievements as an incentive to progress even further and use it as the driving force to excel. The motivation and drive are at different levels for each individual player but can change over time. The amount of motivation and drive will determine the improvements and accomplishments of each player at any level of the game and does become more important as players strive to become advanced or pro players.

Determination and Willpower

Becoming a successful tennis player takes many years of hard training and competition. It is a long and laborious task of repeating strokes, exercises, and drills to hone the skills necessary to rise up through the ranks. In order to reach your goals, you have to be willing and able to give up a lot of your free time to dedicate yourself to a purpose and to push yourself during difficult situations in practice and competition to succeed. This strength of mind drives a person to dig deep when things get tough to never give up and to show grit in coming back from behind. That can only be done with a certain level of intensity and energy that we call determination and willpower. The level of determination and willpower is different for everyone but does determine the amount of energy that a person is willing to spend to reach their goals.

Discipline

This mental quality can be an intrinsic aspect as well as a learned behavior. When it is portrayed as an intrinsic value, players are able to naturally regulate and control their behaviors and tasks without much interference or guidance. They can show great restraint and self-control to follow a certain instruction, execution, or sequence so that it becomes routine and part of their normal performance. Players with good disciplines have an advantage over others since they can reproduce the performance with more ease as they become automated functions over time. It will take less energy as they become more efficient with the capability of spending the energy in other parts of their game.

Confidence

This mental aspect is usually the last aspect to evolve, but it also has the largest influence on the performance in competition. It is determined by how the person feels about themselves, their performance, and their accomplishments. Confidence takes time to develop since improvements and results don't happen instantly. With a highly technical sport like tennis, it usually takes six months to show improvements and results of training. It is possible to improve confidence with more improvements and better results, but it can also work the other way round by how you feel about yourself with a positive demeanor and attitude. Persons who don't have much confidence in themselves will struggle to stay positive and often need much encouragement from others. Their passion for the game—combined with their motivation, drive, and willpower—can help them to succeed against all odds as long as they receive positive feedback and encouragement. An outward attitude of confidence and sheer stubbornness to reach your goals can lead to inward confidence and accomplishments. In fact, having little and reachable minigoals can improve the confidence of players who otherwise struggle with confidence. The minigoals can vary from stroke improvements for that day to a tactical execution that has improved, etc. All these minigoals will eventually provide a player with positive feedback in accomplishments and enhance their confidence. The people who are close to the player can also improve confidence. The parents and the coach play a large role in this. Positive feedback and encouragement speak louder than critical and negative feedback. These comments have to be realistic in content, and players still need to know right from wrong, but the delivery of the message is important here. You can look at it this way: if a player is constantly thinking of the negative things that happened in the previous point, they cannot play well in the present point. The same is true in teaching subjects to students by parents and coaches; it will affect their confidence in practices and matches over time. Be positive and encouraging to enhance their confidence and performance!

C. Reasonable Mental Aspects

These are the logical and rational aspects of the mental game that are necessary to play with consistency and strategy. They are definitely trainable and can be improved over time. They are listed in a specific teaching/learning order from easy to more difficult in a progression from intermediate to advanced player. The more you can get players to buy into these mental training concepts, the more results they will achieve. Let's look at these mental aspects in-depth.

Concentration and Focus

Without concentration and focus, it is virtually impossible to become an advanced player in any type of sport. Concentration and focus show itself in the ability of players to absorb new material and in the level of attention to apply it with deliberate actions into practice. The length and level of the concentration is dependent on the motivation and determination of each player. There are many ways to train concentration and focus. Some obvious examples of the training of concentration and focus are the education we receive from a young age in school. It is no coincidence that the concentration and focus of young children is declining with more tennis players being homeschooled. There are some other forms of concentration that are mostly based on some form of long-term consistency.

Practice

- A simple way to train concentration is with the use of a jump rope. Set a certain number of times they have to make in a row. The consistency of movement and the focus needed to execute and reach a certain level of intensity and performance take great concentration.

- You can demonstrate to students the difficulty of concentration and focus by making them look at a small object or a spot on the wall for as long as they can. Make them record how long they can do this before they lose focus, look away, and think of something else. This will make them aware of concentration and gives them a tool for practicing this on their own.
- Hitting a certain number of balls in a row within a target area and with a certain pattern trains their concentration to perform in competition.
- Playing longer points (serving to eleven) or sets (three to five) in a row will train the consistency of players.

Discipline

This aspect is also trainable by creating routines at home and at practice. Parents are well aware of creating discipline at home, and it should be no different with obtaining a level of discipline in practice sessions. A practice session for players should always be fun, informative, and challenging while building routines to create automated functions. Discipline in tennis players can be as simple as how they organize their tennis bag or being on time for practice or how they stick to certain tactical concepts as shot choices in tactical situations. Some players understand these forms of disciplines more easily than others. In working with competitive players, it becomes important to teach these at an early age to eliminate these in later stages of development. It is possible to train discipline in practice and competition in many different ways. I have listed some below:

Practice

- Make a practice of teaching players to be on time for practice and competition by being twenty minutes early. This will always provide players time to relax, prepare any last-minute items, warm up, and get ready for action.

- Make every practice enjoyable, fun, and challenging in content. Competition and practice should be fun, but passionate players who seek higher levels of play crave a tough workout that makes them feel accomplished.
- Players need to learn to eventually do certain things on their own to perform to their best ability. This includes a good diet, plenty of rest, and a good preparation for practice and competition with a warm-up and stretching. Their physical workout has to become their own responsibility as well in time.
- Make players know the rules of the game! Without proper knowledge of the rules, it is very difficult to become a good tennis player. Knowing the specifics of the rules and how to deal with them creates confidence and avoids confusion.
- Make players aware that you want them to become the best they can be and that hard work does pay off in the end. Challenge them to become better every day by grading themselves in technique, tactics, and physical and mental aspects.
- Players need to learn to take responsibility for their rackets, drinks, food, and all other equipment and make sure they are always prepared.
- Teach them self-discipline by taking initiative and thinking of goals and tasks they can set for themselves. It will provide them with a sense of responsibility for their own improvements in practice and competition.
- Have them make notes about the training and competition. This provides them with feedback on the quality of their performance and solutions they found in dealing with different aspects.

Routines and Habits

In creating a high level of intensity and consistency in performance, it is important to have routines and habits. These are very visible in many top performers just before they start an action. With tennis players, this can be looking at the strings of the racket, walking to the towel to dry off before playing the next point, bouncing the ball a certain number of times before the serve, or moving it a certain way before a return. These routines are important to create a familiarity and comfort before the action to stimulate confidence. It also creates a moment to focus on the action that is about to follow. Some players will create these routines on their own, but if they don't, it is important to teach them for a higher level of performance. Below are some routines that can be trained.

Practice

- Create a warm-up routine that is always the same and includes loosening up the arms and legs, jumping rope, doing specific tennis movements and some sprints, and stretching.
- Being prepared for all circumstances during practice and competition will help players to feel confident. Have a routine in preparing drinks and/or food before every workout or match. Bring extra clothing, a towel, Band-Aids and tape, and extra string and have all the racket's strung that are needed.
- Just before the start of the match, you can do some shadow tennis by mimicking the strokes with a racket and movements you are about to use in the match.
- Make sure to bring a towel that you can go to in between points. Its function is to dry off your hands, but it can also be used to focus for the next point. It prevents players from playing points too fast one after another and rushing themselves.
- Looking at the strings keeps players focused and in the moment. This way your eyes do not get you distracted in looking at something else and losing focus.
- Walking back to the back fence before playing the next point makes players take their time to prepare and focus for the next point and makes them walk up to the starting position the same way.

- Bouncing the ball the same number of times before the serve creates rhythm and timing. The movement has to be uniform to create a feel of comfort and familiarity.
- The movement just before the return has to be uniform and similar in intensity and execution. Most players bounce around and then take position while shifting their weight side to side before skipping forward and making a split step.

Problem-Solving

In every practice and match, there are many problems that arise that need to be solved by each individual tennis player. Once a problem is solved and a solution has been found, it will create a great sense of accomplishment that leads to increased confidence. Some players are able to solve certain problems on their own if they have been given a greater sense of responsibility from an early stage. Others need to be taught to take on this task themselves in order to become successful in solving these problems on their own. I will list several practice options below to enhance and improve the problem-solving skill.

Practice

- Ask plenty of questions during the training to make sure players have understood what is asked of them and let them provide you with the purpose.
- Ask them to solve a problem on their own without giving them the answer. If they don't know it right away, don't be too hasty to provide them with an answer and let them think about it. These problems can be of a technical, tactical, physical, or mental issue; and it is important to touch on all of them.
- Keeping a record in a notebook on their performance during practice and competition can lead players to realize certain tendencies and habits that they need to correct.

- Solving strategic and tactical problems in practice and competition is ideal to train the mind and improve confidence. Let them find the solutions on their own.
- Make sure players know all the rules and how to deal with arbitrary decisions in specific situations that often occur during a match. This type of problem-solving will increase self-belief and courage to step up when decisions need to be made.

Stress Management

Pressure during competition, or even practice sessions, is dealt with in a variety of ways by each player; but there are some guidelines and training methods that can relieve the pressure substantially. We call this stress management. Most of the stress during practice and competition is self-inflicted and brought on by frustration of performance and/or the score in point or match play. Players become distracted with their thoughts and focus and start thinking of the past or the future instead of staying in the present. Worry and frustration become very negative and lead to unproductive thoughts, actions, and behavior. This can lead to a down-spiraling performance and intensity, or even, in the worst case, a complete shutdown. The trick to stress management is to keep the focus on positive thoughts, possibilities, and outcomes and to concentrate on the strategy and execution with a point-by-point game plan. This keeps players on task by only focusing on the next point. See the practice of stress management.

Practice

- *Whenever players seem to lose their calm during match play, try to remind them of where their focus needs to be and why. Keeping their thoughts on the strategy and execution of the tactics is an excellent way to stay in the present and keep their focus on the task at hand. Players need to only think of the next point.*
- *Teach players to slow down when things are getting out of control and/or stress is increasing. This is possible by taking their time in*

between points and going to the towel to take more time to think about the next point.

- *It is also possible to change strategy and slow down the opponent with a higher and slower trajectory. This type of trajectory not only neutralizes the opponent but also makes it much more difficult to hit attacking shots. The higher trajectory gives you extra time to cover the court and get set for the next shot.*

- *By playing games or sets with different scores, it is possible to increase the pressure of play while up or down in score. Training these scores in practice matches makes players less sensitive to the score, and they will learn to focus on the task at hand.*

Temper Control

Many kids struggle to keep their emotions in check during practice, match play, and tournament. This was also the case when I started working with a group of boys born in '87. It started at the fourteen and under international junior tournaments: Teen Tennis in England and Les Petits As in France. The boys were throwing their rackets at every occasion when they were dissatisfied with their game. I was thinking about how to solve this when an idea came to me. I decided to take their racket away whenever they threw it. At that age, most of the kids play with their favorite racket, and I felt they would soon learn not to do it anymore. I also discussed with them the advantages of controlling their anger and how to channel this energy back into their game. The results were dramatic. They definitely stopped throwing their rackets, and in a short while, it had a profound effect on their game. They started concentrating on their game by controlling their anger.

Another factor that has to be taught to players growing up is the respect they show to the tools of their trade (in this case, their racket). In some cases, the better kids are sponsored by racket companies and need to know how to respect this by not taking their anger out on their rackets.

What I didn't realize was that I was carrying all those rackets! I ended up with ten rackets from everyone in my bag, but I soon found an answer for that by letting the guy who threw the most rackets carry the rackets!

To improve mentally in character and maturity, players need to grow in mind-set. Without this growth, there will be no mental improvements. Here are ten ways to develop growth in mind-set:

1. Value the process of improvements over the end results.
2. Acknowledge imperfections in execution.
3. Embrace struggle and discomfort in difficult situations.
4. View challenges as opportunities to grow and improve.
5. Place effort before talent.
6. Reward your actions and executions, not the outcomes or behaviors.
7. Take feedback and criticism as positive and helpful to your development.
8. Replace what you see as failures to learning.
9. Cultivate grit and develop the courage to take risk.
10. Take ownership over your attitude and show great character.

If everything was going smooth all the time, you would never build character.

—Maria Sharapova

Maria Sharapova

Mental Improvement Tips

Making improvements in mental attitude and toughness takes great commitment from every competitor. Most often, they don't realize the impact and importance it has on their performance until they have mastered them. The key is to set a certain standard from the start. It will make working on these topics much easier when it becomes a daily routine. These mental improvement tips will assist players, coaches, and parents to enhance the attitude, toughness, resilience, and confidence of any competitor.

- **Create a Healthy Work Environment**
  The standards of the workouts and practice should be set by the coach, but they are influenced by the player and parents. Practice should always be a fun experience for players to improve in every aspect, especially their mental abilities. By creating a fun environment with disciplined exercises and specific practices, players are challenged to improve their mental attitudes and toughness in a natural way. Coaches and parents can assist in this process by how they communicate in being encouraging and supportive with their instructions, comments, and remarks. Constructive instructions and comments are positive directions on how to change or execute a subject rather than negative remarks on the performance.

- **Prepare for Competition**
  To play in a competition effectively, players need to prepare appropriately. The practice needs to be specific to the demands of the game with technical, tactical, physical, and mental aspects to create a well-developed player. You also have to practice mental toughness, intensity, and focus before you can see results in matches. The experiences and accomplishments in practice matches will eventually develop the confidence in competition. A telltale sign for well-prepared players is how they prepare mentally. You will often see them seek a secluded spot to warm up physically or to focus (going over the important points of the match) on their own just before playing their match.

- **Get In the Zone by Improving the Focus**

  Enhanced focus and concentration will keep players in a mental zone for optimal results. This zone helps players not to get distracted by opponents, umpires, spectators, and external factors. By improving the focus, it will also improve the players' technical, physical, and tactical consistency. Players will be able to execute their strokes with more uniformity, keep up their physical intensity, and play with more tactical awareness. The focus can be improved in practices and matches by staying in the moment and learning to concentrate on the execution of strokes and strategy at all times (see "Being In the Zone").

- **Concentrate on the Execution and Strategy**

  By concentrating on the execution rather than your feelings or the score, it will be easier to focus and stay in the zone. Feelings are usually not helpful with an increase of nervousness, and it distracts you from concentrating on your strokes or strategy. The score will usually create a higher level of nervousness, either when up in score or when down in score. It is much more helpful to concentrate on the executions and adjustments of the strokes and strategies to enhance the consistency and reliability of both these factors. As players become more proficient and advanced with the strokes, the executions and adjustments become automated. This will free up their mental energy to concentrate solely on the strategy and tactics of the game.

- **Develop Routines**

  The routines of players create a comfort level in match play to enhance the focus and concentration no matter where you play or what the circumstances are. The routines are developed by creating a pattern of activity in preparation, in between points, and at the changeover. This can involve going to the towel, drinking water, looking at the strings of the racket, walking in preparation to the next point, etc. All these routines will enhance the consistency and performance of the execution.

- **Stay in the Present by Playing Point by Point**

  Staying in the moment is important to enhance the performance not only in match play but also in practice. By playing each point with a renewed preparation and intensity, it is possible to stay focused on the task at hand. As soon as the point is over, players recap the point very briefly. There is a short-time (few seconds) feedback on how the point was executed in order to use this information for future points. It does no good to dwell on prior points too long, no matter if they are won or lost. They can distract you by thinking about your performance or the score. Feelings usually lead to worry or from playing the proper way into becoming tentative or overly aggressive. You cannot change the past; you can only influence the future with the next point!

- **Never Quit and Run for Every Ball**

  Players who have the mental attitude to never quit and run for every ball have an advantage over most other players. Talent and tactical aptitude can help a player to succeed, but the willingness to run down every ball is a powerful weapon to overcome. The never-ending pressure will eventually wear down the opponent mentally and physically, apply pressure on the consistency, and/ or force them to take more risk with their targets. Quitting (also named tanking) in competition can become a bad habit and make losing a bad habit as well. Never quitting in competition enhances the mental toughness and the pride in accomplishment. This will greatly enhance confidence.

- **Improve Confidence, Self-Belief, and Determination through Visualization**

  Confidence and self-esteem are important factors to execute with determination and commitment. Believing in oneself is the primary catalyst to improve the confidence in a player. Doubts can creep in slowly and undermine the feelings, which leads to lesser effort and intensity. Visualization can make a real change and difference to your confidence and enhance self-belief. This method is an internal thorough process in going through the actions and motions of the match in sequence. Closing your eyes can greatly increase the focus and impressions in your mind. It is comparable to programming your brain in order to create a road map on what to do in each situation. When it is time to execute, the actions will be easier to perform with more determination (see "Visualization").

- **Mental Toughness through Physical Conditioning**
  It is no coincidence that players who are physically in great shape are also mentally tough. It takes hard work, sacrifice, and determination to stand out beyond the norm. It gives any player great confidence and applies tremendous pressure on the opponent. The physical effort will help players to push through difficult situations and keeps them focused on their goals rather than their feelings. These types of players are usually less likely to get nervous or choke in stressful situations. This is why physical conditioning can play a big part in helping you to become more mentally tough on- and off-court.

- **Knowing Momentum and When to Strike**
  All good competitors understand very clearly how and when to apply pressure on the opponent to keep the momentum of the match in their favor. They raise their intensity to a higher level and take initiative to attack with continuous pressure until the opponent folds. They understand how to use their footwork and strokes as a weapon to keep the opponent off-balance and out of position. The timing of this pressure is at key points in the game and will have a devastating mental effect if they are successful. Keeping the momentum going when points are going your way is another example of knowing when to strike. If you have ever experienced this used against you, you should also be able to learn this valuable tool for yourself!

- **Pride Yourself on Being Competitive**
  Mental attitudes of being competitive can be natural instinct of a player, but it can also be taught to a degree. The amount of competitiveness depends largely on the confidence and excitement a

player feels from their accomplishments and results. By choosing the proper tournaments and competitions, a player can improve their results and self-belief and gain some pride in their accomplishments. Through the improvements of the physical intensity and passion for the game, players will be able to take pride in their competitive spirit. Taking pride in accomplishments can be a valuable tool to push you to higher levels of competition.

- **Keep Track of Your Mental Improvements**
  The only way to optimize your mental toughness is to start tracking it by making notes on your performance and methods of improvements. By writing notes, you provide feedback to yourself that will enforce you to change behavior. You might be able to discover trends in your attitude and your actions that can be adjusted with a different method or way of thinking. Identifying the problem is important, but fixing it is imperative for optimal performance.

- **Train Your Mental Toughness with Specific Competitive Situations**
  By frequently putting yourself in specific competitive situations, you can mimic match situations that improve the mental toughness. Especially if you know situations that seem to cause mental problems on a regular basis, this method can enhance the performance through continuous repetitions under pressure. Don't shy away from pressure situations during practice. It will only have a positive effect on the confidence of any player in the long run.

Rafael Nadal exemplifies mental toughness.

Being In the Zone

Being relaxed. Research has proven that peak performances will occur when you are just slightly above your normal state of arousal rather than at the extreme end of the spectrum, as once thought. This is called being in the zone. As you endeavor to be in the zone, you are energized yet relaxed in a subtle balance of quiet intensity. Your mind is calm, and your body is ready to go.

You are confident. When you are playing well, you feel confident no matter what you are up against. You exude great confidence and pride, and it is evident in your performance.

You have no fear. You are not going to let a momentary lapse in performance undermine your belief in your overall abilities. Inner confidence is outwardly exhibited by your posture, your walk, and your facial expressions. You are not just hoping or wishing to be successful, you are expecting to be successful. You have adopted a confident winning attitude. You are prepared and can trust in your ability to do the right thing at the right time. Your mind-set allows you to know that you are going to do everything necessary to be successful.

You are completely focused. You are totally absorbed in the moment. You are not troubled by the past and have no qualms about the future. The only thing you are concentrating on is the task at hand. You are oblivious to everything else going on around you. You have no real sense of time, and before you know it, the game is over. It seems to have flown by, yet everything you did was perceived to have happened in slow motion, with great precision and utmost concentration. You understand that having the ability to stay in the moment is descriptive of all peak performers, and that frame of mind is your goal every time you participate in your sport.

Your performance feels effortless. You notice that things just sort of happen with little or no effort whatsoever. All your moves are smooth, and while in the zone, your sport seems like the easiest thing in the world. Your mind and body are working in perfect unison. Your grace and ease make your every move seem to be the most natural thing in the world. You have a sense of finesse and competency, even when the task proves to be most grueling and demanding. Everything is coming automatically. There is no interference in your performance that stems from your thoughts or emotions. Things are simply happening, just as equally without consent as without protest. As a result of your practice and mental preparation, you are on autopilot (but mindful of all details), fluidly reacting to whatever comes your way. Your body just seems to know what to do without mentally plotting it out.

You are having fun. When you are in the flow, you realize that your enjoyment is incomparable. You are relishing your sport with pure and innocent delight. You believe that your sport supplies something valuable that you can't get from anyone or anything else. You know that your love of the sport is the key to advancement within it and in your life.

Visualization

Visualization is one of the most powerful tools of your mind. When players use imagery—visualization—to its fullest potential, this can accelerate their progress and help them immensely in their mental preparation for the match.

Tennis players also use visualization extensively but usually not in their best interest, and they are not even aware what they are doing. It's when they are thinking about negative consequences of their play that they are basically visualizing failure and feeling in the present how that will probably feel in the future. This makes them nervous; they are not focused and are expending precious energy.

They need to reverse this process and start visualizing their success and how good they will feel when they achieve it. This will fill them with lots of positive energy and program them for success.

Where Can Visualization Be Used in the Game of Tennis?

It can be used in all four major areas of tennis:

1. **Technique**—when players are still learning a new stroke or improving existing ones, they first need to see the correct execution in video or in demonstration and then visualize how to perform this stroke perfectly. This will greatly speed up the learning process.

2. **Tactics and strategy**—when players are planning the strategy before the match, they can visualize how to hit certain combinations of shots. They can visualize good and precise serving, returning, and all other areas of the tennis match. When they play, they react and decide much faster because they already have preprogrammed decisions and directions.

3. **Physical abilities**—the same way other athletes visualize how they can jump higher or longer, tennis players can also visualize how fast they are, how they are able to withstand fatigue, and how strong they are in the third set. Mental images have incredible influence on our bodies when we use them consistently.

4. **Mental preparation**—the most effective way of visualizing in the mental area is when players imagine how they play in the finals or in front of many people. It can happen many times that players get nervous before or at the beginning of an important match because they are not used to pressure around them. If you visualize these situations beforehand, you get used to them in your mind; and when they happen in reality, you will be ready

Martin van Daalen

and relaxed. Another very effective way of visualization is when players *anticipate* situations in the match that could potentially cause them to lose focus or to get upset. You can then visualize these situations and *how* to handle them. That way you can prepare for when they happen in reality and immediately know how to respond because of the previous programming in your mind.

How to Visualize Effectively

Sit comfortably on a chair in a quiet spot and take a couple of deep breaths to relax first. Then in your mind, put yourself on the tennis court and try to see all the surroundings. Try to see the shapes of the objects on the court: the net, the lines, the fence, etc. Then try to hear the sounds that you would normally hear on the court—the sound of hitting the ball, your breathing, and other sounds. Then try to feel your movements and your strokes. Make a forehand topspin in your mind and try to feel how that would really feel. Then try to feel your movement on the court from left to right and so on. The last and most important component is your emotions. This time try to feel the emotions of how good you would feel if you hit a certain shot, won a match, or reached your desired ranking. When you include your positive emotions (enthusiasm, happiness, and satisfaction), the results of visualization will be much more effective and longer lasting.

Another very effective and useful use of visualization is immediately after you make an error on the court. As soon as you miss, you turn away, walk back to the back fence, and in your mind, see how the ball hit the target. See exactly how high over the net, where on the court, and how fast and with how much spin you played it. This has double effect: it takes you away from your negative thinking since you are not seeing successful, and it also trains your body for the next similar situation when you will have to play a similar shot. This way it will be already stored in your mind.

How to Practice

Practice the following ways of visualization for one week:

1. After you make an error, imagine how you actually hit the ball. Write down some of the mistakes and how you imagined them later.

2. Rate yourself from 1–10 on how good you are at this. The rating of 10 means that you can do it clearly and immediately; 1 means that you can't do it and that you don't see anything (yet).

3. Every night before you fall asleep, visualize for five minutes one of the elements of the tennis game that you want to improve— technique, tactical play, physical or mental abilities.

There is a lot of chance that only after one week of practice, you may see significant results. Be open to this possibility. Visualization is a tool often used by high-level athletes to increase calm demeanor and focus during their performance. The only limit is your own mind.

19—COMPETITION AND TOURNAMENT PLAY

Competition is usually the driving force for any player to develop their game. The passion for the game makes you want to work harder to achieve your goals. Teaching and coaching the game of tennis also requires coaches to instruct players how to play and conduct themselves during competition. This is where all the training of technical, tactical, physical, and mental aspects needs to come together. Learning all these components gives you the knowledge on how to execute during practice but not always the capabilities to execute during competition. The reason for this is the level of pressure and expectations.

During competitive practice sessions, players are usually more relaxed. They are having fun, and there are fewer expectations on the outcome of winning and losing. In team events and tournaments, it becomes much more serious, and many more people are involved. Coaches, players, parents, and other spectators can extensively raise the level of anxiety. Players are very aware how people around them react differently during match play in practices versus tournaments. Take for instance the difference in attitude when playing a friendly match, a team tennis event, and a national tournament. The attitudes and reactions of players, coaches, parents, and spectators in all those events are different. This effect can be even more extreme when we are dealing with advanced players or pro players. They really shouldn't be since they are all forms of competition with the goal of improving your game. They are all perceived to be different as the expectation levels and importance of the matches change (money). It can become much more serious, and players can feel this pressure significantly. So how can we as coaches influence their performance for optimal results? The answer is this: keep it fun and challenging.

Making It Fun and Challenging

Making practice sessions and competitions fun is largely accomplished through positive and stimulating feedback. The type of instructions you provide as coaches and parents is crucial to the attitude toward practice and competition. Positive and stimulating feedback will be perceived as helpful to players, whereas the negative and/or derogatory comments will be perceived as irritating. Repetitious remarks or patronizing comments will eventually start to bug the player, and resentment and frustration can set in. Coaches and parents can alter the mood of a player by the tone of their voice. Keeping the mood light and encouraging will stimulate players to relax and perform better. Encourage and praise students whenever you find an opportunity. Be helpful by showing and reminding them how to execute rather than chastising their mistakes. The facial expressions of the instructor can become an important tool as well. A pleasant and relaxed expression will be perceived as stimulating and encouraging, while a stern or angry expression will often cause confusion and self-doubt. Making it fun for players to compete in team and/or individual events changes their outlook of the game in general and fuels their passion to excel. By challenging a player to reach a certain goal, you make them focus on the goal rather than their fears. It is a very good method to stimulate their positive thoughts and to create a healthy outlook on competition. Many players who struggle with anxiety in match play or who doubt their own ability can benefit from this method.

Preparation

Being successful in team and individual events is mostly due to the preparation. Proper training and conditioning can make a big difference to the outcome of any match or tournament. Players need to hone their skills by improving their technique, their strategy and patterns, their physical ability, and their mental toughness. Preparation for tournaments starts on the practice court long before a match is played. This process of preparation should be founded by a long-term plan with an ongoing development of all the skills. It takes a long time to develop a top player; and coaches, parents, and players should work toward those goals set forth together. They need to be on the same page with their plan and expectations, and patience will be a key factor to the success of all involved. There are several factors to keep in mind when preparing for a team and/or individual event. Below I will outline the most important factors:

- **Scheduling**
  The scheduling of tournaments and events needs to be organized in a logical and progressive manner to enable players to reach their goals each year and in the long term. The best way to do that is to start with the goals for the current year and compare that with the available yearly tournament schedule. Before completing this schedule, you need to look at the timeline of practice and competition and determine if the proper ratio is preserved for optimal results at the most important events. We call this periodization. You can make this even more detailed by inserting practice sessions for technical, tactical, physical, and mental aspects. However, when you plan your practice sessions, make sure that the preparation is functional to your short- and long-term goals.

- **Coaching**
  The buildup and preparation to an event is important to achieve the optimal results. The development of a player should be the main goal. When they are in a stabilizing phase, they can usually build on their results with the continued improvements. But there will also be weeks when the player has to improve by learning new topics. There are obviously subjects that are counterproductive to results. One of these can be an improvement or change to a stroke, but it can also be a progression of a strategy. Both developments can take away from the short-term results but will have a long-lasting effect on the improvements for future events. The trick is to use the

proper events to practice new subjects, to find other events to stabilize and improve confidence, and to finally peak at the major events.

As players become more advanced and proficient with their developments, it becomes easier to introduce changes and subjects. The changes are usually small adjustments, and the new subjects are usually improvements or progressions from previous methods. The subjects and type of practice will change as the event nears. The focus will change from a learning phase to a stabilizing phase then to a match phase. In the learning phase, the player is still experimenting with the topic. The stabilizing phase is the time to try out different methods to execute and to improve consistency and confidence. The match phase is when the player is solely focused on the execution during point or match play.

The preparation for team and individual events should include all facets of the game with technical, tactical, physical, and mental factors. The focus in the learning and stabilizing phase will be more on the technical, tactical, and physical aspects; whereas the focus changes to the tactical, physical, and mental aspects in the match phase, right before the event. As a final preparation, before the event, you do not want to have players focus on technique anymore. But instead, let them focus on how to play the game. This will require them to have an overall game plan or strategy for the match and for them to prepare a strategy before each point is played.

- **Preparing a Strategy**
  Being prepared for competition means you also have a game plan. This is where coaches can play an important role in teaching players how to be tactically prepared. This form of coaching becomes more important as players progress to intermediate and advanced levels of play. The strategy of how

to play the game can become a deciding factor in winning matches. Therefore, the only logical progression is to teach players how to analyze their opponent so they can develop a good game plan or strategy. By going over the strengths and weaknesses of both players, they should be able to find a strategy that can lead to specific tactics and patterns. Teaching players to make their own game plan will enhance their confidence once those plans come to a good conclusion.

- **Team Coaching versus Individual Coaching**
  The preparation for team events is somewhat different from individual tournaments. For team tennis events, you are dealing with all the different characters of the players on the team. It also requires individual strategies for each player and a lineup from top to bottom. The coach or captain has to make a choice on the double combinations in teaming them up properly to complement one another's game. Creating a good team environment, where each player is supporting one another, can be a deciding factor once the competition gets close in score.

- **Team Coaching**
  Coaching a team is quite different from coaching individual players. When coaching a team, the instructions and comments are most often directed at the whole team (but can also include some private sessions). This can be an advantage in the teaching and learning process. Corrections and improvements can easily be introduced by having the players demonstrate the exercises to one another. They learn from one another's mistakes and accomplishments and will be able to quickly adapt those in their game. Coaches will still have to individualize the instructions and corrections to the style of each player to optimize their performance. Discussing results and strategies afterward can be useful in team events, but it should also be done separately in a private conversation. Some subjects of match discussions are personal, and it is never a good idea to embarrass players by

bringing this forward in team discussions. Many times, there is on-court coaching involved with team tennis—think of college coaching or team tennis, the way they play in Europe. This method of coaching is very educational for players since they can obtain strategic advice on how to play. Coaches are able to provide advice during the changeover. Often, it is easier to see what strategy to play from the side than when you are playing yourself.

Knowing the Rules

Knowing the rules can work in your favor. This was also the case when I was coaching in the sixteen and under Junior Davis Cup competition played in Germany the summer of 2003.

It was a fierce competition, and we had advanced to the semifinal playoff against the host country, Germany. As a national coach, I was allowed to sit on the bench, just like regular Davis Cup, and coach the boys during their match. The boys on the team were Alex Kuznetsov, Timothy Neilly, and Michael Shabaz. Timothy Neilly started off as second singles, and it was a hard-fought match up until 3 all in the first set. I knew this was going to be a tough match for him to win and had to keep my wits about me. The opponent was serving, and at 15–30, the German hit the first serve out. The referee called it out as well but was not very vocal about it. I saw Tim look at me as he returned the ball and kept on playing. I looked up at the referee, but he showed no sign to stop the point. I knew then that that was the edge I was waiting for!

Timothy eventually lost the point, and I looked up at the referee and commented, "That point needs to be played again."

The referee looked at me perplexedly and answered, "But they played out the point." Now I already knew that if the ref had not stopped the point after he called the ball out, I could always ask him to replay the point, win or lose. I asked for the head referee to come to the court, and it was confirmed that the point needed to be replayed.

They replayed the point, and Tim won the point and was up 15–40 on the opponent's serve. That was all the leverage he needed and pushed ahead to win that game. The German boy got so upset that he had trouble keeping his emotions together, and it ended up being an easy victory after that game.

Now you could say as an observer that I unfairly took advantage of the situation. However, keep in mind that I, as a coach, am not able to stop the point; only the referee can do this. In this case, I had nothing to lose. If Tim had won the point, the other coach might have asked for the same ruling from the referee!

So you see, when coaching a match, it sometimes pays off to know the rules of tennis. It definitely paid off in that match!

Alex Kuznetsov is now working with Maria Sharapova, and Tim Neilly is a coach at a country club in Boca Raton. It's fun to see them every time we meet.

A Defining Moment

During international league tennis matches, I have been involved with many strange situations. Sitting on that bench can be very frustrating. This next story is a good example.

I was coaching the international league team to play another team in the Netherlands. The surface was red clay, like most of the surfaces in Europe. The number 1 player on our team was Glenn Schaap, a challenger player from Amsterdam. After arriving at our destination, I strolled over to the courts to look over the opponents. There was a Swedish guy on their team, and I had heard he was pretty good. I only needed a short while to see he had lived up to his reputation. I made some mental notes on his strengths and weaknesses and went back to the locker room. I had a little chat with Glenn and reported what I had seen. I started to tell him what I thought he should do against this guy, but he seemed not very interested and told me, "I got this one!" This comment worried me. I never liked to see a player become too cocky. I added a last comment: "You better be ready for this guy." And the guy I was talking about had just entered the top hundred ATP under the name of Jonas Björkman!

We went to the court, and they started the match. I was still somewhat uneasy about his casual and cocky attitude. I must say that Glenn surprised me in a big way. After just one game, Glenn had seen enough and sat down at the changeover (they still had the break in those days) and asked me, "So what do you want me to do?" I had already worked out the strategy against Jonas and proceeded to discuss this with him in detail.

To my surprise, he was very disciplined in his execution of the strategy, and the match started to turn in his favor. He slowly started to grind him down, and the mistakes were piling up for Jonas. Glenn was slowly gaining control over the match and won the first set with a score of 6–2. After the set, he sat down and said, "So what now?"

"Now you start attacking him," I said. "I want you to attack his return and throw in a few serve and volleys."

He looked at me in surprise. "Serve and volley on clay?"

"Absolutely, don't slow down," I added. And to his credit, he didn't and played flawless tennis to beat Jonas Björkman (6–2, 6–1). It was one of the best matches I had seen him play.

To me that was a great example of the player understanding very quickly that he had made an error in judgment and better take all the help he could get. To me that was a defining moment for Glenn Schaap, and it served him well. You either define the moment or the moment will define you! Glen is working as a coach on the pro tour, and we regularly run into each other at tour events.

On-court coaching takes some getting used to. It takes just as much training to do as any other skill in tennis. Knowing what to say, when to say it, and how to say it are the important skills a coach needs to learn through practice in life situations. A player is not always used to having someone talk to them during a match. In most cases, the player uses that time to focus and think about their strategy. In some cases, the player uses that time to relax and not think about too many topics at all. Either way, if they are focused and on their game, they feel invigorated and motivated. They are like in a trance, also called in the zone. With on-court coaching, this state of mind is more difficult to reach when coaches are talking too much (overcoaching). Sometimes it is better not to say too much, especially if things are going well. Being supportive and encouraging can be important to keep the momentum going. If you see some problems arising in their game, try to analyze it first for yourself and decide how to communicate this information as clearly as possible. Your directions should be focused on strategy, unless there is an easy fix to a problem that is causing the strategy to fail. Giving players too much information will confuse them, so keep your advice short and to the point. You will be more successful with on-court coaching, and your players will soar in performance.

Team events can be very inspiring to players and can lift them to higher levels of play. The group concept can alleviate the fears players might experience when playing their tournaments on their own. Being part of a team provides mental support from the other team members in practice and competition. The concept of playing for a team instead of yourself can be very liberating and stimulating. The fear or anxiety is often replaced by a sense of responsibility toward the group. There have been many players who initially struggled with their performance in individual events but later on improved their game in team events. In many cases, this was achieved through the camaraderie and support they experienced from the other team members. Confidence is the key here. (The same can be the case with improving your singles game through the improvements you make in doubles play.)

Individual Coaching

Coaching individual players is easier to organize since you only have to deal with one player. You can fully focus your attention on this individual and make easier adjustments in practice, scheduling, and coaching during matches. There is more pressure to perform as a coach, and parents and players expect instant results. This quicker progression is not actually true. Players don't always get more results in working individually with a coach. It is possible but not a guarantee. It mostly depends on the character of the student and their learning traits. Some work better in groups, and some better individually.

Private coaching can be very boring for players when they have little interaction with other players. The competition against other players of the same level is important to practice strategies, patterns, and shot choices. Physical training works well on an individual basis, but with younger students, they work harder when some form of competition is included. So this requires other students joining in.

In my career, I have had many individual coaching jobs. Some of the jobs were in coaching players on the ITF junior tour, some on the professional tour, and then there were also the special assignments of getting players in college positions. Here are some testimonials of their experience:

I started working with Martin the summer after my junior year in high school. He immediately gave me an evaluation of my strengths and weaknesses and what I needed to change off the bat. We then went on to training four hours a day along with physical training for the next two months, in preparation for tournaments. Throughout the time that I got to know Martin, we became closer and had experiences that we still laugh and joke about to this day. Not only was he a great tennis coach but also a great chef! Martin cared so much about me, and really wanted to develop me as a player but also as a person. He took interest in my life to make sure not just the tennis aspect was good but also my emotional and social aspect of growing up. Without him, I would have never reached my goals in tennis and in life. When it came to recruiting and going off to college, he really helped with talking to coaches and pushing me to the best school I could go to. Now that I've been studying at Indiana University for two years, I still call Martin a few times a month to discuss how I'm playing in practice, as well as matches. During summer breaks I love to go down to Miami Beach and train to get feedback as well to improve my game. His new academy has great coaches and is a great environment for upcoming junior players! I loved being part of the academy and am excited to see its development!

—Madison Appel, Indiana University

Madison Appel

I grew up playing competitive tennis in Southwest Florida. I had always known that I wanted to play Division 1 tennis at the highest level and needed to prepare the right way in order for this dream to become a reality. I met Martin van Daalen right before the summer of my junior year when I was coming off multiple injuries. For those of you who want to play college tennis, you know this is a crucial time as you start to get recruited by college coaches. Naturally, this was a very stressful time for me as I had a lot of pressure to perform this coming year. Martin was able to help me during my time of need not only with my physical game but also my mental game. I was able to reach number 2 in Florida and top 30 in the nation and was recruited by coaches all over the country as Martin has a vast network and a good relationship with many of these coaches. I ultimately ended up committing to the University of Florida under Martin's guidance. Playing at the University of Florida has been one of the best experiences of my life. I was ranked top 100 collegiately in both singles and doubles, part of a team top 5 in the nation, reached the elite 8 in the NCAA tournament, and I was part of a team that won the Southeastern Conference Tournament Championship. None of this would have been possible without Martin.

—Josh Wardell, University of Florida

Martin van Daalen played an instrumental role regarding the success of my tennis career. With a very strong coaching background, Martin is able to portray his message to his students in a unique, custom-to-the-student way. With his even keel, "take it easy" mentality, Martin gave me some of the push necessary to become a scholarship collegiate tennis player for the University of Florida. Collegiate tennis is some of the most fun I've had as a tennis player. Going to school at the early age of 17, I played number 6 as a freshman. Remembering some of the useful tools Coach van Daalen gave me as a junior, I was able to work my way up the lineup to eventually playing number 1 as a senior. Thank you for everything MVD!

—Spencer Newman, University of Florida

Coaching players individually at tournaments can be a difficult task that requires a lot of patience. Coaches have very little influence, coaching wise, once the match starts. Unlike the on-court coaching, coaches are not able to communicate with the player. Corrections and instructions are only possible before and after the match. Nevertheless, it is still very much a common practice with parents and coaches alike to coach during matches. In many ways, the coaches, parents, and spectators can be distracting to a player, making it more difficult for them to focus and to get in the zone. Whenever a player starts listening to the comments or remarks from the side or starts wandering with their eyes, it usually will avert their attention and focus off the court rather than on the court. There usually will be a loss of concentration that causes players to change the way they play or play without a specific strategy. Encouraging a player during a match can be supportive, especially when they have just hit a great shot. Support during a match can also be useful when a player is feeling disappointed after playing a bad point, game, or set. As long as the encouragements and comments are positive and not made too repetitive, they can assist a player in their efforts. When they become too frequent in nature, it becomes more distracting and detrimental to concentration. So the key to successful coaching is to be supportive with positive encouragements when appropriate.

Match Analysis

The most important part of coaching players at tournaments should be done after the match with a match analysis. This is where the learning process begins for every player.

If both player and coach have done their preparation properly, they have trained to get ready for competition and figured out a game plan for the match. During a match, there are several factors that will influence the outcome of a match:

The technical aspects of the game are influenced by the execution of the strokes. The technical quality of the strokes can have positive and negative effects on the execution of the strategy (tactical aspects). Players with higher technical skills will have more consistency and more options in choosing different strategies. More consistency in the strokes will reduce the fear of failure and stress level of a player (mental aspects). Good technique will also help the efficiency of the strokes and save much more energy over the course of a match (physical endurance). So as we make an analysis of the match with a student, we need to discuss the technical execution and how it influenced all the other factors during competition.

The tactical aspects of the game are determined by the execution of the strategy or game plan. A game plan or strategy is made up of different tactics and are executed with patterns and shot choices according to the defensive, neutral, or offensive situations and options of play. A player with high technical, physical, and mental skills will have a higher chance of executing the strategy with success. The analysis of the tactical execution during a match needs to be discussed with the player after the match in order to learn from possible mistakes. Players have to learn to be objective without taking the comments and remarks personally. Explaining how the strategy can work better in a nonjudgmental fashion can alleviate emotional feelings and responses.

The physical aspects have become much more prevalent in today's tennis matches. With the advancements in racket and string technology, the game has sped up tremendously. The increase in speed and tempo of the rallies has amplified the importance of the speed and agility of the footwork in combination with the strokes. The training of tennis athletes has become part of everyday workouts to improve explosiveness, coordination, strength, speed, stamina, balance, and flexibility. Part of the analysis after the match has to include the physical aspects and how they affected the outcome of the match.

The mental aspects have a large influence on the technical, tactical, and physical execution during a match. Keeping the emotions under control during practice and match play will assist a player greatly to control the strokes during the rallies. Staying calm will keep a player relaxed so they can execute the strokes without muscling the movements of the body and to increase coordination, fluidity, and efficiency. Being in a state of relaxed alertness provides a player the possibility to play the points in match play with controlled aggression and to think clearly on tactics and shot choices. The moment this mental state is disturbed, it will negatively affect the execution. The mental aspects and its effects on the rest of the game need to be a large part of the analysis and discussions after the match to enhance the performance in competition.

<u>MATCH ANALYSIS</u>

Player   :   Game style   :
Date   :   Age   :

	<u>Strength</u>	<u>Weakness</u>
Technique		
Tactics		
Mentality		
Conditioning		

The form above is a great tool to structure the match analysis of a player. They are able to create a method of thinking by filling in the blanks and discussing it later with their coach. Rather than providing them the information upfront, players have to think about all aspects of the match and reason what went well and what topics need improvement. In using this method, you are teaching players to coach themselves and to make better strategy choices in future matches. They also can use this documentation as a reference when playing the same or similar opponents.

Recap on Coaching

Coaches often make many mistakes. Not necessarily on purpose, but because they don't have the proper coaching education or don't have enough experience. The sad thing is that many students suffer in their development because of coaches making mistakes in coaching and teaching with their behaviors and attitude. Here are some of the most common mistakes:

Mistake No. 1—Being Too Nice
Have you noticed when students don't listen to their coaches? I am sure you have seen kids who act rude and/or talk back. Some of this is the change of behavior in school, but it definitely has to do with creating a friendly relationship instead of teacher-student relationship. They don't have to like you, but they have to respect you as a coach and possible mentor. You should not seek their approval on what you are trying to teach. Players don't work hard because you are nice to them. They work hard and win because of their skills and their mental toughness. Being nasty is not the answer either. Just be your pleasant self but be tough by example in what you want to teach. You can't manipulate students by being nice, but you might be able to if they see you don't demand anything from them you haven't done yourself.

Mistake No. 2—Being Negative

This is the opposite of the attitude and behavior of mistake no. 1. Instead of being too nice, you see the coach berating his students. Yelling all the time and belittling them is also not the right way. We see this coaching style in old football movies, but this is not a coaching style that will make your students respect you. I actually know many coaches who have adopted this conditional love method to toughen up players. A large percentage of them will fold under this negative approach. I am not saying you should never raise your voice. It will be necessary at times, but the words don't have to be negative. Just be firm and tell them to pick it up and do a better job. If you are too negative and you criticize too much, they will go from bad to worse.

Mistake No. 3—Trying to Help Athletes Perform Better by Correcting Them

What do most coaches do when they see an athlete make a mistake? They correct them right away. The coach is obviously trying to help, but it rarely works like that. It's true that about 5–10 percent of athletes (usually the best ones) will take a verbal correction and implement it immediately. The rest will nod, smile, and say, "Okay, Coach!" and then pretty much go back to exactly what they were doing. This is maddening.

Here is the proper approach: wait till they fail multiple times and then ask them what they think about their execution. They might never say they are doing any of the things wrong that you might notice. There is the problem. So when you are mentioning to bend their knees, they might feel they are already doing that. The only way you are going to make a change is to make them feel the difference in bending their knees. Show them by example and make them do it to feel it. The vast majority of verbal corrections don't work. Find out what your athlete responds to and use it more often.

Mistake No. 4—Failing to Believe in Your Athlete

When you give a struggling student extra attention and compliments to boost their confidence, you might actually get the reverse results. How many times have you given a struggling athlete extra attention, pep talks, and compliments to boost their confidence, only to watch them get worse and worse? You can't make a quick fix by giving them more attention or a pep talk. If you do this in an obvious way, kids perceive it as not believing in them. Treat them the same way as others so they don't think of themselves as inadequate.

Mistake No. 5—Not Knowing How to Get Your Athlete Out of a Slump

Every athlete gets to be in a slump sometime or another. Telling them to be positive is not the answer to the problem. There is always a reason why a player gets to be in a slump. The way out is to find out the reason why this happened in order to fix it.

Mistake No. 6—Not Getting Help

This is the worst mistake of all. This is the mistake that prevents most coaches from achieving the kind of success they really want. As a coach, you are used to having all the answers. That will not work all the time, and being stubborn will not solve the problem. Sometimes there is a necessity to get advice from others to get a better perspective.

Tournament Play

1. Preparation

Being prepared for competition is the key to success for any tennis player. Proper preparation means being ready for any situation that might occur. The only way you can do this is by training and playing practice matches to gain experience. Here are the various ways you can prepare for the tournaments and matches:

A.   preseason preparation
B.   pretournament preparation
C.   match preparation
D.   rest (active rest) and recovery

And all these training sessions have to include the following items:

- technical preparation   - by training and mastering your strokes
- physical preparation   - with intensity on on-court and off-court training
- tactical preparation   - in many practices and match situations
- mental preparation   - with practice sessions with points and discussions
- match preparation   - routines developed in practice matches

When you are a tournament player, you need to be ready not only to win a match but also to win multiple matches in a row. For juniors, this means playing at least two singles matches and possibly two (pro set) doubles matches. As a college player, you could play a double header (meaning playing a pro-set doubles), followed by a singles match, and then doing that again in the afternoon. When playing ITF juniors or pro events, you could play one singles and one doubles match in a day. But that all changes if it rains. And in playing ITF juniors and pro events, you often play three weeks in a row. Winning tournaments in a row is the most difficult achievement. In order to do that, you have to be in great physical shape and have mental stamina to last several weeks.

Preseason Preparation

In this particular training period, you lay the groundwork of your tournament and match preparation. The training is quite rigorous, and the better the work ethic, the better the results. Tough training often leads to mental toughness and stamina. The training program needs to be precise and diverse to reach your goals while at the same time being educational, stimulating, and maintaining a pleasant training environment and having fun. The focus in the preseason is on coordination, strength, stamina, and flexibility. Speed and intensity can be involved in the afternoon sessions and in the practice matches but are not the focus in the training sessions. Speed and intensity are more trained in the physical training and with footwork drills and on the track. Coordination is best trained when the maximum power is not above 60 percent. Therefore, much time needs to be spent in grooving the strokes while practicing patterns and tactical situations to create familiarity and efficiency in movement. The program should look something like the one below:

Day	Time	Type	Time	Type
Monday	9–11 and 1–3	tennis/match play	4–5:30	weight training
Tuesday	9–11 and 1–3	tennis/match play	4–5	footwork/track
Wednesday	9–11	tennis	1–2:30	weight training
Thursday	9–11 and 1–3	tennis/match play	4–5	footwork/track
Friday	9–11 and 1–3	tennis/match play	4–5:30	weight training
Saturday	9–11	match play	1–2	footwork/track
Sunday		rest		rest

With a program like this, the basis is laid to improve the technical, tactical, physical, and mental aspects of the game. The body and mind are both prepared to compete at the highest individual level possible. With the technical training, this means improving the fundamentals of all strokes. With the physical training, this means improving the coordination, stamina, strength, speed, and flexibility to its optimal performance. For the strategic training, this means practicing patterns and shot choices in many different tactical situations in point and match situations. The mental training starts with tough training and competitive match practice to enhance the resilience during tournaments. The tougher the player trains, the tougher they are in competition. It is possible to do too much in not taking a break in the middle of the week and/or not taking a day off to physically and mentally recover. Overtraining is not only unusual but also avoidable when training is fun and done together with other players. A shared burden is much easier to take than working alone!

Pretournament Preparation

The preparation right before playing a tournament is different from preseason. The pretournament preparation is much more competitive-specific. The training is not so much focused on duration of training (stamina) but should be more focused on the intensity, strategy, and point play. So practice times will be reduced to one-and-half-hour sessions, but intensity is high, and focus on performance should be higher. Physical training is also reduced, and all motions and practices are focused on speed and the intensity of performance. This change of the training duration gives players the opportunity to relax and focus before a high-level competition so performance can be most optimal.

Match Preparation

Getting ready for a match takes discipline and years of training. You don't want to go unprepared into a match. (I found that out the hard way when I played my first match at the age of twelve. I played the number 1 seed and lost first round 6–0, 6–0.) Obviously, you need to do some scouting to find out more about your opponent. Second, you need to make a game plan and discuss this together with a coach and player. And then the day of the match arrives. You have to make sure all your equipment is ready and your rackets are freshly strung and the grips on your racket are new. Make sure you have brought food and drinks and plenty of replacement clothes and towels. You need to arrive at a time that allows you to do a physical warm-up, a warm-up on court, and some time to eat and replenish fluids before your match.

a. Physical warm-up (twenty to forty minutes)
The physical warm-up is extremely important to be optimally prepared for matches. You need to start off slow and increase the intensity over time. Warm up all muscle groups (legs, trunk, shoulders, and arms). The warm-up should include dynamic stretching, running, footwork and arm exercises, change of direction drills, and sprints. You can also use tennis balls to toss around to speed up your footwork and increase hand-eye coordination in catching the balls.

b. Strokes warm-up (thirty to forty minutes)
Warming up your strokes for competitive play is an important part of the match preparation. You have to take it slow and be very deliberate with your execution to ensure automation and consistency during the match. Focus on consistency to increase the confidence in your performance. Keep the intensity of the strokes and footwork to a level where you can easily control the ball at all times.

The quality of the strokes during the warm-up can positively influence the quality of play in the match, but it should not be used as a grade for winning or losing the match. You make your own destiny by how you respond to all the situations and how you adjust to them with the decisions you make.

c. Prematch (ten minutes)
Right before your match is called and you go on court, the anxiety can get very high. Nerves can be good to enhance performance, but it can also get to a point where they decrease your performance. To offset the increase of anxiety, you should have the routine of

Martin van Daalen

running some sprints and performing some form of shadow training to mimic the movements of your feet and the strokes. This type of routine will assist the muscle memory in the beginning of the match when most errors are made due to a lack of rhythm and coordination. Make the movements as realistic as possible in your mind by visualizing point play, starting with a serve or return, and then playing out the point.

Rest and Recovery

Getting sufficient rest and recovering from matches and tournaments are just as important as the training itself. Without sufficient rest, there is no performance increase. With the body exerting energy through training, the body will adjust during the rest period by supplying more energy than what was previously available. This cycle is called training compensation or supercompensation (see chapter on training).

If the training units follow one another too fast without proper rest for the muscles and nervous system, the reverse will be the case, with less energy available. If this cycle is repeated many times, it can lead to overtraining.

Active Rest

After completing a tournament or tournament series, it is advisable to take some time off to let the body recuperate and recharge. Taking two or three days off is totally fine, but active rest is the best way to recover. With active rest, we mean an activity that is fun and requires less energy to perform. This could be jogging, swimming, or biking. These types of active rest heal the muscles and tendons much quicker and take away stiffness and soreness. Yoga, massage, or any other form of relaxation is obviously also a great way to recuperate while stretching all the muscle groups.

2. Game Plan

Having a game plan is always better than not having a plan. A game plan provides the strategic structure to your brain and in turn increases consistency and rhythm. By making a game plan, you increase your chances of success in competition. You would be surprised how many players do not have a game plan before they start their match. So if you construct a plan, you are already ahead of the curve. A game plan should include serve and return tactics, what patterns to use, what to watch for from your opponent, and a plan B, in case your first plan does not work.

3. Pressing

Pressing is a common factor in competitive play when players pressure themselves to higher performance beyond their control and comfort level. They often start hitting harder, playing faster, and taking more risk than necessary. As tennis players, you will all experience this at one point. As a less-experienced player, you will not recognize it so easily. Learning to stay at a level where performance and execution of your game is optimal is the key to good play. Overexerting yourself or forcing the situation can lead to many more unforced errors and losing momentum in the match.

Pressing can occur in many different ways. It is possible to start pressing when the opponent starts increasing the speed and intensity of play. Instead of using the speed and redirecting the ball, it is easy to be drawn into hitting the ball at a faster pace and doing too much. When you are playing regular rallies, it is normal to accelerate the ball to surprise the opponent by changing the rhythm. When young or less-experienced players accelerate the ball, they have the tendency to stay in that rhythm and end up pressing too hard and not slowing down to rally speed again. The experience of match play will teach you over time what your speed of play should be and how to increase it slowly (without pressing) as you improve your game. Most players try to hit too hard, and most juniors believe that ball speed relates to being a better player. Nothing could be further from the truth. Yes, applying proper pressure on your opponent is necessary to keep them from constantly attacking you or putting you in difficult situations. But pressing too hard only puts more pressure on yourself instead of on the opponent.

4. Playing Up

As you progress as a player, you will start playing in different age groups or levels. You should try to play three different levels of tournaments:

- tournaments to win
- tournaments to finish in quarter- or semifinal
- tournaments to qualify at higher level

By playing the different levels, you can experiment with your strokes and tactics to enhance your performance at all levels. Playing up can help you to play more freely since there really is nothing to lose when playing with older players. You can learn from them and gain experience on how to play at that level. Playing up does generally increase the speed of play and teaches you to focus more on footwork, strategy, and early preparation. You might need to play more consistently at a higher tempo and react quicker to tactical situations. Not being used to these things could mean losing some matches to gain experience. As long as you understand this and are willing to invest in your game, playing up is a good thing to try. If you are not quite ready for this level change, it can be a traumatic experience. So how do you know when to play up? It's quite simple actually: first dominate in your own level before playing up! You can also watch your win-loss record and decide to play up based on that.

5. Creating Momentum in Your Matches

Momentum in a match is the flow of winning points to keep the advantage in your favor. Momentum is important to keep the pressure on your opponent and to make them think they have little chance of beating you. Momentum makes you feel you are winning most of the points and gives you confidence throughout the match that you will be successful in the end. The scoreboard is one of the key factors to create momentum. Here are some factors that influence momentum:

- having a game plan
- commitment of play
- intensity
- focus on certain points in the game, set, and match
- not slowing down

To gain momentum, you have to use a game plan with commitment and intensity. Having a game plan gives you direction and strategy to combat your opponent and win the majority of the points. Starting a match the proper way with high-percentage play creates momentum through consistency and taking advantage of unforced errors from the opponent. The intensity during play ensures the speed and tempo of the rallies to decrease the opportunities for opponents to take initiative. At the same time, it creates pressure and options to open the court and score points. When losing points, players have to increase the intensity in the next points to ensure they don't lose the momentum. A good rule of thumb is to not lose two points in a row and to try to do the opposite to your opponent. Winning certain points in a game is very advantageous to gaining momentum. The first points in each game create a scoreboard pressure. Some players are really focused on this, and if you are not, they will take advantage of you every time. The 30–0, 30–15, or 30–30 are important points as well since the following point creates a game point. The same goes for 40–0, 40–15, or 40–30. Don't slow down on these points. That will only help your opponent gain their confidence and renew their efforts to compete with you. The moment you slow down, your opponent will play stronger. Juniors make this mistake all the time, and instead of finishing the game, they end up playing multiple extra points, with no security to win the game. The score in the set also has a momentum. The seventh game is the magical game to watch (5–1, 4–2, and 3–3). Winning the seventh game will give you the momentum in the set, with a higher percentage chance of winning the set. Many of the coaches and experienced players are aware of this. So if you don't pay attention to this fact, you will often be on the losing end. When leading in score, don't slow down. Too many times, you see players taking a physical or mental break only to pay the price later. Become a good front-runner when leading in score and finish the match before relaxing. It will save you a lot of grief, make you play with momentum, make you play more efficiently, and give you the opportunity to not only win more matches but also win more tournaments. When things are not going your way and the momentum is not flowing your way, there are several things you can do:

- increase your intensity to apply more pressure on your opponent
- change your strategy to gain advantage with a different method
- slow down the game with high topspin or slice to deregulate your opponent
- take more time in between points to make your opponent lose their rhythm
- control the moment before the moment controls you

6. Performing Under Pressure

Performing in high-level competition can be quite stressful. Learning how to deal with this pressure is a skill that needs to be mastered over time. The pressure you feel just before you go on the court is real. The pressure you feel when you step on the court to play the first game is reflected in the weakness and sluggish feeling in your legs and arms. The pressure of playing in a large stadium and not wanting to fail in front of all these spectators makes you anxious. You have to ask yourself what you are afraid of most: losing the match or making a fool of yourself in front of all these people. The answer is, you should not be afraid of either! There are matches you will win, and there are matches you will lose. And all those people don't really know you or your capabilities. They are there to watch good tennis, and you are going to show them what that looks like. As you can see, it is all about perspective and attitude. Here are some points for you to consider concerning performing under pressure:

- a positive perspective and attitude
- give it a 100 percent effort all the time
- make every pressure point a fun challenge
- prepare for optimal performance
- practice under pressure
- keep your strategy simple
- be committed to your strokes

The positive perspective is that you can win any match if you give yourself a chance. Playing with fear is always a bad recipe and will lead to disaster. The attitude of a performer is to give your best possible effort. Giving less than a 100 percent effort gives you less chances to succeed. Every player knows when they play their best matches, and they always include 100 percent effort and a competitive and fun challenge to beat your opponent. In those circumstances, players forget about their fear of losing and try much harder to win. So how do I recreate that environment by myself when I play? First of all, I have to prepare properly to set the tone and focus. Being ready for competition gives confidence and self-belief in your performance. Sometimes players become so nervous before competition that they make all the classical mistakes in preparation. They are chatting with other competitors, and this can increase anxiety by worrying about other subjects. They lose time in their preparation and don't warm up enough or sometimes not at all. So it is better to do the warm-up alone, focus on the points of your strategy, and make some goals of improvements in your game. By secluding yourself a little bit before the match, you bring your brain at rest, and you can even meditate to calm yourself down with slow deep breaths. And then right before the match, jogging and running some sprints will greatly reduce any fear you might have before the match. Many top players also use some shadow tennis and meditation as if they are playing some points without the ball.

Martin van Daalen

"Emotional players don't make smart players."

"Practice makes perfect." And the same goes for performing under pressure. The practice matches are the place to learn how to deal with pressure. To do that, you have to take the outcome of the matches out of the equation. If you are too worried about losing, you will be too emotional. And emotional players don't make smart players. They make nervous players who don't perform well under pressure. Keep your focus in your practice matches on your strategy and try to perform even better and more disciplined on important points in the games, sets, or matches. You will only start competing better in tournaments after showing emotional control in practice matches.

Once on court and starting the match, keep things simple! It is a golden rule that is broken by many—even by experienced players. Keeping it simple means having a simple game plan on how to play against your opponent and playing big targets to execute your strategy. Opening up the angles on the court and playing too close to the lines will only bring unforced errors (or in junior tennis, the opportunity to call balls out). This simple method actually forces your opponent to take initiative (and risk) first while providing you with angles to strike back. The commitment needed to act is the last factor of importance. Being brave to hit the ball to the selected target takes courage. The courage to commit is a character trait of champions, and you can recognize the ones who have this as a natural gift. They are not scared to hit the ball hard when needed and are committed to hitting passing shots or hitting winners to the open court. They don't feel these shot choices as fearful shots but more as challenging shots to pull off in a crucial situation. They hit enough of them to know that the commitment to the shots is necessary to be successful. Once you follow these methods long enough, the confidence in your shots increases and you are able to perform under pressure.

7. How to Compete without Fear

Like most athletes, every now and again, you'll get hit by the unpleasant feeling of performance anxiety. Even if you are the most positive athlete out there and you have not experienced this ever before, it could suddenly hit you. Most often, your anxiety happens because of a change in your expectations or because you start to focus on the outcome (results) of the match. Obviously, you cannot control the outcome of the match, so your anxiety grows. If you are able to control this emotion, you obviously would become a much better competitor and enjoy your game a lot more. So what should you focus on instead? Instead of being obsessed with winning and rankings, you should strive for a much higher goal—becoming the best competitive tennis player you can be. Most top players in the game are doing just that. They don't play for the money; they play for the excellence of their performance! If fear of performance is your weakness, you could turn it into your strength. You can start off by choosing performance goals in each match that need improvement. For example, you could set a goal of making a certain first-serve percentage, or it could be to try to make every first game point or make every overhead. There are obviously many goals you can set for yourself. They all will make you focus on improvement rather than results!

8. Building Self-Belief and Confidence

Building your confidence and self-belief is an important factor to learn and maintain in every sport, but especially in tennis. Competing in tennis is complicated, as you are alone out there, with no coaching or guidance. On the big stage, at Grand Slams, it is like being in a gladiator arena; but in this case, it's the athletes fighting it out, dueling one on one for the big prize. All tennis players experience doubts and the fear of losing when competing at any level; but it is the mentally tough players with grit, character, and perseverance who prevail. Understanding what you need to focus on is the key to controlling your nerves and believing in your skills. Some of the things you can't control are these:

- winning or losing (depends on skill level and experience)
- how good you play (depends on skill level and form of the day)
- who you play against (learn to focus on your game plan, not the opponent)
- when you play (the schedule decides the time, so prepare accordingly)

But there are a lot of factors you can control. They might not have an impact on the results, but they definitely have an impact on your performance. Those factors are as follows:

- preparation (your preparation has a large impact on performance)
- game plan (have a plan on how to combat your opponent)
- intensity of play (the physical and mental intensity should be optimal)
- try 100 percent (always give yourself the most chances to win)
- show competitive attitude (positive attitude, grit, perseverance)
- have competitive goals of improvement (improvement versus results)

Focus on the things you can control rather than focusing on the things you can't. If you do these things, you will become a great competitor and excel beyond your wildest dreams. Your confidence and self-belief will soar when your plans and goals work out the way you planned them. Confidence and self-belief also will increase as your results follow. They are linked together. But it is possible to turn it around with a skill called visualization. This skill teaches you to see yourself the way you imagine. This could be in the form of visualizing how you perform your strokes or copying a certain player's style and imagining yourself playing like that.

9. Visualization

Most tennis players don't use visualization, and the ones who use it probably don't know how to do it properly or have never been taught how. Golfers use this skill all the time to envision the ball flight before they step up to the ball and make their stroke. Most athletes don't believe in it, and very few actually have the skills to use it to their advantage. Visualization is imagination in your mind. It is a very useful resource to improve your performance to a high level.

> I used to do it myself all the time with my preparation before the matches. I would find a quiet spot in the locker room, where others could not disturb me, and close my eyes to enhance my inner thoughts. I would imagine the way I would start the match and how I was moving and hitting the ball. I would imagine how confident I was in striking the ball with commitment, how intense I was, and how consistent I would play. What strategies I would use and what improvement goals I had. All these took no more than five minutes, and by then I was ready to play. It always had a positive impact on my game, and I used it throughout my playing career.

Visualization is of images happens the following ways:

- memory   (recollecting how you execute stroke or movement)
- imagination   (envisioning yourself in a future or previous situation)
- environment   (visual example or demonstration)

In working with young national players at the moment, you see them struggling with their confidence, attitude, and emotions all the time. They always focus too much on their results, overanalyzing their problems and focusing on the things they can't do. Instead they need to focus on the road ahead and their goals and necessary improvements. I will have to teach them how to visualize better!

10. Winning When Playing Bad

Very rarely will you play your best tennis when you want to. The form of the day can fluctuate a little, and every day, one factor in your game can work better than others. So how do you win your matches when you are playing bad or performing beneath your normal level of play? There are certain things you can do to not make matters worse and not beat yourself up:

- Have a simple game plan. Keep your strategy and style of play simple to eliminate unforced errors as much as possible.
- Play big targets. By sticking to large target areas, you eliminate easy errors and opportunities of opponents calling balls out. This also keeps angles smaller for opponents to strike winners.
- Slow down your style of play with higher topspin or slice strokes to slow the tempo of play and make it more difficult for the opponent to hit winners or open the court for more angles.
- Hang in there and stay close in score to keep the opponent under pressure. You never know when the opponent will make mistakes or get tired.

I have witnessed many matches where players were not playing their best tennis but were able to eventually win by keeping the pressure on the opponent and not giving up. Grit and perseverance are important mental skills to win matches when you are not playing your best tennis.

11. Coaching Yourself

An important mental skill in tennis matches is self-coaching. Learning how to coach and what to say (think) at the right time is a skill learned through experience. Self- coaching can help you support yourself in difficult situations. It helps you to push yourself on and to persevere in tough situations, when everything seems to go against you. Self-coaching should not be confused with negative self-talk (comments) that you often see players do when they are frustrated with themselves and make bad comments on their performance. Self-coaching is supposed to be positive in nature and is helpful to make you perform better. Here are some examples of self-coaching:

- "Come on, keep playing tough."
- "You can do this."
- "Focus on your strategy."
- "Pick up intensity."

All these forms of self-coaching are quite normal with competitive players. You can often see them softly discussing situations and strategies with themselves. Make it a habit to do this in a positive way to win more matches.

12. How to Play Against Better and Weaker Players

Besides your own level of play, you will compete against different levels of play many times. Sometimes the opponents will be weaker, and sometimes they will be stronger in skill level. There are some classical mistakes that players make in these situations. Below are some of those examples.

Against weaker opponents
- sloppy or careless attitude
- less intensity
- tentative commitment to strokes/strategy
- unforced errors caused by anxiety

Against stronger opponents
- overhitting
- risky target choices
- pressing (muscling) strokes
- unforced errors by self-imposed pressure

The mistakes players make against both skill levels are quite common and can be avoided by using the proper intensity of play with the appropriate strategy. Take both matches seriously and don't try to press too hard against the better players or try to play it cool against the weaker players. Respect all players in their skill level and try to take all matches seriously. That way you will have more success overall.

13. How Routines and Habits Help Your Game

Routines and habits in competitive play assist players to keep their focus. Routines are customs developed over time to stay on track and to play efficiently. Habits are behaviors during competition that help the players feel a rhythm and familiarity of play by repeating the same behaviors over and over. Here are some examples of *routines* that have a positive effect on play:

- taking your time in between points by going to your towel to focus and relax
- looking at your strings in between points so as not to get distracted
- walking back behind the baseline after each point to strategize the next point
- setting up before each point in an athletic ready position to react better
- bouncing the ball before the serve gives rhythm and focus before execution

Here are some examples of *habits* that have a positive effect:

- being on time for practice sessions and preparations for matches
- having a warm-up routine before matches
- having your equipment and drinks/snacks ready for matches
- scouting your opponent for a tactical game plan
- cooling down after the match
- discussing feedback with the coach for details on performance

As you can imagine, all these aspects will have an effect on the performance of the matches and results in tournaments. It is advisable to train these routines and habits with your students. With young players, it can be helpful to videotape their routines in between points so that they can see for themselves what their body language and general attitude looks like. I promise you, they will be surprised!

14.   Learning from the Champions

You can learn a lot from watching top players in practice and competition. It can teach you how they practice and what their routines are. It can teach you how they deal with different game styles and strategies with their patterns and shot choices. You will be able to see how they start matches, when they accelerate, and how they finish off games, sets, and matches. You can view how they deal with tough situations and what their attitudes and demeanors are in match situations. Try to not only copy their strokes but also study their strategies, movements, and footwork. But most importantly, try to copy their professional behavior; it will make the largest difference in your play and results.

15.   Professional Attitude

Your attitude and behavior will have the largest impact on your performance in practices, matches, and tournament plays. It requires you to have a mature approach with your conduct and be able to stay calm at all times even though there might be some frustrating situations. Keeping your cool at all times opens up the possibility for discussions and learning. A professional behavior and mature attitude speed up the process of development exponentially. Not only do you learn and perform better in practice but the learning process will also extend to your matches play as well. The ultimate learning tool of champions!

20—TRANSITIONAL PLAYERS

Transitional players are the competitors in between junior and pro levels. They strive to compete at the highest level in their age group and often have to make a choice between going to college or playing future and/or challenger events. Most top college players also compete on the pro tour whenever their schedules permit. In this phase, not everyone can start playing pro events. There are several problems to overcome. Here are a few to consider:

- Financial - It is very expensive the first few years to travel and play the twenty to thirty weeks necessary to move up the rankings. Even if you progress in these events, it does not cover the costs you are making.
- Ranking - Your national or international ranking has to be high enough to enter into the pro events or next-level events to progress. Your ranking determines, for a large part, if you can compete or not.
- Physical - Many players are not ready to play a higher level yet and get hurt. Some players need extra time to develop their bodies.
- Mental - Not all players are ready for the stress of playing on the tour. When money and points are involved, it can play tricks on your mind and influence how you play.

Turning Pro ... or Not

Many juniors who play at a high level nationally or internationally ask themselves at one point what the next step to take would be. You are maybe playing the highest-level tournaments, playing Grand Slam juniors, or maybe even playing some future-level events. You might have an ATP/WTA ranking, but that still does not mean you will succeed. The combined factors above make up your possibilities and choices. This is when you have to decide to turn pro or go to college.

College Tennis

When all, or several, of these factors are involved, it is worth to consider college tennis. There are several advantages to playing college tennis:

- All your practice sessions are arranged for you—groups and private instruction.
- You can get part or whole scholarship to pay for tuition and training.
- You can play on a team and get on-court coaching and support from teammates.
- You have athletic trainers to organize your physical training each week.
- You have trainers at your disposal for injuries or massages.
- You have housing in the dorms with other athletes.
- You have special mess halls for athletes only.
- All equipment and clothing are organized, free string and stringing.
- You have many practice matches and college matches for competition.
- All travel and expenses are paid for.
- The coaches take you to pro events with all expenses paid.
- Even if you leave school to play pro tennis, you can return and finish schooling on your existing scholarship.

So what do college coaches look for? If you are a good player and you play national and ITF events, they probably already have you on their radar. Besides that, they look at your rankings and your UTR (Universal Tennis Rating), and they look at your head-to-head results to compare you to other players they might know. If they are interested in you, they will come and see you play. Don't be surprised if they don't introduce themselves since they are not allowed to talk to players in competitions (NCAA regulations). Once you are done in the event, they can approach you. The ages they start looking at your results is between sixteen and eighteen.

If you are interested to going to college, you would do well to write the coaches and give them a small outline of your tennis career. Make sure to mention your coach and contact info so they can call and inquire about you. Some players also send a small video to show their strokes. If the college coaches are interested, they will invite you for a visit at the campus to meet the staff and the team.

What College Do I Choose?

There are many good schools to choose from. So how do you make your picks? You have to do your homework. You have to ask some college players and their parents you know about schools you are interested in. You can also find out about the reputation of the coaches and their program. And you eventually have to talk to the coaches and develop relationships. Then you have to find out if those schools you are interested in are recruiting for the year you are graduating. It's quite a process as you can see.

Many schools also recruit foreign players. In fact, tennis happens to be the college sport with the most foreign athletes (see next page). As you can see, tennis has the highest percentage athletes in their programs with 30 percent women and 32 percent men. This does not make it easier for US students to get a spot on the team. There are some teams that are made up entirely of foreign players. (On a personal note, I think this is one thing the NCAA should look at changing. Maybe only two players max should be allowed on a team.)

Nevertheless, there are still many colleges that are recruiting US players and value the relationship you build with them. There are some events that you can visit here in the US that are visited by almost all the top schools every year. Here is a list of events to keep in mind so you can get in touch with them for a face-to-face meeting.

- all national level 1 tournaments, ages sixteen and eighteen
- This includes national clay courts and hard courts.
- All ITF level 1, 2, and B1 events in the US
- The Easter Bowl 16 and 18 in Indian Wells
- The US Open junior event
- The Orange Bowl 16 and 18

If you happen to compete in these events, that is even better. But even if you don't and you are only fifteen, start introducing yourself and let them know who you are. It is not always what you know but who you know!

Number of Foreign Athletes by Div 1 Schools in US (2013-14)

	4%	8%	12%	16%	20%	24%	28%	32%
Tennis							X	O
Ice hockey					O	X		
Skiing				X				
Squash			OX					
Golf			O	X				
Field Hockey		X						
Soccer	X		O					
Water polo		X						
Basketball	X	O						
Swimming	X							
Fencing	O X							
NCAA Average	O X							
Beach Volleyball	X							
Rowing	X	O						
Volleyball	OX							
Cross country	X O							
Track and field	XO							
Lacrosse	X O							
Gymnastics	O X							
Rifle	X							
Bowling	X							
Sync. Swimming	X							
Equestrian	X							
Baseball/softball	O							
Sailing	O X							
Football	O							
Wresling	O							

As you can see in the graph above, tennis has the highest percentage participants of foreign students in D1 schools of all the major sports (boys—O, girls—X).

Martin van Daalen

Schooling and Acceptance

Never forget that your school results are just as important as your tennis results! If you desire to go to college, you had better make sure that you have good grades. Your SAT results count heavily for your acceptance into college. You should start taking your SAT from the time you are fifteen, if possible. Some schools have higher acceptance levels as others. It is advisable to find out from the coach what they are. If you are homeschooled, you should also find out what the policies are concerning acceptance. Not all colleges accept homeschooled students, and the trend seems to be going that way for many other schools.

Even after receiving a scholarship, you have the responsibility to keep your grades up during your four years. If you fail to keep passing grades, they could take your eligibility away till you get your grades up again. The coach can provide you with tutors if you request it, so if you are homeschooled or your grades are not so high, make sure to request tutors in a timely fashion. The coach wants you to play and will help you with whatever problem you may have.

Training and Coaching

The schedule for college players is set by the coaches. You basically have group training every day followed by physical training several times a week. Usually there are two private training sessions per week, but you can ask the coach or assistant for extra help (initiative has to come from the student—NCAA rules). The college schedule is pretty much the same each year:

August–December: preseason practice session, NCAA tournaments
January–May: college matches, NCAA championships
June—August: ITF pro events (future and challenger)

There are many opportunities, especially over the summer, to play ITF pro events. The colleges that take pride in developing players take their top players to these events in the US and provide coaching and travel expenses. Not every player takes advantage of this situation, but even while in college, you can improve your ATP or WTA ranking. If you are one of the top college players, there are some opportunities to qualify for a USTA college team and receive some wild cards into future and/ or challenger pro events over the summer.

Futures and Challengers

The future events are the lowest level pro events. They are governed by the ITF (International Tennis Federation) in London and the starting point for every top national and ITF junior player on the international pro tour. Everyone with a top ITF junior or national ranking can apply for the qualifying events (once you apply for your IPIN [international player identification number]. Everyone has started this way at one point or another. Once you get through qualifying, you receive ATP or WTA points (for WTA, you have to acquire three main draw results before you get a ranking). As you acquire more points, you will be able to play challenger-level events, with more points and prize money.

Prize Money

As a college player, you have to declare your amateur status each time you play a pro event to keep your eligibility for college. You can, however, take some of the prize money as expenses (up to a certain amount per year) as long as you are not receiving expense money from college. The moment you declare yourself pro, you lose your college eligibility status and cannot go back to amateur status.

Pro Tennis

Once you make a commitment to pro tennis, you can start organizing your training and tournament schedule and have to budget your finances for the year. There might be opportunities through the federation, if your age and ranking are appropriate. The federations of each nation have traveling teams with the best juniors or prospects. It is advisable to have a conversation with them first and to think this through before turning pro and weigh all your options.

21—PRO PLAYERS

Pro players are competitors who play for money. Every top junior player might dream about playing on the big stage one day. But there is a lot more to it than the glamorous lifestyle they perceive. Pro tennis, like many other pro sports, is entertainment. And you make your money by entertaining spectators with your skills. So there are a lot of responsibilities that come along with the status of pro player.

Professional Attitude

Your attitude toward the game has to change. You are not only playing tennis for your own satisfaction but you are also playing for the spectators and the media that come along with it. You have to develop a professional behavior and attitude toward all involved in the pro world (coaches, managers, officials, spectators, media, and sponsors). If you are able to do this well, it will benefit your business and your career as a pro player. As a junior player, you did not need to think about all these things; but as a professional tennis player, you definitely do!

Playing on the pro tour requires you to follow certain rules and etiquette. There have been some bad examples of players who did not understand this at all. The reasons for this can be found in the training they received from an early age and when they transition to a pro career too early. Coaches, mentors, and managers have a responsibility early on to guide and train young players how to behave. One of the responsibilities of young pro players is to be able to do press interviews. This takes some media training and time to get used to. Good coaches and managers will think of this early to protect their protégé and make sure they get the proper preparation.

Developing Pro Players

Developing top junior players into pro players takes time and patience. It is a long process that requires a lot of dedication from all involved. The average age for players to reach the top 100 just moved up from twenty-seven to twenty-eight years of age (2019). That should tell you how difficult and long-term this process is. Becoming a top national or international junior alone is complicated enough. The days of turning pro as a teenager have become very rare. Besides being physically and mentally talented to reach the pro levels at a young age, you have to be lucky that everything goes your way. Finding your confidence against other talented players, playing against opponents you can beat to move ahead in the draw, getting the help with wild cards, getting noticed by management companies for sponsoring, and not getting injured too often are just some of factors that play a role in your success.

Management and Sponsoring

There will be a moment in your career when you need a management company. This could be when you are still a top junior or later on when you have made your mark on the tour. The management companies have all the contacts with sponsors and can also assist you with financing your career. There are many management companies out there on tour, and it is not always easy to find the right company that fits you.

They all are a little different in their approach and what they can offer you. But one word of caution: management companies are out to make money too! If they like you as a prospect, they will all make many promises to get you to sign with their company. You might be wise to have your own personal lawyer to look over any offers they might present to you. You don't have to make any decisions right away. Walk away and talk it over with your lawyer, coach, or mentor—whomever you trust with these matters and has your best interest at heart. I have helped many players obtain a contract with management companies, and there are some basic rules to use when dealing with them:

- Talk to many management groups and let them know you are considering all the other companies as well. Don't choose one too quickly.
- Gather all the information from each one so you can make comparisons among all of them. It also gives you talking points from offers already made.
- Have them all give you a written offer instead of only a presentation. This can be important later on when promises are made to services.
- Everything is negotiable. You don't have to decide on the day you meet or any other day. This is totally up to you.
- Have all written offers checked legally by your own attorney.

When management companies make you an offer, they have already checked the deal they can make with the major sponsors. For tennis, the major sponsors are the clothing companies and the racket companies.

Pros and Cons

There are some pros and cons of management companies that you need to be aware of when deciding what company to go with. Some things they do well, and other things they don't do well. Here are some examples:

Pros of Management Companies
- They are able to get you the best deals from the major sponsors.
- They have the contacts and confidence of the sponsors.
- They take care of all the contract negotiations.
- They have the ability to finance contracts upfront.
- They can organize wild cards with major tournaments.
- They can manage your finances if necessary.

Andy Murray

Cons of Management Companies
- They are in management to make money.
- They have their own interest above your interest.
- They often suggest racket change that can lead to loss of confidence.
- They often suggest a change of coach that can lead to loss of confidence.
- They often change the schedule for contracts instead of development.

All these aspects can make a difference on the player's development or career. As long as you remember that they work for you, you can never go wrong!

Major Management Companies

There are some major management groups that have the majority of the top tennis players in their company. Below is a list of most used ones:

- CAA
- IMG
- TEAM8
- Octagon
- Lagardère

Equipment

For management companies to make a deal, they have to persuade you to use a different clothing company and racket company than what you are currently using. The reason for this is that the clothing and racket companies don't want to pay you for something you are already wearing or using. This is where it becomes difficult for you, as a player, to switch rackets, especially if you like the equipment you already have at the moment. Changing equipment can be dangerous if you are still a transitional player or a young pro player. You can seriously damage your confidence if you don't like the rackets.

Support Team

Going on the pro tour is not something you start out of the blue or without a support team. To organize it properly, you need a few basics to build your career on:

- a training base to work from
- a primary coach who is going to guide you
- an inner circle of advisers (parents and mentors)
- a management team or sponsor group
- a fitness coach
- an athletic trainer or physiotherapist
- a group of colleagues that you can train with
- a stringer where you customize your equipment

As you can see, the support team can be quite extensive. When you are just starting out, your support team stays home. As you progress and become a top player, you will slowly start to add persons on tour from your support team to travel with you. As you have seen with most top 10 players, their support team on tour is like a traveling team. They go along to all the major events and provide the player with whatever he or she needs.

Training

The training program for pro players is very different compared to the program for juniors or transitional players (college). Those programs are all designed with a higher degree of discipline and authority. The way you communicate with pro players is cooperative. You are part of a team. As a coach, you might be the main person to dictate the training, but there are others on the team you have to cooperate with.

You have to communicate with them on training and tournament schedules so they can coordinate physical training and physio/massage treatments. Coaches also have to coordinate with the player's management on all special arrangements that are made on their behalf. This could vary from appearances at events to media or sponsor meets/commercials. It becomes a puzzle of dates and events that need to be scheduled around training and tournaments. All players have a base they like to work from. Sometimes it is a familiar place they like or are used to. But it could also be a training site on the road, as preparation for a series of events. Pro players have to gauge how much they do according to the number of matches and time spent on court. They need to learn to train on the road and become immune to the attention from fans and the media. Learning how to focus on the job at hand and taking no notice of their surroundings is a skill learned over time.

The type of training depends on the preparation for the tournaments. For example, the month of December is the preseason period for the new year. The training done at this stage is much different compared to that after each Grand Slam in preparation for the next series of tournaments. The preparation for Grand Slam events is different in the sense that the tennis training changes to a longer session of three hours instead of two tennis sessions. This is to get ready for the possible best-of-five-set matches played there. The fitness training can be done in the afternoon after lunch and a good rest.

Types of Training

- preseason (November to December, on-court, weight training, track)
- presurface change (hard, indoor, hard, clay, grass, hard)
- pre–Grand Slams (top players take a week before each Slam at the site)

I have witnessed some different types of training over the years of pro tennis. Years ago, I saw John McEnroe prepare for Wimbledon; he had organized three different players for the training so they would play at a high level each set. They followed one another after each set so that practice would be tougher for him. The other two warmed up before starting each set so they would be ready to go full pace from the start. I saw Nadal do the same training method on the practice courts at Wimbledon. There will always be coaches and players trying to find new training methods to prepare better for events. The bottom line is, you need to be extremely fit, very tough, and 100 percent committed to compete at the top. The training gets you ready to do your job!

Coaching

Coaching pro players can be a very gratifying job, but it's also quite frustrating at the same time. Not all players were trained in a disciplined environment; in fact, they probably have been told how talented and how good they are their whole life. If their junior coach did a good job instilling discipline and respect for each other, your life as a pro coach will be much easier. A pro coach has many tasks, but not all of them have to do with coaching on the court. Below is the list of their duties:

- discuss and organize training and tournament schedule
- organize training and sparring and schedule physical therapy and recovery (physio)
- discuss and organize travel with team and management
- organize practice partners during tournaments
- coordinate with management (schedules, appearances, sponsors, media)

Preseason

The coaching during preseason is much more hands-on since that is when all the major training and preparation has to happen. There are more instructions on the technical, tactical, and physical aspects of the game. Mornings are usually reserved for drilling of strokes and patterns, whereas the afternoons are more filled with point and match play. Special attention is given to changes or improvements that need to be made. This is the most intense and rigorous training part of the year.

Instructions

The focus is on the execution of the strokes during drills and exercises as the players are trying to train the automation of the strokes (muscle memory). As preseason comes to an end, the focus will turn to the ability to use strokes in points with strategic and tactical situations.

Pretournament

In this phase, right before the event, you will see players warm up for thirty minutes and then focus on playing points for the remainder of the training. For a top player, it is most important to feel the rhythm of the points and games and mimic what happens in tournaments. The coach will try to help with instructions during play but stay in the background, in the back corners of the court. It is best not to interfere too much so they don't get distracted. Being out of direct sight helps players to focus. In some cases, the coach does not need to say anything. It could be that they give feedback in the middle of the game, but it's also possible that they give it right before or after the game is over. Instructions should be short and to the point so that the flow of the points is not interrupted. With better players, you don't need to say so much; and most of the time, it could be a praising comment: "Good shot," "Good rally," etc. If you are going to make a comment, try to say something motivating first: "That was a good start to the point, but try to play this way after …" Competitors are more likely to listen when they hear a compliment first.

Instructions

The focus is on match play and how to construct points. There are less drills and more match situations and point play with predetermined start of the point and open end. And there will also be sets played against different opponents. All the instructions will be geared toward strategical and tactical solutions.

Tournament Coaching

Your job as a coach becomes more defined during actual tournament play. This is the phase where you want your player to succeed most and where all the hard work from preparation is supposed to pay off. The coach sets up practice sessions against other participants. The hitting partner is sometimes involved when the player needs more grooving of the strokes, but mostly, the practice involves a warm-up and point play. Time is limited at the tournament sites, and sessions usually last up to an hour. The top players do have some preferential treatment in being able to train on center court (sometimes for longer sessions). You can get some indication on the next-day schedule from the tournament desk to plan your match day better.

If you are not playing a seed and have a lower ranking, you will probably play during the day schedule. If you are a seed or a top player, they will likely schedule you on the center courts and you could also play at night. This information could be important if you want to prepare your practice session at night under the lights. It is quite different to play at night or during the day. The warm-up consists of a physical part and a hitting part. The physical part (thirty to forty minutes) can be running or biking, some stretching (dynamic), and some movement drill (sometimes with catching a tennis ball). The hitting part (thirty to forty minutes) is more for coordination and timing of the ball than anything else. Players don't try to hit too hard and play as smooth as possible. Right before the match, there is a possibility to do some sprints or shadow tennis (mimicking the strokes without the ball).

Day Matches

Matches on the pro tour usually start at 11:00 a.m. Occasionally, they will start at ten in the morning, but that has more to do with weather circumstances. This gives players plenty of time to prepare for their match even if they are the first one on. The game plan is sometimes discussed the night before with short reminders on the day of the match. The focus of the game plan is on specific strategies during the serve and return games, the patterns to find the weaknesses of the opponent, and maybe some improvement goals.

During the day, players would have to deal with the sun and hot weather. The ball flies faster in hot weather, and the heat can become a factor in long matches. Being prepared for hot weather and longer matches means special sports drinks (electrolytes) and snack food (bananas) on court during match play. Take your time in between points to recover physically after each point from the beginning of the match. Go to the towel, dry off, quickly evaluate the previous point (two to three seconds), and think about what strategy to use in the next point (twenty seconds).

This time management is something you see experienced players do well. There is recently a play clock introduced so that players on court can see how much time they have after the score is called. The service motion has to start before twenty-five seconds have passed. You will see players use less time when they are winning points easily, and you'll see them use more time on longer and tough-fought points. Whenever serving, you can use the play clock to your advantage by pressuring the return player in taking less time. Since the return player has to play to the rhythm of the server, the returner has to follow and be ready to play, taking away time to recover. This can be a strategy when you see that your opponent is getting tired or having trouble with the sun and the heat.

Recovery after the match is important to prepare for the next day. In hot weather, it can be advantageous to stretch, cool down, and then take an ice bath. (Most of the larger pro events have several trainers and physiotherapists on staff to take care of the needs of the players.) After the ice bath, take a massage to get rid of the lactic acid that builds

Martin van Daalen

up in the muscles from strenuous exercise. Sometimes players like to do their media interview first, in the cooldown time, and then see the physiotherapist afterward. It all depends on the length of the match and how tough it was.

Discussing the match afterward is important feedback for players. The timing of discussing depends on the player and how they deal with wins and losses. It works best to remind the player what the game plan was and how that worked in the match. This way you get an idea what their feelings are about their performance. Junior players are usually more defensive when receiving feedback, so be careful to not be too negative. Start by saying what went well and then mention the topics that need improvement. Finish by deciding how changes can be made for future matches.

Night Matches

Playing matches at night, under the lights, takes getting used to. If you know your match is scheduled at night, you can prepare by practicing at night the days before. Obviously, the lights are much better at pro events than at your local club, but it still is a much different environment with stadiums and spectators. The air is much cooler at night, so the balls move slower. You might need to bring a jacket and some extra towels for the changeovers. With no sun and cooler temperatures, matches are not so easily won on stamina. Strategies need to be clear, and weaknesses exploited. You would do well to organize your hitting warm-up closer to the start of the match and have your food intake in the late afternoon.

Instructions

The focus will be on the basic strategy of serve and return, combined with patterns of play in the rally. Most coaches like to give their player a plan A and a plan B in case plan A fails to work. The coach has a scouting report of the opponent with strengths and weaknesses, likely

shot choices and patterns, and habits on first and second serves, returns,
break points, and specialty shots.

Coaching at Grand Slams

In these major events, you play one match every other day. However, the matches are best of five sets for the male players and can last three to five hours. Preparation and tactics have to be adjusted to this type of competition. The stamina in matches becomes an important factor, and knowing how to manage your energy in the different sets is an important strategy to learn.

Whenever possible, it is best to win in three sets (in best-of-five-set format). But there can be circumstances that force you to rethink your energy output in each set. Winning the first set is important in this format (best of five) but not as important in the shorter format (best of three). Getting the upper hand early gives you more chances of winning the match, but in five-setters, it is not a deciding factor. You could lose the lead in one of the following sets and have to decide whether to push hard to come back or to put more energy in the beginning of the next set. Make sure to discuss the possibilities with your players so they can decide when the situation arises. They alone can make these choices since they are the ones playing and they can feel how much energy they have left. The performance at the beginnings of each set can influence the outcome dramatically. If players coast through the sets and just hold their service games, the decisions fall on the tiebreak. Tiebreaks can go either way and should be avoided, if possible. They are very inefficient ways to win sets and take a lot of energy from players. Not only are you playing more games to get to that point, but the mental stress is also much higher and drains your energy level even more.

Understanding time management and the use of taking breaks to change clothes is another strategy that needs to not be overlooked in Grand Slam matches. Sometimes taking a break can change the momentum in a match either way!

Days Off

After your singles match, you get the following day off from play (unless you are playing doubles or mixed or there was a rainy day in the schedule). Using your day off the proper way is something you need to learn through experience. It is not a good idea to do nothing. It is a day to get a light workout in the gym to loosen up the sore muscles, a light hit to keep your timing up, and some massage and stretching. Use your day off as recovery. If you are playing doubles and/or mixed, it can be tough to keep up physically. Usually the players who have a chance to go far in the tournament will not play doubles and/or mixed doubles. As a female player, this does not need to be an obstacle; but as a male player, the best-out-of-five format makes it tough to combine.

Coaching During the Match

As you might know, there is a no-coaching rule during Grand Slam events. The WTA tour allows coaching during breaks at the smaller events. For male players, there is no coaching at any time. Even though it is against the rules, it doesn't mean that coaches don't try to make a few comments. You can witness it all the time when watching TV and they do a close-up on the player's box. The referee might not be able to hear anything, especially right after the point has finished, and the spectators are clapping and cheering. It is during that time that coaches or their support team will try to coach their player. Cheering on your player is allowed, and you will see the support team take good advantage of this. When there is a close point and their player is able to win, you will see them cheer loudly not only to promote the player's performance but also to get the crowd into the match. The support and comments can be more subtle with one-word instructions or by making the player aware of an important point by clapping the hands twice (with or without a comment). In the case of a rain delay, coaching is allowed in the locker room. This is where a strategy change can make a big difference. Learning when to make comments and when not to (not distracting the player and letting the player focus) is a coaching skill that is obtained over time in real live matches.

> While working for the Dutch Tennis Federation, I was coaching a group of girls at a challenger event in Portugal. My top player at that time was playing against a high-ranked girl from Spain, and the coach was obviously coaching during the match. I got up and walked around the court so I could lean over to talk to the chair umpire during a changeover. I told him, "The coach of the Spanish girl is openly coaching. Can you please put a stop to that?"
>
> The chair umpire replied, "No, he is not saying anything of value for the player."
>
> Now my Spanish is not so good, but I do know when there are tactical instructions given to a player on court. The umpire was not going to help me, so I decided to try a different method. I went to sit next to the other coach, on the seat directly beside him. He looked at me, surprised, but did not say anything. When his student came close to our side of the court, I could see he was about to give another instruction. At that moment, I turned to him and said, "Hi, my name is Martin. What is your name?" He had to disengage from his student, hesitated a bit, and then told me his name. Every next time he wanted to say something, I would ask him another question. His student on court understood what I was doing and was furious and started shouting and cursing at me. Of course, that resulted in a warning from the umpire. The Spanish girl became so mad that she ended up losing that match in three sets. It was also a good lesson for my student to never give up!

Scouting

Observing future opponents during matches can give valuable information on the habits and strategies of the player. Every player has a certain style of play with strengths and weaknesses. For any coach, it is important to provide their player with the best possible information so they are forewarned on their opponent. Here are some of the aspects that coaches look for:

- style of play
- strengths and weaknesses
- basic strategy
- favorite patterns
- shot choices when in offensive position
- shot choices when in defensive position
- habits on serve
- habits on return
- habits on break points
- specialty shots

When making a scouting report, you don't have to give all the information you have gathered. It depends on the player. Some players like concise information on their game plan, whereas others like to discuss their opponent's strategy in more detail.

There are many aspects to coaching on tour. I have seen many great coaches get the best out of their players, but it is also possible to hurt your player if you make bad decisions at crucial moments. Experience is the key to success in this case, and you can't learn how to do this without making some mistakes along the way. So don't be too hard on yourself when something fails to work. Learn to stay calm, be flexible, learn from your mistakes, and move on to do it better in the future!

Media Training

When turning pro, you will be confronted by the media. There are interviews before the match and also after the match. The spectators are interested in the players and their personal lives. So how do you deal with this? Media training.

In guiding many juniors from junior to pro, it has always been a factor I was aware of and always had management companies include in their contracts. Young pros have to learn how to sell themselves in order to get sponsor contracts. If they are able to excel in the communication with the media, they will be able to increase their popularity for even larger contracts.

In guiding several players through this process of turning pro, I was able to coordinate with the management companies to prepare them for the media with special training for interviews. Many times, I was present when they performed the training so I could assist them better at pro events. Some of the subjects at this training were as follows:

- *Your life story.* Have your life story ready to tell when asked. It is an important way to sell yourself to journalists and TV. What you say should be a carefully prepared script that you rehearse many times so it becomes natural for you to repeat. It is a perfect time to shine and reveal what you would like people to know about yourself.

- *A script when you win.* You should learn how to talk about matches when you win. Staying humble in your own efforts and praising the efforts of your opponent are always good points to endear yourself with the spectators and journalists. Make sure to focus when specific questions are asked about your opponents and your opinions of other players and stay neutral in your answers.

- *A script when you lose.* Learning what to say when you lost the match can be difficult if it was an emotional match. Stay objective and don't let yourself get drawn into controversial conversations. Be complimentary of your opponent with comments and remain sportsmanlike.

Martin van Daalen

- *Changing the subject.* Be ready to change the subject from a topic that you don't want to talk about by having-ready-to-go topics you *do* want to talk about. By having these special topics ready at all times, you can change any topic and eat up the interview time so that you dominate the conversation.

The media training is especially important for young pros coming on to the pro tour and for players who need to enhance their popularity to sell themselves. For young pros, it is also very important to follow the ATP and WTA training programs. These help you get all the necessary information to assist you on the pro tour. Even top players practice the interviews to enhance their popularity and support in the sport.

If you compare Novak Djokovic with Roger Federer on popularity, Roger is by far the more popular figure. So is Novak so bad at interviews? The answer is, not at all. In fact, he is very charming, just like Roger. He is also very funny with some of his answers, just like Roger. So "What is the problem?" you might say. Yes, he is a little less humble on the court, but the real answer lies in all the interviews Roger does in comparison to Novak. He goes to all the networks and actually has learned to enjoy the interviews. Novak does the interview on court and in the pressroom, and that's it! Roger has understood how this works and takes time for everyone to be an ambassador for the tennis sport. If you ever make it that far, take an example from him and follow his lead. As you do more interviews, you will become much better and do these with ease to finally look like a rock star.

Grigor Dimitrov

Martin van Daalen

22—EQUIPMENT

There are many types of racket, shoe, and clothing companies. All of them want you to use their products, but let's be honest, these are very personal items. Not everyone likes the same rackets, shoes, or clothing. Here are some percentages of the market shares of the top 30 men and top 30 women clothing companies:

CLOTHING: TOP 30 WOMEN

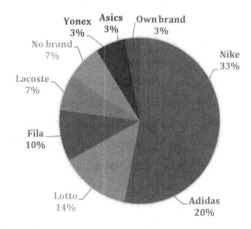

CLOTHING: TOP 30 MEN

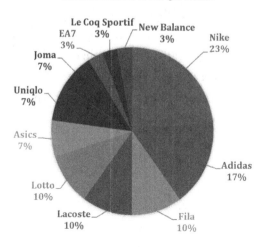

Rackets

The average racket is now about 28 in. (71 cm.) long and weighs from 9.5 to 14 oz. (270–397 g.). There have been many recent innovations in racket technology, not all of which have caught on with players. One maker markets a hexagonal racket, while others are making rackets with extra wide bodies. A racket made of a new material—graphite fiber-reinforced thermoplastic viscoelastic polymer—was designed to have variable flexibility, depending on how hard the ball is struck. A design to alleviate tennis elbow employs small lead bearings enclosed in plastic chambers inside the head frame. The movement of the bearings as the racket connects with the ball is supposed to cushion the vibrations that might cause pain to the player's arm. But the most common rackets are now made of aluminum or of a composite of graphite, fiberglass, or other materials. Aluminum rackets are usually made of one or several alloys. One popular alloy contains 2 percent silicon as well as traces of magnesium, copper, and chromium. Another widely used alloy contains 10 percent zinc with magnesium, copper, and chromium. The zinc alloy is harder, though more brittle, and the silicon alloy is easier to work with. Composite rackets may contain many different materials. They usually consist of a sandwich of different layers around a hollow core or a polyurethane foam core. The typical layers of a composite racket are fiberglass, graphite, and boron or Kevlar. Other materials may be used as well, such as ceramic fibers for added strength. Other materials found in tennis rackets are leather or synthetic material for the handle grip. Old wooden rackets usually used a leather handle grip, but modern rackets generally use a leather-like replacement such as vinyl. Rackets may have plastic parts too, such as the yoke at the base of the head and the cap at the bottom of the handle.

RACKETS: TOP 30 WOMEN

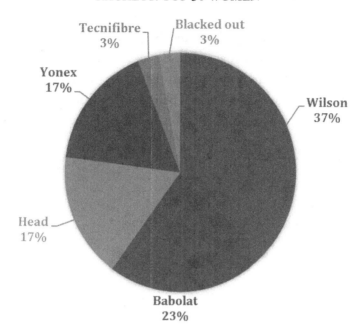

Tecnifibre 3%
Blacked out 3%
Yonex 17%
Wilson 37%
Head 17%
Babolat 23%

RACKETS: TOP 30 MEN

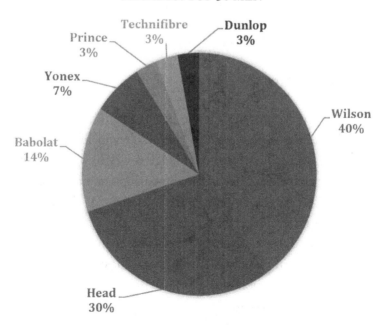

Prince 3%
Technifibre 3%
Dunlop 3%
Yonex 7%
Wilson 40%
Babolat 14%
Head 30%

Specifications (Specs)

Every racket is a package deal and is made up of several different specifications, also known as specs. Besides the length and size of the racket head, it has a variable of aspects that make the racket very unique. Every change to the racket makes it play and feel different when hitting the ball. The various aspects of racket specification are as follows:

- length
- weight
- head size
- grip size
- swing weight
- twist weight
- balance
- stiffness

Every combination of the specs has consequences on the performance. Experience and playing with different rackets will give you feedback on what you like most.

Weight and Power

Does a heavier racket always hit the ball faster? The answer is no. It is true that adding more weight to the racket will hit the ball faster, depending on where the weight is added, but weight in itself is not the only deciding factor of power when comparing one racket to another. Experimenting with the amount and positioning of the weights will produce some different performances. You can see that some really heavy rackets produce relatively less speeds compared to lighter rackets with a different total combination of specs—most significantly, specs concerning the distribution of the weight. Below is a coaching story of how not to use extra weight.

When I was working for the USTA as a national coach, I took three players over to the international sixteen and under team championships. Alex Kuznetsov was the number 1 player on the team, and he decided to show up with lead on all his rackets. Now having some weight added to the rackets could be a good thing, but you don't experiment with that at an important event like this. He had put lead all around the inside of the racket. It was way too much and not suited for someone his age, size, and strength. I begged him to take it off, but he would not listen. Even in practice, you could see that it was much too heavy, and he had trouble getting the racket to move forward and lost tremendous amounts of racket head speed. This affected his timing and his topspin. As it turned out, he lost some matches that he normally would win. Even though they had two match points to win the semifinal against Germany, he was not hitting his normal way. They ended up losing that semifinal match and were so disappointed that they also lost the playoff for third place. It was a good lesson for him, but it was at a tremendous price for the team. After this team championship, I took him to a professional to have his rackets customized.

Alex went on to become a top junior and played the final at the junior French Open, playing against Gael Monfils in the finals. He turned pro at seventeen but, unfortunately, broke his leg in a car accident. He is now coaching Maria Sharapova on tour, and I see him regularly on TV and at events.

Balance and Power

Balance is an indicator of weight distribution, though not a particularly useful one when it comes to power. You can have a low-balance, high-swing-weight racket or a high-balance, low-swing-weight racket. Similarly, you can have a very high-balance racket with a very low weight and vice versa. A one-ounce racket can have the same balance point as a fourteen-ounce racket. Or you can have rackets with the same balance with all the weight located near the middle of the racket or all the weight located at the two ends. The latter will be much more powerful than the former even though they have the same weight and balance. In fact, as you try different combinations in the program above, you will find many lower-balanced rackets with the most power. In such cases, it is not the balance that is creating the power. It is the total distribution of each little piece of the weight. Of course, balance is relative to the length of the racket also.

Swing Weight and Power

Swing weight is a two-faced property. If low, you call it maneuverability. If it is high, you call it stability. More than any other spec, swing weight will demonstrate a general trend of more is better when it comes to power. Swing weight is a measurement of a racket's resistance to being rotated about an axis going through your hand. A low swing weight makes it easy for the player to swing the racket (maneuverable). But it also makes it easy for the ball to move the racket, resulting in loss of power. Racket movement is the biggest culprit in loss of power. Swing weight is determined by both the amount of mass and its distribution in the racket—distribution being much more important. The farther an amount of mass is located from the hand, the more effect it will have on stabilizing the racket.

Stiffness and Power

A stiffer racket will not bend as much as a more flexible one. Bending loses energy because the frame does not snap back by the time the ball leaves the strings. By using the program above, you will notice that frame stiffness seems to matter least just below the center of the racket and most near the tip. Near the center, specifically at the so-called node of oscillation (or no-vibration sweet spot), the racket will not bend when the ball hits it. Therefore, at those locations, the program will list a few very soft frames with a lot of power closer to the top of the list. At the tip, where the frame wants to bend the most, stiffness is more important; and you see stiffer frames at the top of the list for advanced players.

Twist Weight and Power

On off-center hits, the racket will spin like a top. The frame's twisting occurs due to more or less torsional frame stiffness. Twisting is an acceleration of the entire racket around its central tip-to-butt axis (longitudinal axis). Twist weight works the same way as swing weight but about a different axis. Rackets with lower twist weights will twist more than those that are higher. The farther off-center you hit, the more obvious the loss in power is. Also, the larger the head size, the less obvious is the loss in power (because the weight is located farther from the axis or rotation). But as usual, when it comes to actual power performance, our rules of thumb are only that. For example, a high-twist-weight, large-headed racket may also have a low swing weight. So even though it is stable right to left, it is unstable tip to butt. When it comes to power, movement in one direction can cancel stability in another, or stability in one direction can more than make up for instability in another.

Head Size and Power

Head size goes hand in hand with twist weight. A larger head puts the weight farther away from the long axis and makes it more difficult to move the racket about that axis. That is why the sweet spot is bigger on larger rackets; off-center hits generally cause less twisting at a given location compared to smaller rackets but not always. Smaller head sizes may not have the weight located as far from the axis, but there may be more of it, making up the difference. On centerline hits, a larger racket in and of itself should not make any difference in power. In fact, you will notice many midsize and midplus rackets near the top of the shot speed list along the center of the racket. That is because they have high swing weight. In fact, many so-called player's rackets are near the top. These are usually characterized by higher weight and swing weight and lower head size, balance, and stiffness. It is the swing weight that more than makes up the difference to result in higher power potential.

Strings

"Strings are the soul of a racket."

Strings may be the soul of a racket, but for too many players, they are just an afterthought. Players will spend months trying rackets yet only minutes choosing a string, the very object that contacts the ball and greatly determines what the player feels. Fortunately, the nongut synthetic string universe (mostly nylon- and poly-based) has improved *dramatically* over the last few decades. Today, there is so much diversity in the string market that any player, with a little research, can zero in on a desired set. Here are a few guidelines to make your string and tension selection easier.

Playability

It's very difficult to obtain consensus on what makes a string playable. Some players like a crisp, firm playing string, while others equate playability with softness and comfort. Historically, a playable string is one that is gut-like in its feel and resilience. Natural gut is the only string made from a natural product—thin ribbons made from beef intestines, which, when twisted into a tennis string, create a comfortably crisp feel that is simply unmatched. Natural gut is the oldest tennis string and remains the benchmark for playability.

Durability

Most tennis players want a string that offers everything. Unfortunately, increased durability in tennis strings is usually at the expense of playability, especially on shorter strokes, which feel stiff and dead. Thicker gauges and abrasion-resistant materials will be more durable, but they are less elastic and resilient than their thinner counterparts (see gauge table below). If a player is breaking a 16-gauge nylon string (synthetic gut), we might suggest they switch to a 15L version of that same string, if available.

String Gauges

Generally speaking, thinner strings offer improved playability, while thicker strings offer enhanced durability. Tennis string gauges range from 15 (thickest) to 19 (thinnest), with half-gauges identified with an *L* (15L, 16L, etc.), which is short for *light*. A 15L string is thinner than a 15-gauge but thicker than a 16-gauge string. Thinner strings also provide more spin potential by allowing the strings to embed into the ball more.

String Gauges and Diameters in Millimeters

15	= 1.41–1.49 mm	17	= 1.20–1.24 mm
15L	= 1.34–1.40 mm	17L	= 1.16–1.20 mm
16	= 1.26–1.33 mm	18	= 1.10–1.16 mm
16L	= 1.22–1.26 mm	19	= 1.00–1.10 mm

String Materials

Nylon—Synthetic gut or nylon? Truth be told, most synthetic guts are made with nylon (sometimes referred to as polyamide). There are different grades of nylon, with varying levels of feel, so don't be afraid to try different synthetic guts until you find the right fit.

All in all, synthetic gut delivers a good combination of playability and durability at a great price. In the old days (wood racket era), any self-respecting player used natural gut. Today, an impressive number of nonprofessional players use nylon-based strings, which have greatly improved in the feel department.

Nylon multifilaments—They offer truly impressive comfort and power. Unlike the more basic synthetic guts (which have a single solid core), multifilaments are comprised of hundreds or thousands of ultrapliable, elbow-friendly fibers and are bundled together with flexible resin-like polyurethane.

Natural gut—This is the ultimate in playability, feel, and tension maintenance. Often overlooked because of its cost, natural gut is the best choice for players with arm problems or those who crave its sublime comfortably crisp feel. Formerly, this is the number 1 choice of ATP and WTA tour players. It is now used more in hybrids, combining polyester mains with natural gut crosses (with some players using gut in the mains for more power and feel). Natural gut offers maximum feel and control due to its ultrahigh flexibility, which provides phenomenal ball pocketing.

In coaching one of the top US players at the Italian Open in Rome, I had a situation to solve with a sore arm. The player was complaining of his arm being sore and stiff after play. I suggested to have a blend of natural gut string and his own string. You can string one type on the top to bottom while stringing the other on the cross strings. I told him we should try to get some and try it out in practice. We didn't have any gut string available, so I went to find his agent, and together we were able to get six sets of string from Babolat. I was happy to tell him I had found some gut string and that we should string all his rackets for tomorrow's match. He said, "No, let's just string one to try first."

I replied, "That is a bad idea. What if it breaks?"

He didn't want to budge on this, so I let it go but feared the worst! The next morning, he was ready to play and was scheduled to play against Paul Haarhuis, a top 30 ATP player. I had given him the tactical information on Paul since I knew him well and went to sit in the stand. The first set went well, and he was competing and clearly liked the new string! It came down to a tiebreak, and then the string broke! He looked at his racket and then up at me in the stand. I kept a straight face and shrugged my shoulders. I could so see him winning that match, but then I was not sure at all. He grabbed another racket out of his bag, with the old string, and was ready to play the next point. I was sitting on the edge of my seat in anticipation. It was Paul's turn to serve. He hit the return, and the ball flew all the way out and hit the back fence. He looked at his racket and then up at me in the stand. Now I could not keep a straight face and looked down to hide my smile. He lost that match and always strung up all his rackets the same way after that incident.

Polyester—It is a very durable string designed to provide control and durability to players with long, fast strokes. Polyester is the number 1 choice on the pro tour because it allows advanced ball strikers to maintain surgical control on their fastest, most aggressive strokes. The incredible stroke speed enabled by polyester also translated into categorically higher level of spin, which literally changed the trajectories and angles available to the player. Polyester also served to harness the immense power that came with graphite era. While it used to be too stiff and dead for recreational players, a growing number of string manufacturers have devoted the lion's share of their R&D to creating softer, more elastic polys so that a wider cross section of players can enjoy its benefits. Another way to get the benefits of polyester is through a hybrid, which is also very popular on the pro tour. This is typically done by combining polyester (usually in the mains) with natural gut or multifilament crosses. This setup provides the durability, control, and spin of polyester with the comfort, power, and touch of a softer string—otherwise known as the best of both worlds. Because of its high stiffness and relatively low power, polyester is not recommended for beginners or players with arm injuries.

Kevlar—This is the most durable string available. Kevlar is very stiff and strings up very tight. Therefore, it is usually combined with a soft nylon cross to reduce string bed stiffness. Ultimately, Kevlar hybrids are the least powerful and least comfortable strings currently available. Players trying Kevlar hybrids for the first time (from nylon strings) are recommended to reduce tension by 10 percent to compensate for the added stiffness. It is not recommended for beginners or players with arm injuries.

String Tension

String tension is the final piece in the racket-string-tension triad. It's also the least understood by most recreational players. Let's start with the basics: lower tensions provide more power, while tighter tensions provide more control. This is a very general rule of thumb and assumes a certain level of player ability (especially the control part). A beginning player may need more control, but tighter string tensions aren't the solution. This player needs a soft, forgiving string bed that lower tensions provide due to the frequency of off-center hits. Advanced players who swing fast and hit hard usually need more control and will therefore benefit from tighter tensions. There are, of course, always exceptions; but these generalizations apply to the majority of players. Each racket has a recommended tension range. This range has been determined by the manufacturer as a result of extensive playtesting by real players. If a player doesn't have a specific need (more power, arm problems, etc.), he should start at midrange and make any adjustments from there. Otherwise, here are some specific guidelines for selecting a string tension.

String Tension for Power

As we stated above, if a player is seeking more power from his racket, he should try dropping tension a few pounds. The string bed will deflect more (and the ball less), returning greater energy to the ball. There is a point of diminishing returns where the string bed turns into a butterfly net, but it's well below any racket's recommended tension range.

String Tension for Control

A tighter string bed deflects less and deforms the ball more, providing less energy than looser strings. This means the ball won't fly as far when you hit it. Beginners who are shanking the ball in every direction won't gain any advantage by increasing tension, but intermediate and advanced players who are hitting a lot of long balls will be able to reduce the depth of their shots without changing their swing. It is also generally accepted that spin potential is enhanced with higher tensions, which provides even more control for topspin and slice players.

Arm Injuries

Lower tensions result in a softer string bed and a larger sweet spot, reducing the amount of shock and vibration transmitted to the hand and elbow.

Switching Rackets

Too many players are stuck on a tension ("I always string my racket at sixty pounds") and don't make allowances when changing rackets. Whether changing head sizes, brands, or buying a new titanium racket, a player will need to make the corresponding tension change. If sixty pounds was midrange on his old racket and the new racket's tension range is fifty to sixty pounds, he should start at fifty-five pounds with the new racket.

Switching Strings

If a player changes from a soft string (natural gut, synthetic gut, multi) to a poly-based string, we suggest reducing tension 5–10 percent to compensate for the higher stiffness. This is more art than science and may require trial and error to get the feel exactly right. When switching to Kevlar, be advised that this material is much stiffer than nylon synthetics and quite a bit stiffer than most poly-based strings, so tension accordingly.

Shoes

There are several types of shoes for different surfaces. The sole of the shoe determines the playability of that shoe for that surface. The profile on the bottom is specifically designed to provide grip and proper amount of slide availability. The types of surfaces are hard court, clay court, grass court, and indoor rubber or carpet.

The profile of the shoes can vary according to the make and level of play. For example, the clay court shoes for Roland Garros need a sharper and deeper profile in order to grip on those clay courts since the clay substance is a much finer grain than other clay courts. Regular clay court shoes do not work well there. Grass court shoes have a bed of nobs on the bottom profile to grip the grass. The number of nobs on the bottom of the shoes is regulated by the Wimbledon tournament. Try out the different types of profile and decide which one fits your playing style.

23—DRILLS FOR TOURNAMENT PLAYERS

The drills on the following pages are exercises you can use for competitive players. Each drill explains how the exercise is set up and how to use it for tournament play. Try to repeat these on a regular basis; you can play most of these in point forms to get you ready for competition. Below are the keys to the court diagrams. They give you a better idea on positions and hitting directions.

Keys to Court Diagrams

●	Player Position
▯	Coach Position
○	Target
⟶	Coach Feed
- - ➤	Hitting Direction
- · -➤	Player Movement
◄ - ➤	Rally Direction

Drill 1—Baseline Direction and Recover Drill

The coach feeds the balls to the corners of the court. The students move to return the balls to alternate targets. The students recover to the middle of the court.

Practice

The purpose is to practice the recovery and movement back to the middle of the court. The combination of movement and accuracy of the strokes is important to construct a point. Alternate with recovery in drill below.

Drill 2—Baseline Movement and Rhythm Drill

The coach feeds six to ten balls to the corners of the court. Each student then retrieves the balls and plays two balls cross and two balls down the line.

Practice

The purpose is to give students a rhythm and feel for the rally by running them side to side. The coach can observe movement, balance, ball control, and recovery footwork. Consistency is key to make many rallies in a row.

Drill 3—Inside-Out and Wide Forehand

The coach feeds balls to two targets on the baseline. The object is to control the court with the forehand stroke and footwork. Use crosscourt and inside-out forehands. After three to five repetitions, switch players.

Practice

The coach adjusts the speed, spin, and trajectory of the balls. Students focus on the different footwork and direction control from both sides of the court.

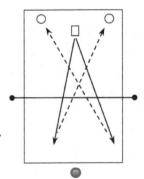

Drill 4—Inside-Out and Running Forehand

The coach feeds the first ball inside out, followed by a wide ball for a running forehand along the baseline. Afterward, they run around and join at the back.

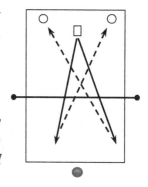

Practice

The coach adjusts the speed, the frequency, the height, and the spin of the ball. Players need to learn how to prepare quickly and play the different targets on the court. Same drill in reverse with forehand and running backhand.

Drill5—Running Forehand and Backhand

The coach feeds several (six to ten) balls wide to forehand and backhand. The players try to neutralize the opponent with the target in the middle of the court. Afterward, they run and join at the back. Practice control, spin, and trajectory.

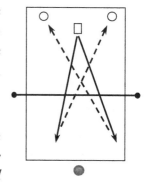

Practice

The purpose is to get players used to running down the ball and returning it in the proper direction. The coach can gauge the speed and the direction of the feed to the capabilities of the player.

Drill 6—Baseline Consistency During the Rally

The coach feeds the balls to the players on the baseline. They can only play to one side of the court. One player can play anywhere. Make the rallies as long as possible. This drill is also possible with points.

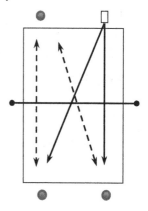

Practice

The purpose is to improve directional control from all players and to improve consistency with the change of direction from the one player. Can play this drill against two players are alternate players separately or together.

Drill 7—Baseline Consistency in Two-on-One Play

The coach feeds from the side of the court to the players on the baseline. The players can play freely to each direction. This drill is also possible with points. Use different shots.

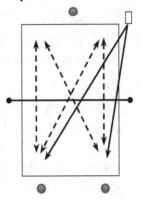

Practice

The purpose is to simulate play against a strong opponent. The coach has influence of speed and angle of the feed in moving the players around the court. As errors occur, the coach feeds in the next ball.

Drill 8—Volley Movement and Direction Drill

The coach feeds to the players at the net. Players step forward to volley. Alternate directions to the targets. The coach can adjust the speed and angle of the feed.

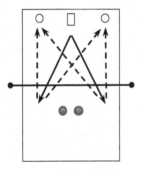

Practice

The purpose is to train movement and direction of the volley. Players train both forehand and backhand. Recovery footwork becomes essential to the volley.

Drill 9—Volley Direction and Movement

The coach feeds the balls across the court to the net players. They will move continually closer to the net position. The coach can vary the speed and interval of the balls. Practice in both directions.

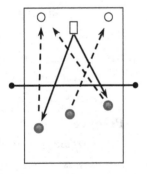

Practice

The purpose is to train closing the net with the volley. As players progress, they learn how to close more rapidly, in approaching the net.

Drill 10—Volley Poaching Drill

The coach feeds one ball at a time through the middle of the court. Players intercept (poach) the ball as they move across the net. The coach can vary the speed and direction of the feed. Close in closer to the net on every next shot.

Practice

The purpose is to learn to intercept the ball for doubles play. The players move around and repeat the action from both sides.

Drill 11—Combination Approach Drill

The coach feeds three balls in sequence. Start with a baseline stroke, then an approach shot and a volley to finish. Practice this drill from both sides. The coach can adjust speed, spin, and intensity.

Practice

The purpose is to hit a variety of shots to mimic a match situation or rally in approaching the net. Coaches need to watch for recovery and balance during the execution of this drill.

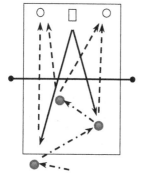

Drill 12—Approach Shots and Passing Drill

The coach feeds short balls so players can approach the ball down the line. The passing shot can go crosscourt or down the line. Coaches can adjust speed, spin, and height of the ball. Play out the point after the approach.

Practice

The purpose is to increase control/consistency of approaches and passing shots under pressure. Make sure the players maintain consistency with large targets.

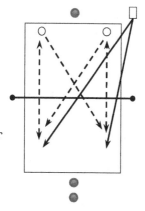

Drill 13—Two-on-One Volley and Baseline Drill

To start the rally, the coach feeds the ball to the net players. They only return the volley to one side of the court. Coaches can vary speed, angles, and overheads. Play with points.

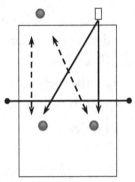

Practice

The purpose of the drill is to train automated responses from the players to rally under pressure. The coach should provide a wide variety of shots and keep the students adjusting to different situations.

Drill 14—Two-on-One Volley and Baseline Drill

To start the rally, the coach feeds the ball to the players on the baseline. They only play to one side at the net player. Coaches can vary speed, spin, and direction with the players adjusting to point situations.

Practice

The purpose of the drill is to train automated responses from the players to rally under pressure. The corrections are made to stroke production and footwork. Play this same drill with points (volley, lob, and overhead).

Drill 15—Two-on-One Volley and Baseline Drill

To start the rally, the coach feeds the ball to the net player. Players can rally the ball around the whole court. Coaches can adjust speed and spin with lobs to create match situations for the students.

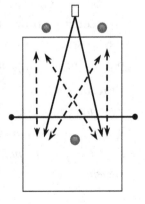

Practice

The purpose of the drill is to train automated responses and movements from the players under pressure. Coaches should watch to see if the players demonstrate recovery, balance, and control. Play with points starting the volley at the service line.

Drill 16—Two-on-One Volley and Baseline Drill

To start the rally, the coach feeds the ball to the player at the baseline. The players can play the ball around the whole court. Coaches can vary speed, spin, and depth of the ball.

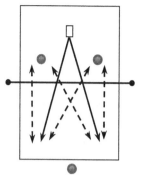

Practice

The purpose of the drill is to train automated responses and movements from players under pressure. Coaches should watch for recovery and control. You can play this same drill with points.

ACKNOWLEDGMENTS

Foremost, I have to thank my parents for introducing me to this wonderful sport. They have always tried to guide me and encourage me to work hard and to be the best I can be in whatever I attempted to do.

Acknowledgment and thanks go out to my two sons, John and Tom, for being my biggest supporters in my career and in writing these books.

I am grateful for all the wonderful coaches who taught me the game. Their teaching has brought out my passion for tennis and instructing others to enjoy the game as much as I have. My thanks go to Mr. van der Berg, Jan Hordijk, and Eric van der Pols for being so patient and diligent in teaching me the intricate parts of the tennis game.

In my playing days, there was one person who took an interest in teaching me the tactical and mental aspects of the game. Henk Korteling was a mentor to me, and he was instrumental in teaching me how to control the mind and enjoy the game.

As a student coach, I attended several teaching courses in the Netherlands. There are, however, some coaches who take a special interest in stimulating you to reach a higher level of coaching. Tom de Goede was one of those coaches, and my thanks go to him for pushing me to excel.

Lynne Rolley has been a friend and colleague in coaching and guiding players. She always has been a great support in helping me with players and difficult situations. Her clear vision and experience in the management of players, coaches, and parents has been instrumental to me and taught me to look at many different perspectives of coaching and teaching. Thanks, Lynne, for all your advice over the years.

Rodney Harmon has always supported me in many ventures and ideas as a coach. He has become a close friend and adviser over the years of working together. I have to thank him for stimulating me to write and create these books of teaching tennis. His passion for tennis instruction combined with his insight for the game and his positive attitude has been an inspiration to me. Thanks, Rodney, for the advice, the many suggestions, and inspiring me to write these books.

Magnus Norman was a great friend and colleague in working together in Finland. I was always impressed with his professional approach to coaching and his attitude to other players. I appreciated his support in helping me with the high-performance program in Finland and his efforts in educating the coaches.

Many thanks have to go to David Kenas in helping me with the photos' sequences.

REFERENCES

Bergeron, Michael. *Playing Tennis in the Heat.*

Gosselin, David C. 2002. *Coaching Different Gender.*

Hodgkinson, Mark. 2016. *Fedegraphica.*

Kovacs, Mark S., Todd S. Ellenbecker, and W. Ben Kibler. 2010. *Tennis Recovery.*

Love, Page. *Nutrition.*

Martens, Rainer. 1990. *Successful Coaching*, tennis edition.

Pankhurst, Anne. 2008. *Periodization for Tennis Players.*

Tennis Profiler. 2018.

USTA. 2001. *USA Tennis Parents' Guide.*

USTA. *Sports Psychology Guidebook for Coaches.*

Van Daalen, Martin. 2011. *Teaching Tennis Volume 1.*

_____. 2017. *Teaching Tennis Volume 2.*

Van Fraayenhoven, Frank, ed. 1995. *Guideline and Training Book for Coaches KNLTB Part A and B.*

INDEX

A

aggression control, 316, 321–22

analysis
  competitive, 130
  goals of, 125
  methodology of, 128–29
  types of, 127

angle shot, 244, 266

anxiety, 236, 353, 366, 372, 374

Art of War, The (Sun Tzu), 145

assertiveness, 93

attitude, mental, 148, 175, 183, 314–15, 334, 336

Australian formation, 257

B

backhand, 100, 103

backswing, 191–93, 201, 206, 210, 222

balance, 270–71, 277, 358, 410, 412

ball rotations, 150, 174, 200, 217, 219, 225, 238

C

character, 21, 66, 86, 104, 107, 312, 332
  building, 35, 44, 73
  competitive, 73

coaching
  competitive, 19
  individual, 354, 357
  on-court, 350, 353
  private, 354
  progressions of, 39

coaching mistakes, 360, 362

college players, 363, 385–86

mental aspects for, 63

college tennis, 37, 356, 382
  advantages of, 37, 382

communication, 90–93, 104, 110, 314

concentration, 43, 325–26, 335, 357

confidence, 35, 66, 69, 86, 96, 103, 218, 233, 313–16, 318–19, 324, 336–37, 353, 375
  building, 35, 52, 115, 154, 172, 215, 374
  low, 35, 313

consistency, 24–25, 48, 55–56, 59, 70, 77, 107, 146–48, 150, 156–57, 188, 314, 422

control, emotional, 28, 44, 61, 74, 86–87

coordination, 25, 273–74, 364
  hand-eye, 68
  ways to train, 274

court diagrams, 421–26

court surfaces, 230–31
  clay courts, 57, 123, 137, 168, 217, 219, 222, 420
  grass court, 168, 217, 222, 231, 269, 420
  hard court, 168, 217, 222, 284, 420

crosscourt, 147, 204, 221, 224

D

depth, 149, 176, 178, 224–25

diet, balanced, 289

discipline, 323, 326

Djokovic, Novak, 12, 133–37, 241, 405

E

endurance, 31, 56, 222–23, 269, 272, 274, 278
errors
  forced, 215
  mental, 223
  physical, 221
  primary, 128–29
  secondary, 128–29
  strategic, 219
  tactical, 219–20
  technical, 218
  unforced, 215–16, 218–20
  types of, 218
execution
  consistency of, 43–44, 47, 57, 64, 201, 218, 224
  discipline of, 43, 45, 57, 85–86

F

fatigue, 117, 216–17, 221
fears, 318, 374
  ridding of, 319
Federer, Roger, 12, 78, 133, 136–37, 241, 405
flat serve, 173, 175
flexibility, 276, 287
forehand, 50, 77, 79, 83, 187–88, 190, 245
  developing a dominant, 188, 190
  inside-out, 165, 422

G

game plan, 65, 229–33, 245–46, 259, 358, 368, 370, 375, 398
  constructing a, 184, 229, 231
goals
  long-term, 98, 103
  outcome, 96, 107, 113
  performance, 96, 113

process, 97
  short-term, 97, 103
growth periods, 80

H

Hingis, Martina, 12, 15, 17, 144

I

I-formation, 258
injuries, 294
  achilles tendon, 298
  ankle sprain, 297
  back, 303
  blisters
  feet, 294
  hand, 306
  bruised heel, 296
  calf, 299
  cramping, 309
  hamstring, 301
  heat exhaustion, 309
  hip, 302
  knee, 300
  neck sprain, 305
  plantar fasciitis, 295–96
  shin splints, 298
  shoulder, 304
  stomach muscle strain, 303
  tennis elbow, 307–8
  wrist, 305–6
intensity, 8, 25, 27, 53, 72–73, 106, 282, 364
  training, 53
ITF (International Tennis Federation), 31, 54, 60, 386

J

junior players, 44, 52–53, 139, 264, 388, 399
  training of, 51
  training program for, 280

L

life-ball situations, 188
lob, 193, 195, 197, 254, 265–66

M

management companies, 389–90, 392
    pros and cons, 390, 392
match analysis, 357, 360
media training, 388, 403, 405
momentum, 227–28, 232, 237, 268, 337, 353, 369–70
motivation, 43, 107, 323–25

N

Nadal, Rafael, 12, 70, 133–38, 150, 187, 339, 395
net partner, 260, 264

O

open events, 114
overhead, 206, 208
    backhand, 78, 206
    jump, 59, 206
    regular, 206–7
overtraining, 121, 310, 365, 367
    signs of, 121

P

passion, 9, 90, 107, 322, 345
patterns, basic, 242
peak performance, 119, 121, 340
percentage play, 154
periodization, 117, 279, 347
plan, developmental, 8, 53, 95
    outline of, 95
players
    advanced, 59–60, 103, 113–14, 125, 142–43, 150, 155, 171, 174, 214, 247–48, 282, 322, 325, 418

diet of, 289
aggressive baseliner, 159, 249
    tactics against, 249–50
all-court, 159–60, 250–51
baseline, 266–67
competitive, 74, 378, 421
diet of, 289–91
counterpuncher, 161, 215, 251–52
defensive, 160, 163
inexperienced, 214, 226, 247
moonball, 247–49
    tactics against, 247, 249
net
    tactics against, 211
physical components of, 72, 216, 219, 271
recreational, 44, 292, 417
return, 171, 173, 180, 196, 246, 254, 257–58, 260, 264, 398
transitional, 46, 61, 139–40, 381
positioning, 56, 198–99, 255
post-analysis, 127, 129
practice matches, 49, 160, 334, 373
preparation
    match, 365
    pretournament, 365
pressing, 368
pressure points, 70–71, 73
problem-solving, 44, 87, 329
pro coaches, duties of, 395
program
    running, 286
    stretching, 103, 276
pro players, 37, 64, 140, 228, 278, 282, 323, 345, 388–89, 393–94
    mental aspects for, 66
    weekly program of, 65
pro tennis, 36, 38, 140, 155, 386, 388
pro tour, 38, 388, 393, 397

R

racket angle, 25, 189, 208, 210
racket head speed, 82–83, 189, 201, 207
rackets, 307–8, 408, 410, 412–13, 418
    balance of, 410, 412, 414
    composite, 408
    specifications of, 410
    sweet spot of, 69, 413
rallies
    long, 32, 100, 213–14, 274
    medium, 213
    short, 212–13
rankings, 3, 36, 115, 381, 386
recovery, 82, 202, 398
redirection, 202
rest, active, 367
return
    defensive, tactics of, 179
    for doubles, 263
    high, 174, 203, 266
    low, 174, 204, 254
    neutral, 239–40
    neutralizing, tactics of, 178
    offensive, tactics of, 178
    priorities of, 157
    tactical objectives of, 177
rhythm, 74, 115, 171, 188, 329
routines, 65, 74–75, 327–28, 335, 379

S

scouting, 151, 365, 379, 402
self-coaching, 377–78
server, 156, 171–73, 177–79, 185, 196, 238–40, 257–59
service box, 156, 260, 284
short ball situation, 195, 202
shot choices, 86, 157–58, 164–65, 167–68, 182–83, 185, 221, 235, 373
shot selections, 199–200
side spin, 174
skills, intangible, 68

slice, 147, 150, 191, 245
    backhand, 190–93, 239
specialty shots, 59, 78
speed, 25
spider run, 276, 283
spin, 49, 147, 150, 174, 179–80, 189, 202, 225
split step, 148, 209, 234
sports drinks, 32, 291, 310
sportsmanship, 73
statistics, 133, 136–38
    first set percentage, 137
    four-ball rallies, 136
strategy, 27, 142, 145, 231–32, 348–49
    basic, 28, 40–41, 57, 146, 151
    fundamental, 45, 55–56, 232
strings, 414
    materials
        Kevlar, 418, 420
        natural gut, 414, 416–17
        nylon, 415
        nylon multifilaments, 416
        polyester, 417–18
students, types of, 20
Sun Tzu, 145
    The Art of War

T

tactical fundamentals, 146
tactical priorities, 224
tactical situations, 49, 63, 76, 169, 171, 182, 190, 195–96, 203, 223, 235
    approaching the net, 195
    baseline play, 182, 186, 215
    net play, 203, 263
    return, 176–77, 191–92, 197
    serve, 171
tactical skills, 60, 62, 254
    camouflage, 62, 189–90, 201–2
    risk management, 62, 157, 210
tactics, 142–43, 146, 225

Martin van Daalen

tennis match, crucial points of, 226
tennis parenting, 89
tiebreaks, 228, 400
topspin, 57–58, 150, 167, 174, 179
tournament levels, 114
tournament plan, 98, 104, 113–14, 116–17
tournament schedule, 58, 113, 386
training
    flexibility, 287–88
    yoga, 276, 288
    mental, 104, 312, 365
    movement, 26
    physical, 37, 63, 65, 269, 271, 292, 354
    plyometric, 278, 282
    speed, 26, 283
    strategic, 365
    strength, 274, 278–79

weight, 26, 80, 276, 283, 301
training plan, 98, 104–6

V

visualization, 341, 343–44, 375–76
volley
    drop, 208
    half, 208
    high, 204
    low, 204

W

warm-up, 232–33, 397
weapon development, 77, 79, 81, 100, 212
weather conditions, 169, 217–18, 222–23, 231
winners, 214

Printed in the United States
By Bookmasters